Tales of a Sojourner

a Memoir

by

Ken Miller

Candy —

With love

Ken

Tales of a Sojourner

Copyright @ 2016 by Ken Miller

Cover Photo by Cole Miller

The names and identifying details of some individuals have been changed to protect the privacy of those involved.

All rights reserved. No part of this book may be used without the written permission of the author except in the case of brief quotations for critical articles and reviews.

Printed by Create Space, an Amazon Company

Available from Amazon, Create Space, and other retail outlets

ISBN – 13: 978-1530266005

Novels by Ken Miller:

Evening of Pale Sunshine
Weep Without Tears
Return to the Bosque
Beware the Abyss

Dedication

The dictionary defines a "Sojourner" as someone who resides temporarily in a place. That description really applies to everyone; we are all here on earth temporarily, some longer than others. It may be more applicable to me than most because I have resided temporarily in so many places in the United States and in Iceland, Vietnam, Thailand, Taiwan and other countries and territories.

Through all my travels, from my birth on a house built on the back of a truck in Utah, to lands far and wide, and to the present day in Texas, I have held two people up in my life as true heroes: my father, Charles, and my mother, Ruth. I was one of the seventeen children they brought into the world, and their light will shine brightly down through the generations to come.

Contents

Introduction   1

Chapter 1.	From Diapers to Bombs	16
Chapter 2.	Why Not Canada	21
Chapter 3.	The Lights in the Sky Are Stars	39
Chapter 4.	From Basic to Sun Holidays	42
Chapter 5.	Deadly Old Cape Cod	47
Chapter 6.	Land of Fire and Ice	62
Chapter 7.	Giant Leap For Mankind	81
Chapter 8.	Evening of Pale Sunshine	93
Chapter 9.	Tobacco Road	116
Chapter 10.	Kraits and King Cobras	120
Chapter 11.	Aloha Hawaii	130
Chapter 12.	Oysters and Hushpuppies	146
Chapter 13.	Cowboy Boots and Camels	152
Chapter 14.	Johnny's Salt	156
Chapter 15.	Angel Falls	164
Chapter 16.	Goats in the Bathtub	175
Chapter 17.	The Tree of Life	188
Chapter 18.	No Feng Shui	199
Chapter 19.	Japan, Sorry Dad	215
Chapter 20.	The Devil's Highway	218
Chapter 21.	Real Aussies Don't Drink Fosters	226
Chapter 22.	A Sense of Time and Place	237
Chapter 23.	Rule of 72, Sorry Dad, Sorry Mom	243
Chapter 24.	What's Under the Kilt	248
Chapter 25.	Katrina Was No Lady	255
Chapter 26.	Return to the Bosque	262
Chapter 27.	She's Squirting Oil	268
Appendix	Author Listing	276
About the Author		299

Introduction

Like most of us, I was unsure how to start to write my memoirs. How does one tell one's life story? Has mine been interesting enough to publish a book about it for everyone to read?

The premier newscaster of CBS News in the 1960's and 1970's, Walter Cronkite, who was remembered by many for breaking the news of the death of President John F. Kennedy, used to say in his famous network sign off of the historical educational television series, *You Are There*, "What sort of a day was it? A day like all days, filled with those events that alter and illuminate our times... all things are as they were then, and you are there."

My life has been filled with those things that alter and illuminate our times, and I was there. I was raised in the mountains of North Idaho, the ninth of 17 children of Charles and Ruth Miller. I was fortunate enough to graduate from Washington State University, which was paid for by the U.S. Air Force. I served for 20 years in the military and was an executive in the aerospace industry. I lived in the Far East for five years, Iceland for a year, and in many of the United States. My careers and personal travel have taken me to all 50 states, 45 countries, and a number of territories.

As a young lieutenant in the Air Force I was a base reporting officer for Project Blue Book, the U.S. government official UFO investigating, analysis, and reporting agency. Later, I had the pleasure of being assigned to the NASA Apollo Program, which included the first moon landing. Supporting the conflict in Southeast Asia took me to Vietnam and Thailand and an assignment at USAF Pacific Headquarters in Hawaii. My career in the aerospace industry as a product support engineer, training center manager, and product support director afforded me more opportunities to travel world-wide and to meet many people in different countries and of different religions.

To share my life story, the joy, sadness, accomplishments, and failures; the events that altered and illuminated my time, I decided to start that journey by giving the reader a tour of the apartment I now occupy in Fort Worth, Texas.

On the wall at the top of the stairs leading up from the garage is a photo of my oldest son, Alan, taken when he was in the marines. He was training in the Nevada desert with his squad in preparation to go to Iran to attempt to rescue the 52 Americans taken hostage when the Shah of Iran was overthrown in 1979, but he sprained his knee during a night exercise and had to stay behind. The mission was aborted because of bad weather, and one of the helicopters on the rescue mission, perhaps the one Alan might have been on, ran into a C-130 tanker aircraft and crashed, killing eight U.S. servicemen and injuring several more. Inserted into Alan's picture is a cloth badge from the Atlantic Beach, North Carolina Police Department where he served until retiring to teach police science at the local college and one from the Carteret County Sheriff's Office where Alan established and supervised their Special Response Team (SRT).

Next to Alan on the wall is a high school photo of the grandson of my life companion, Candace (Candy) Gillen. His name is Jacob, and he now works in Austin, Texas.

To Jacob's left is a high school graduation photo of my grandson, Blake, now a fireman in Cypress, Texas. He was recently recognized at a benefit dinner hosted by the family of a man who was severely injured in a motorcycle accident. Blake, off duty and on his way home, stopped and rendered aid to the victim until the ambulance arrived. The man, who lost his leg, and his family thanked Blake profusely for keeping him alive until medical care could get there.

My desk and work area are just across from the top of the stairs. In front are my computer, printer, and television monitor. Just above, on the first shelf are copies of the four novels I have written, *Evening of Pale Sunshine*, *Weep Without Tears*, *Return to the Bosque*, and *Beware the Abyss*.

To the side of my books is a box photo frame inscribed with the words: *There is nothing on this earth to be prized more than true friendship*. It contains a recent picture of me with one of my lifelong friends: John Dicus. I've known John since early in grade school. He was much taller than I was, well over six feet and, when I would be bullied at school, I would yell for John. His appearance immediately dispersed the harassers. John visited me not long ago with his wife and daughter. I gave him a guided tour of Fort Worth, which has a very interesting history that has led to its nickname: *Where the West Starts*.

On the top shelf is a wood display holding two ceremonial Chinese swords that were given to me when I worked as an engineering advisor in Taiwan. An inscribed placard reads:

Presented to
Mr. Kenneth L. Miller
In appreciation for your Dedication
To the AIDC Logistics Support Division

4 August 1994

On the wall to the left of my desk is a photo of me and my third son, Brian, taken when he attended high school in Taichung, Taiwan where I worked. Brian is now the warehouse manager for an audio/visual company in Dallas, and he is a professional musician playing bass with the Chris Watson southern blues band.

Below the photo is a wooden engraved plaque depicting six of the types of aircraft built by the aerospace company General Dynamics, which was acquired by Lockheed Martin in 1990. On the left are the work horses of the Cold War, a B-36 Bomber and a B-32. Below them, a World War II B-24 seems to come alive in the air. On the right side are the jet aircraft: a B-58, an F-111, and the largest selling military jet airplane in history, the F-16 Fighting Falcon. The inscription is:

> *Presented to*
> *Kenneth L. Miller*
> *In Recognition Of 19+ Years Of Dedicated*
> *Service And Contributions To The Success Of*
> *Lockheed Martin Tactical Aircraft Systems*
> *31 December 1997*

On the right wall of my office is a framed print of a painting that would have made Dad smile if he could have seen it. Titled, *Amazon Dinner Party*, it depicts a dinner table in an outside setting with a river flowing past in the dark background. Seated around the table are John Wayne, Clark Gable, Sophie Loren, Elvis Presley, Marilyn Monroe, and Elizabeth Taylor. A dark haired woman wearing a low-cut red evening gown is handing Wayne a glass of wine. In the background, Ann Margaret is dancing on a small stage.

The artist, and she is the one serving the wine, Pilar Wayne, was John's widow when she painted the picture. I met her one day in the windy parking lot of a Fort Worth grocery store. After John died, Pilar married the president of Radio Shack, which was headquartered in the city. When we met, I was startled to see a cart full of groceries speeding unaccompanied toward my car. I stopped it just before the impact.

A slender, well dressed and dark haired woman rushed up to me. "I'm so sorry," she said with a slight Latin accent. "Thank you."

I wheeled the cart to her Cadillac and put the packages in her trunk. She started to back out of her parking spot, and then stopped and rolled down her window. Writing something on a card she had withdrawn from her purse, she handed it to me with a smile.

After she left, I looked at the card. It was a print of the picture I described above. On the back, she had written, *Thank you! P*, with the title of her painting and her name: *Pilar Wayne*.

I never saw her again, but I have framed the print. I later heard she and her second husband moved to the house in Southern California where she had lived with John. I wish Dad could have seen the card Pilar gave me. He was a great fan of John Wayne. I think his family helped him collect almost every one of the 142 movies Wayne made over the years.

Above Pilar's print is a certificate of completion from the United States Golf Teachers Federation for a course I completed at the Tapatio Springs Resort in the Hill Country of Texas in May of 1995 to become a professional golf instructor. Although I never continued as a teacher, golf consumed a lot of my time as an adult; perhaps too much at the sacrifice of spending more time with my family.

Over the years I chased a little white ball with dimples all over the world, from sharing the fairways with kangaroos in Australia, to putting on sand greens that were whisked with a broom in Bahrain, to teeing off alee a typhoon wind in Taiwan, to struggling out of sand traps on championship courses in Florida, Georgia, California, Texas, Louisiana, North and South Carolina, Tennessee, Arkansas, Massachusetts, Washington, Oregon, Mississippi, Georgia, Colorado, Arizona, Idaho, Utah, Nevada, Montana, Kansas, Wyoming, Oklahoma, New Mexico, Illinois, Maine, New York, Mexico, Venezuela, Panama Canal, Israel, Jamaica, Germany, Scotland, Japan, Thailand, Vietnam (where we had to check the current Viet Cong attack reports before teeing off on the Pentagon East course), Spain, France, England, Italy, Brazil, South Africa, Singapore, and Puerto Rico, and while shooing sheep aside during a summer midnight round on a golf course straddling the Arctic Circle in Iceland.

Next to the golf certificate are two others. One is my discharge from the USAF in 1978 with the regular rank of Major. Beside it is the Bronze Star I received for my service in South Vietnam in 1971 and 1972.

On the same wall is a certificate given to me for my participation in NASA's Apollo Program, specifically for the Apollo 11 mission of July 20, 1969 when the first man, Neil Armstrong, set foot on the moon. When he, Buzz Aldrin, and Michael Collins left the earth's orbit on their trans-lunar trajectory, I was an airborne mission coordinator on an EC-135 aircraft flying on a race track pattern off Mauritius Island in the Indian Ocean. We were relaying voice communications from the Command Module and recording critical data we later downloaded to world-wide NASA ground stations for the engineers and scientists at the Houston and Kennedy Space Centers to evaluate.

Entering the living room, the wall to the left has a photo of my grandson, Cole, below some of his art productions. Cole, now in college in Austin, Texas, is a talented artist, web site developer, and the owner of an internet store selling his original clothing designs and art.

To the right, on the way to the guest bedroom, is a wedding photo of Candy's son, Chris, who is Jacob's father, and his recent bride Joanna. They live in Georgia. Near that photo are one of Blake and his bride Ashley, my niece Kaylin and her new husband Marc.

Just past those pictures is a china cabinet where Candy displays family ceramic collections and wine glasses. To the left of the cabinet, next to the kitchen, is a panoramic photo of USAF Thunderbird F-16 aircraft flying over Lake Powell in Nevada. Inscribed with my name, it was given to me by the commander of the air show aircraft, Lieutenant Colonel Stephan Trent, when I was the Director of Product Support for General Dynamics, the manufacturer of the F-16.

Passing the kitchen in the hallway brings into view several of my favorite photo displays. On the right, next to the thermostat, is a black and white picture of my oldest sister, Eileen, taken when she was still in high school in the 1940's. Everyone seeing it for the first time are taken aback because she is so attractive: dark hair and flashing eyes that beckon above her beautiful face.

When I look at Eileen's picture, I am transformed to an earlier era when young and striking women like Loretta Young, Lorraine Day, Dana Wynter, Hedy Lamar, and Elizabeth Taylor graced the movie screens. I put Eileen's image there so I can smile at her every time I adjust the room temperature. Today, she is in a nursing home in Coeur d' Alene, Idaho where she still graces everyone around her.

Near Eileen are two photos taken during the Miller/Bishop Reunion, which took place in Moyie Springs, Idaho in 2004. Unfortunately—or perhaps fortunately—both of our parents were deceased before we found out the truth about their past and invited family members from Illinois to join our celebration; family we were only to discover from the 1930 Census released in the year of 2002. That eye opening event warrants full coverage later.

In 2015 we had another family reunion in Coeur d' Alene, Idaho and I've added a photo of Eileen holding up one of our reunion t-shirts. Next to it is a display of one of the shirts designed and sold by

Cole.

On the right of Eileen and the thermostat is a three-picture collage of Bonners Ferry, Idaho where I spent most of my formative years. The first photo was taken next to the Kootenai River Bridge from the north side. It looks down on the small town, which only stretched three short blocks before it lifted upward toward a hill on the south. The middle picture was taken of a sign on the north side of the bridge that summarized the history of the town. Finally, the third photo was taken down at street level in the town looking past the Rex Theater.

Below the Bonners Ferry photo is a framed 1988 Idaho auto license plate. When Candy and I visited Idaho in 2006, we accompanied my niece, Drexel Love, when she visited friends of hers, Claudia and Clint, who lived near the Montana border. Claudia had an old car that had not been driven for many years. Its license plate read Idaho 4929. When Candy noticed it, she told Claudia she was born in 1949. Claudia laughed and said she was born in 1929. Several months after we returned to Fort Worth from our Idaho visit, Candy received the license plate in the mail. Drexel told her Clint had died, and Claudia wanted her to have it.

Across the aisle from Eileen, the reunion photos, and the license plate are my parent's wall dedicated to Charles and Ruth Miller. Putting aside for the moment the terrible secret about their past we uncovered, a single black and white photo of Dad and Mom taken at their 50th wedding anniversary shows the love they had for each other.

Something else is clear to me when I look at it now; they gaze outward with love for each of us children and they seem to ask us for understanding and acceptance of who they are. There is pain in their eyes I did not recognize before we found out who they really were; pain that asks for forgiveness.

Above Dad's and Mom's photo is another collage. This one shows events from the days when they lived on the Camp Nine farm north of Bonners Ferry in the '50s and '60s. In one of them, Dad is standing in the front yard next to a pile of logs that need to be sawed into furnace length and split before they can be thrown and stacked into the basement for providing the winter heat.

Another one shows Dad seated next to my second son, Mike, and his grandson Blake. Blake, about a year old at the time, is staring at his great grandfather's pocket, where Dad had a round tin of Copenhagen chewing tobacco outlined through the cloth.

Entering the guest bedroom to the left reveals a group of photos from my son Alan's family: his wife, Donna, and their two children, Keith and Nina, taken when the kids were very young.

Tales of a Sojourner

Next to it is a shadow box with a miniature fishing pole and a photo my son, Mike, took of me catching a large fish in the world renowned San Juan River of New Mexico, a catch and release area that has over 20,000 fish per mile, averaging 17 inches in length. Years later, Mike, and his wife, Jennifer bought a rental/vacation home on Vallecito Lake just across the Colorado border to the north of the river.

On the other wall entry are photos of my Australian family; my brother, Joe, his wife, Alice, and their children, Joel and Kaylin. Joe retired as a master welder and instructor from the aluminum processing plant near Bunbury, and Alice is a therapeutic masseuse.

Joe worked as a welder on the trans-Alaska pipe line from Prudhoe Bay south over 800 miles to Valdez during the mid to late 1970's. His high school classmate, Alice Douglas, meanwhile had migrated to Australia, who at that time needed professionals to fill their workforce. Alice went there as a school teacher and was later joined by Joe. Two children were born in Bunbury, south of Perth in Western Australia.

Joel, a world traveler, who has some of the Miller sojourner genes, is now getting a PHD at the University of Western Australia in Perth, and he is one of the hosts for the annual Technical, Entertainment, and Design (TED) conference in Perth.

Kaylin became a registered nurse, serving with the Doctors Flying Service covering many thousands of square miles populated by a very few who farmed in the Outback of Australia. Some of the sheep and cattle ranches were so large the children attended school over short wave radio. Kaylin flew hundreds of miles with her doctors to tend to illnesses and injuries of the far flung ranchers and their families. Later, Kaylin served as a hospital nurse in Melbourne. After returning to her hometown of Bunbury as a nurse, she married a wonderful man named Marc Phillips, and is now living in Perth.

One of the photos on Joe's wall shows me standing with his family in an elevated park overlooking Perth when I went to visit them. Several years later, my sister, Carole, and I went back to spend some time with Joe and his family. It was in December, and I have a picture of a banner hanging over a Bunbury street proclaiming the Christmas holiday season. It was a little strange, since it was summer down under not the winter time we had left behind in the United States.

Beside Joe's photos is a striking, framed cloth painting of a Chinese Panda Bear. It was presented to me by Colonel Wang Ting of the Aerospace Industry Development Corporation (AIDC) of Taichung, Taiwan. I was assigned as a technical advisor to Ting in the early 1990's. The Chinese tradition is to give the family name first, followed by the given name. I set across from Ting in an adjoining desk for three years, sharing my experiences in supporting aircraft development and support and listening to him cough while he chain-smoked cigarettes.

Below the painting is another gift given to me by Ting just before I departed Taiwan. He took me to a factory where they made ceramic vases. While there, the department supervisor, accompanied us down the production line while a beautiful white vase with several inlaid layers lined with gold paint was being manufactured. At the end of the line, the supervisor lifted the vase off the conveyor belt and handed it to Ting who, in turn, presented it to me. I will always cherish it because it was made just for me.

While in Taiwan, I helped establish a Society of Logistics Engineers (SOLE) chapter that was later acknowledged by the international SOLE parent association. At my going away dinner, I was given a plaque engraved on metal that read:

To Ken Miller
Good Luck and Best Wishes
To The Happy Rice Eater
You Have Been a Good Friend
A Good SOLE Brother
And A Great Advisor
SOLE Chapter 14-01, Taiwan

My name, Ken Miller, translated into Chinese is *Happy Rice Eater*.

Next to the plaque is a beautiful display dish engraved through a dark patina of a flower pattern with gold etching:

From the Turkish Officers
To
Ken Miller

It was given to me when I was the manager of the General Dynamics Logistics Training Center. We provided training on the F-16 systems operation and maintenance to the U.S. Air Force and 25 foreign countries who have bought over 4,500 of the aircraft since 1976.

Not only was I able to welcome hundreds of enlisted men and officers from around the world to our classrooms and laboratories, but I was also fortunate to travel to many U. S. and foreign air bases and support facilities.

Next to the commemorative plate is a large placard developed for the book signing of my third novel, *Return to the Bosque*, at the Friends of the Fort Worth Library Book Store on October 20, 2007. I hosted a monthly book forum for the Friends, and the director was gracious enough to sponsor my book signing.

In the left corner of the bedroom is a built-in four shelve area. In addition to photos of Candy's and my family, I have placed several of the special books I've accumulated on one of the shelves. There are original copies of *Gone with the Wind*, c1936; *Grapes of Wrath*, c1930, (This book belonged to my niece, Drexel Love. She got it from her father's estate, Pete Turner, after he passed away and gave it to me); *The Works of Haggard*, c1928; *Lost Horizon*, c1933; *A Tree Grows in Brooklyn*, c1943; *Marshall's Life of Washington*, c1832; *Whispering Smith* by Frank Spearman, c1912; *The American* by Henry James, c1907; *Lonesome Dove* by Larry McMurtry, c1985; and James Michener's autobiography *The World Is My Home*, c1992.

These are but a few of the many books I have in my bookshelves, closets, and stacked in the garage. I also have several hundred e-books available on my Samsung tablet, iMac computer, and smart phone. I can't even estimate the many hundreds of thousands of books I have read over my life, although I will later list some of those that have influenced and intrigued me over my lifetime.

When I was a management instructor in the U.S. Air Force teaching mid-level officers, I took a speed reading course and was able to skim through books very quickly. I still do that for some writing, but when I get into a book that really interests me, I slow down; often re-reading passages, descriptions, and dialogue as one would savor an excellent meal.

When I finish a book, I have an empty, longing, hungry feeling until I start another one. But that defines a voracious reader like me; it is a trait I inherited from Dad along with my sojourner proclivity. I am an eclectic reader of fiction, science, biography, autobiography, politics, and other genres. In a pinch, I even read the writing on toothpaste and shampoo containers when I can't reach a book or a magazine. Reading is a transcendental experience. I think it is a terminal condition, once afflicted with it you have it for life.

During my days and nights as a sojourner wandering the world, I have dined in many places. I prefer the company of others but, of necessity, I often dined alone. Actually not alone, because I always carried two items with me: a note pad to write in and a book to read from.

One time in San Francisco, while wearing my Air Force uniform, I was eating at a seaside restaurant by myself. A man sitting near me with his wife, approached my table and asked me if I would like to dine with them. "You look lonely by yourself," he said.

I smiled and held up the paperback book I was reading: James Michener's *Tales of the South Pacific*. "I'm not alone," I said. "I'm sharing my meal with Nellie Forbush, Emile de Becque, and Bloody Mary." The man smiled knowingly and returned to his table. I think he was also a voracious reader.

During my U.S. Air Force tour supporting the Apollo Program, we often flew to Johannesburg, South Africa before staging over the Indian Ocean to support the trans-lunar trajectory blastoff of the Command Module and the Lunar Excursion Module (LEM). I was dining one afternoon by myself while reading a well-worn copy of *Grapes of Wrath* by John Steinbeck. An elderly, elegantly dressed woman approached and asked me to join her and her husband at their table.

"I can see you are a Yankee," she said with a smile. "And also a reader."

"How did you know I am an American?" I asked as I rose to meet her husband.

"You cut your food with the knife in your right hand," she said. "Then you transfer your fork to that hand to pick up your food and eat it. Only Yankees do that."

I also received tutoring in culinary dining from others around the world. In Italy, a young man who spoke no English, showed me that you don't cut spaghetti into small pieces with a knife, you wind it up on a fork against an open spoon before chomping on it. In Hong Kong, a Chinese waiter, who understood English, showed me how to eat with chopsticks and how to lay them on my plate without offending fellow diners at the table.

On many other days and nights, I have dined with Einstein, Shakespeare, Moby Dick, Winston Churchill, Sherlock Holmes, Yuri Zhivago, Count Dracula, Scarlett O'Hara, Jane Eyre, Milo Minderbender, Uriah Heep, Robinson Crusoe, John Galt, Jeeves, Ichabod Crane, Ebenezer Scrooge, James Bond, Fagin, Kim, Holden Caulfield, Atticus Finch, Yossarian, Tarzan, and so many other interesting real life and imagined characters. I have never been bored or alone as long as I something to read, or someone to share a meal with.

Next to the book shelf is a beautiful antique roll-top desk built by Thomasville. On top are several small photos of members of Candy's and my family. One of them shows Candy and her three sisters, Jamie, Annette, and Holly. The inscription on the frame reads:

Life made us Sisters...
Love made us Friends

Beside that is a family photo of my oldest brother, Charlie, with his wife, Lilly, and their children Joann, Jim, and Linda. Charlie, who passed away in 2009, was a rare, spontaneously naturally funny person. He could tell some of the most outrageous and hilarious stories.

When asked if he was making them up, he would flash an enigmatic smile, reminiscent of my mother's, and say, "Truth is stranger than fiction."

Mark Twain expanded on Charlie's statement by stating, "It is no wonder that truth is stranger than fiction. Fiction has to make sense."

Another brother, John, has a picture next to Charlie's. Taken while John was serving in the U.S Army just before his assignment to the American Embassy in Ethiopia, it shows a strong yet compassionate young man who was a wonderful brother and a loving son. He would later become a much respected owner of a food distribution business in Fort Worth before he was murdered in his home in 1982. It would take nearly thirty years before his killer was identified by a cold case detective and sent to prison. We'll meet John again in a later chapter.

On the wall next to the bedroom window is a small black and white photo of a thin, distinguished looking man with a mustache wearing a dark suit and tie and holding a narrow brimmed hat in his right arm as he looks off in the distance. His left hand is supporting a framed painting on black silk of a white bird above a flowered wreath.

I found out later it is a bier picture that was traditionally placed next to a coffin during a funeral service. It was my maternal grandfather, Edward Bishop, who died in 1954. That was the year I was a freshman in high school and had no idea relatives of my father and mother still lived in Illinois and elsewhere.

Leaving the bedroom, we'll walk through the kitchen. Most kitchens aren't very interesting, they have a stove, sink, refrigerator, pantry, and some cabinets and counter space. This one has real relevance to me.

On the wall just inside to the right is a carved wooden bread board that is an engraving of flowers above a large turtle with *Costa Rica* inscribed above his shell. Candy and I vacationed there with Mike and his family a few years ago. The week spent on the Pacific Ocean side of the country was very enjoyable.

Costa Rica is a beautiful tropical place with high mountains, secluded beaches, and friendly people. It is one of the few countries in the world that does not have any military forces, and has a flat ten percent income tax. Are you reading this, Washington D.C.?

To the left of the turtle is a copy of a plaque Mom kept on the wall behind her cook stove in Idaho. She had a wonderful sense of humor. When someone would ask how old she was, she would just smile and point at the plaque:

> *I Count My Age*
> *By Friends Not Years!*
> *I Count My Life*
> *By Smiles Not Tears!*

The refrigerator in the kitchen isn't just a refrigerator to keep food cold. As Marty Feldman shouted in the movie, *Young Frankenstein*, "It's alive!" Photos give it life. Kept in place with magnets from Costa Rico, California, North Carolina, Fort Worth, and other places, the pictures of our world-wide family members smile back at us. There is my older sister Penny from a photo back in the 1950's, my Aussie niece Kaylin with her dog Huxley named after the famous English author, Kaylin's brother Joel wearing a dark hat with his head tilted down in a moment of quiet reflection, Candy's family at a reunion in Napa Valley, my grandchildren and great grandchildren, and other photos that evoke gentle moments of reflection.

There are three "Save the Date" magnetic backed cards on the refrigerator also. That seems to be the new way to announce upcoming marriages. They don't encourage us to "Save the Titanic," "Save the Lusitania," or "Save the Alamo," all unmitigated disasters. They tell us in no uncertain terms to save the date when weddings will take place; in other words, don't plan anything else that day or the marriage gods will get you. In these cases, they refer to my grandson Blake's nuptials in Cypress, Texas, my granddaughter Nina's in Newport, North Carolina, and my Aussie niece Kaylin's in Singapore.

One of the amazing things about the photos on the refrigerator is that while most of them were printed directly from a digital camera, the rest were downloaded from the on-line social media giant Facebook and other sites, then printed on my computer.

The modern day internet has some positive applications besides the irritations of spam, scam, and requiring passwords. I never thought I would see the day when cameras with film requiring development would go out of style, but it has happened.

Above the dining table beside the kitchen is a large numbered print of a jazz band playing in the Preservation Hall saloon in New Orleans. I bought it during one of my many visits to the crown jewel city of the south. The artist, Tommy Thompson, who had a studio near Jackson Square, signed it to me with the inscription, *Carpe Diem*, which is Latin for *Seize the Day*.

I didn't grow up with music prominent in my childhood. We had several radios, but I didn't listen to music very often. Back then many of the cars didn't have radios. The reception in the valley where we lived was spotty at best with Spokane a hundred miles away past several mountain ranges. Mom loved music, and she had several phonographs where she played old 45 and 78 RPM records, many of them scratched from our many moves.

As I went out into the world, I developed an appreciation for popular, western, classical, blues, and jazz music. I especially came to like jazz after several visits to New Orleans. The haunting and uplifting refrains of jazz bubbles up from the sidewalks and streets of the French Quarter, wafts down from the ornate metal balconies above, and streams out of the doors of the many restaurants and nightclubs.

That has developed into a love for the older masters of the genre like Count Basie, John Coltrane, Dave Brubeck, and others. Thanks to one of my favorite authors, Michael Connelly, who wrote a series of novels about a Los Angeles police detective named Hieronymus Bosch—named for the 15th century Dutch artist who painted the horrifying *Garden of Earthly Delights*, a nightmare landscape of grotesque predators and screaming human victims—I found a real oldie treasure.

Bosch was a lover of classical jazz. One of his favorite performers was Art Pepper who wrote and performed a tune he named *Patricia* in honor of his daughter, because he didn't spend enough time with her while she was growing up and he was out on the road performing. Bosch said Pepper's saxophone sounded like it was crying. I downloaded the passage from iTunes, and Bosch was right: his saxophone is wailing.

I also listen avidly to the great singers of jazz: Etta James, the first lady of jazz; Fats Domino, the soul of jazz, who has a voice that sounds like sluggish water pouring through a rusty pipe but possessing a powerful and mythical resonance uniquely its own; Dinah Washington who has a tremor in her singing voice that brings chills to my spine; and so many others gracing the history of the uniquely American music genre.

As original jazz transitioned into blues and popular music, I came to appreciate artists like Frank Sinatra, who enunciated each syllable of each word with such impeccable mastery, and Tony Bennett, who has such a soulful voice. When Tony sings *I left my heart in San Francisco*, I can feel the pain and anguish he feels from leaving his love behind.

Going into the master bedroom, we pass by a painting of a Shi Tzu that looks very much like our dog, Hollywood, who is now ten years old. Holly is a special pet and friend. Her big eyes reflect her intelligence and compassion. When either Candy or I are feeling down, she lies quietly beside us to give us comfort. Holly has traveled with us all over the United States and to Canada. A most enjoyable travel companion, she watches the roadside fields for cow and horses, rising up to paw at the window when she sees them.

Every morning Holly takes me out for my morning potty walk. She has developed two interesting dances during our outing: a *Pee Potty Polka* and a *Poop Scooting Boogie.*

Unfortunately, Holly suffers from two complications common to her specific breed. Her hair grows so fast we have to take her to the groomer about every six weeks. The other problem is that most Americans pronounce her name incorrectly. The Shi Tzu breed was developed for the aristocracy in China; it means *Lion Dog*. They were bred for their long mane and tiny body structure. The proper way to pronounce her breed is the Chinese way, *Shee Dzu*, not *Shit Soo*.

Despite her small stature, Holly is ferocious when she sees a larger dog from the sanctuary of our patio. As Mark Twain said, "It's not the size of the dog in the fight, it's the size of the fight in the dog."

The bedroom, in addition to the bed, contains Candy's office desk and computer. On one wall are two of the most unusual photographs, taken together, that I have ever seen. To the left is Candy's mother looking toward her left. Candy on the right looks back toward her mother. They were both taken at about the same time in their lives; when they were seniors in high school. They resemble each other so much the photos could be exchanged without changing the perspective. It reminds me of two Rembrandt portraits from the 17th century in the National Gallery of Art in Washington, D.C. that look at each other across a doorway.

I have always been interested in art. I studied the great masters like Rembrandt, Leonardo Da Vinci, Michelangelo, Monet, Cezanne, Renoir (my favorite impressionist artist), and others. Whenever I have an opportunity I visit the museums in the cities I travel to like the

Louvre in Paris, the National Gallery of Art in Washington, D.C., the British Museum in London, the Prado in Madrid, the Metropolitan Museum of Art in New York City, the Vatican Museum in Rome, the Museum of Fine Arts in Boston, and many others around the world.

I look at the great artists as akin to the great authors of history; not only does their art and writing reflect the times they live, but they actually change history itself, and they lift us up out of the stress and demands of our daily lives and allow us to soar high on the wings of their genius.

At one time in my life, I thought I would become an artist. I studied oil, acrylic, and water color painting (which for me was an uncontrolled disaster). I discovered I had a talent for color and linear perspective and taught myself to draw with some proficiency. From one of my seascape instructors in Hawaii, I learned that "a color is a color it is because of the color it is next to." However, after painting some landscapes and wild life art, I decided I would not be another Turner, Rembrandt, Cezanne, or Renoir, and I put my painting supplies aside.

There are other interesting photos and artifacts in my apartment, but I think it is time to get on with my story. As my brother-in-law, Pete Turner, would say, "Let's get on with the rat killing."

One last comment, I don't want to disparage anyone I have met over my years with negative descriptions; almost everyone has become a friend of mine, many for lasting relationships. To avoid any derogative references and to maintain privacy issues, I have on occasion just used letter abbreviations in place of proper names.

Chapter 1
From Diapers to Bombs

Newspapers and radio broadcasts during the summer of 1939 were mostly negative: the depression was still affecting many Americans and the winds of war were about to be unleashed by Hitler in Europe. Although no one suspected it yet, the Rising Sun of Japan was soon to crash down on Hawaii while my father was there.

The average cost of a new house was $3,800, a gallon of gas 10 cents, a loaf of bread 8 cents, and a new car—a Chevrolet or Ford—was $700. An average American, however, could not afford to buy a new house or car. Most of them were still making about a dollar a day in wages.

Some really classic movies came out that year. *Wizard of Oz*, *Gone with the Wind*, *Stagecoach* (John Wayne's first great starring role), *Mr. Smith Goes to Washington*, *Wuthering Heights*, *Goodbye Mr. Chips*, *The Hunchback of Notre Dame*, *Gunga Din*, and *Of Mice and Men* were among the many released.

After six years in the White House, Franklin D. Roosevelt's New Deal policies were helping to lead the country out its economic morass. But not even he could look ahead and see that the world was about to be involved in the most destructive war in the history of mankind.

I was born on August 4, 1939 as the 9th of 17 children of Charles and Ruth Miller. My birth certificate listed Dad's occupation as a "Chuck Tender" in Draper, Utah and his name as Charles Calvin Miller. A chuck tender replaced worn out drill bits in a mining operation. I'm sure it was a dirty, back breaking job that covered him with coal dust until he looked like a black mole emerging from the dark underground.

My sisters told me I was born in a small house Dad had built on the back of a truck. Mom delivered me herself with help from my older sisters.

We didn't stay in Utah very long; and that became the normal way of life for Dad and his bourgeoning family. I think I inherited my sojourner genes from him. Southern Idaho was our next stop as the house built on a truck, the fore-runner of the modern recreational vehicle, rolled into a small town called Triumph.

That part of Idaho was pock marked with mines: silver, gold, lead, and coal. Dad was an expert at mining, as he was in so many endeavors: highway and airport construction, forestry, farming, house and barn building, gardening, and raising children that adored and respected him.

I have a photo from his younger days when he was an irrigation ditch rider in Wyoming during the depths of the depression working seven days a week for a dollar a day to feed his growing family. He personified the strength and character of a movie star who I have always admired: Roy Rogers.

Of course, I have no memories of those early days so I have to rely on family lore provided by my elder sisters and brothers. My oldest sister, Eileen, was born in Wyoming in 1928, and Verna (we called her Penny, because her hair was the color of a copper penny) in 1929. Louise followed in 1931, born in New Mexico, and my oldest brother, Charlie in 1932, and then my sister, Lavina in 1934 in Colorado.

The growing Miller family traveled through the southwest, usually on the back of that rustic RV. The first hushed family mystery occurred in 1935, when a baby boy named Leonard Keith died soon after his birth. He was the only one of our large family not to live into adulthood, which was quite a feat during those days when most children were born at home and not in a hospital.

After migrating to Hailey, Idaho, Mom gave birth to Robert (Bob) in 1936 and Floyd in 1937. I followed in 1939 when Dad pursued his employment opportunities in Utah. Returning back to Hailey, my sister Kate joined our burgeoning Miller clan in 1940.

Eileen told me years later, with her tongue in her cheek, that our mother really did not have that many children. She just kidnapped babies where ever Dad's work took him. That is an interesting concept. If that is what Mom did, why didn't some of us grow up to be Chinese, American Indian, Yugoslavian, or Greek? From my observation, most of us Miller kids had some resemblance to each other and to our parents; well some of us did. I really think Mom just loved children and she and Dad just kept on birthing them as long as she could.

When Mom held a new baby she glowed with an innate light of love, and with a smile that told the world she had found her calling in life: birthing and raising as many children as she could. In addition to her moral and physical strength—she carried a child in her womb for nearly 13 years of her life, that's over 150 months or 4,650 days—Mom had a seemingly inexhaustible amount of energy. Her day started before the rest of the family woke as she stoked the furnace, started the wood cook stove, and prepared the morning meal, which included making tasty high rising soft biscuits from scratch.

Many days the comforting aroma of coffee and baking bread would awaken me. And I knew when I walked into the kitchen, Mom would welcome me with a kind word and her enigmatic smile I always felt was just for me. My siblings said they also felt Mom made them feel special when she talked with them. And her day didn't end until long after we were tucked in for the night.

Recognizing Dad's ability as a miner, the civil engineering and construction company, Morrison Knudsen, hired him and sent him to Hawaii in the fall of 1941. Mom was pregnant with my brother, Paul, at that time. Dad worked on the classified Red Hill Project on Oahu where they were excavating large petroleum storage areas in the mountains above Pearl Harbor.

In one of the unusual ironies of history, when the Japanese attacked, they did not know the gas and oil reserves of the U.S. Pacific Fleet were stored in above ground tanks on Ford Island just off Battleship Row since the Red Hill storage area was not completed. Had the Japanese strike planners known, they could have destroyed those vulnerable tanks, which would have crippled the U.S. Navy and might have resulted in the Japanese invading the Aleutian Islands and the west coast of the United States; most certainly it would have prolonged the war in the Pacific.

We lived in Hailey, near the Sun Valley resort area in another house Dad built for us, on that fateful day that will live forever in infamy when the Japanese launched a dawn attack on Pearl Harbor and other military sites in Oahu on the 7th of December.

Dad was staying in the U.S. Army Schofield Barracks with some of his work mates that Sunday morning. He said he and most of his crew went outside and watched the planes flying low overhead on their way to bomb and torpedo the battleships in Pearl Harbor. The red sun emblem on the aircraft was clearly visible to them, although they had no idea what was taking place. When the planes returned on their way to the carriers off the north side of the island, they flew over the barracks and fired machine gun bullets into the mass of onlookers. Dad was spared, but several of his friends were killed.

The day after the dastardly Japanese attack, President Franklin D. Roosevelt made his famous address to the U.S. Congress and to the world:

"Yesterday, December 7, 1941—a date that will live in infamy—the United States was suddenly and deliberately attacked by naval and air forces of the Empire of Japan. Always will we remember the character of the onslaught against us. No matter how long it may take us to overcome this premeditated invasion, the American people, in their righteous might, will win through absolute victory."

After the Pearl Harbor attack our family had no word of Dad's fate. A news blackout was implemented immediately and telephone service was seriously interrupted. Other families in Hailey brought food and gift baskets to our house. Mom, nine months pregnant with Paul, refused the offerings because she was sure Dad was still alive.

The town's telegraph office was north on the street where we lived. One day, a young man at the office received a telegram. After copying it he ran down the street yelling, "Charlie Miller is okay…Charlie Miller is okay. He is alive." By the time the messenger reached our house, nearly everyone in Hailey had heard the news.

Dad returned from Hawaii in late December on a sea transport that he called a bean boat—perhaps it was a ship used to send vegetables to the Pacific troops. During the voyage, he said he was seasick the entire time. Dad finally arrived home in time for Paul's birth on December 30, 1941.

I was assigned to Pacific Air Forces Headquarters on Oahu in the mid 1970's. Bullet damage from the Japanese aircraft machine guns was still visible on the walls outside the building where I worked. It is there yet and will be as long as the building stands, as a reminder that we have to be eternally vigilant to protect our American way of life.

I asked Dad at that time about his experience at Schofield Barracks. All he would say was, "The Japanese were sneaky bastards." That was one of the few curse words I ever heard from him.

Dad never forgave the Japanese and refused to have anything to do with the many products produced by their factories until the day he died. One day, the hammer he was using broke and he sent Mom into Bonners Ferry, the small North Idaho town near where he lived, to buy him a new one. Mom returned with a one-piece hammer made from steel. She told Dad the store owner recommended it because it would never break. Dad took the hammer and looked it over carefully. When he saw it was made in Japan, he gave it back to Mom and told her to return it and bring him a hammer made in the USA.

After the 2nd World War, which ended in September of 1945 when the Japanese surrendered after atomic bombs were dropped on Hiroshima and Nagasaki, the military governor of Japan, General Douglas MacArthur, helped them rebuild their industries and return to economic stability. Some of the early products shipped to the USA were of inferior quality, but in time, with better quality control under the auspice of the United States, they improved until they could compete with American built items.

One of my sisters, apparently not understanding the depth of Dad's vehemence toward Japan, drove up in his yard one day in a shiny Toyota she was quite proud of and wanted to show to Dad and Mom. Mom really liked it, but Dad, after looking it over carefully, said, "This is a Toyota. Isn't it made in Japan?"

When my sister said it was, Dad pointed down the dirt road leading to the house from Highway 95, which stretched north from Bonner Ferry to the Canadian Border. "Take your car and park it by the mailboxes on the highway. I won't have a Japanese car on my property."

Chapter 2
Why Not Canada

From Hailey, Dad followed his wandering urge and need for employment to the U.S. Navy base on Pend Oreille Lake near Sandpoint, Idaho. He didn't stay there long as he was re-hired by Morrison Knudsen and took his brood to Oakland, California where he worked at the Naval Station for a short time before resigning and moving to the North Idaho town of Bonners Ferry.

The awesome Kootenai River starts its journey in Canada, then flows south through Montana before turning west into Idaho where it joins up with the Moyie River as it thunders north through the town of Bonners Ferry and bisects Boundary County and rolls back into Canada to eventually merge into the Columbia River, which empties into the Pacific Ocean.

The Meryl Streep movie *The River Wild* was filmed on the Kootenai River upstream from the town, where some of the wildest rapids in the United States pour through a narrow Montana valley.

The deep river in the Idaho portion of its journey is home to some of the largest fish to be found anywhere, the massive land locked White Sturgeon that weigh as much as 1,700 pounds. They have inhabited the waters for thousands of years; since the river was first formed during the melting of ancient ice formations.

When **gold** was discovered in southern **British Columbia** in 1863, thousands of prospectors from all over the West surged northward over a route that became known as the Wild Horse Trail. Edwin Bonner established a ferry in 1864 where the trail crossed the **Kootenai River**. In 1875, Richard Fry leased the business, but the location retained the name of the original founder and became the town of Bonners Ferry.

Before the **gold rush**, few visitors came to the region; among the earliest was the intrepid explorer **David Thompson**, a **cartographer** for the **Northwest Trading Company**. He arrived in 1808 to trade with the Kootenai Indians. The local natives gave Thompson's exhausted party dried fish and moss bread. Thompson returned the next year and established a trading post on **Lake Pend Oreille, near the present town of Sandpoint**. He was followed in 1846 by the **Jesuit Priest Father DeSmet**, a missionary to the **Kootenai Tribe**.

With mines to the north, the community of Bonners Ferry flourished in the 1880s as a supplier. The **Norwegian**-built **steamer** *Midge* began service in 1883 and operated for the next 25 years, carrying passengers and freight between Bonners Ferry and British Columbia. The **Great Northern Railway** was built through there in 1892, followed by the Spokane International.

Bonners Ferry was formally established in 1893, along the south bank of the Kootenai River. Scattered along the valley and bench land were a few ranches and homesteads. Numerous mines were developed in the nearby mountains, including the Continental Mine in the Selkirk's. The lumber industry also grew rapidly. Bonners Ferry, perched on stilts to avoid the inevitable spring floods, appeared to be a boom town.

Moving into the 20th century, the town became the center of a lumbering and farming community. The valley land was drained, levees were constructed and farms were cleared on the benches. The rich Kootenai Valley became known as the "Nile of the North," while the Bonners Ferry Lumber Company grew to be one of the world's largest **lumber mills**. The downtown took shape as brick buildings were constructed, replacing those on stilts. Completion of the **Libby Dam** in 1975 lessened the threat of serious flooding and ushered in a period of prosperity and immigration into the mountains and valleys of the county.

When we moved into Boundary County, Mom gave birth to my younger brother John in 1943. We thought Dad's sojourner days were over, but that was not to be. We moved back south to Salmon, Idaho where my sister Carole was born in 1944, before returning to Bonners Ferry. By this time, several years had passed without Mom having any more children. She was soon to rectify that. My brother, Joe, now an Australian citizen, was born in 1946 and Jerry in 1947.

Then Dad's wanderlust led him and some of his family to Saint Francis in the northwest corner of Kansas near the Republican River. Dad was hired to help build a dam on the river just across the state line border near a dot in the road with the appropriate name of Hell, Colorado. We weren't there very long because a tornado demolished a portion of the dam under construction.

Returning to Idaho, we eventually settled on a 180-acre property Dad purchased north of Bonners Ferry near Highway 95 on the Camp Nine Road. We were just over 10 miles from the Canadian border, so the winters were filled with snowball fights, frozen fingers, runny noses, and cabin fever. John Graves, the acclaimed Texas author of *Goodbye to a River*, would have called the farm "a hardscrabble homestead." Much of it was covered with trees and brush, and a large part was on an untillable steep hillside.

Over the years we cleared many acres and planted them in wheat and alfalfa. We kept several milk cows and dozens of chickens to supplement the potatoes, corn, and other vegetables from the large garden. Dad also had his favorite strawberry patch (which was off limits to us kids and our grubby fingers), and apples, cherries, and pears came from an orchard. In the fall and winter, we supplemented our meat supply with venison. The deer were readily available in the fields near the house or on the mountain abutting our farm. I don't ever recall going hungry or without clean clothes to wear.

Dad built a huge barn that dwarfed the house for storing hay and providing a place to milk our cows—with the boys help of course. One day I asked Dad why we didn't get paid for the work we did on the farm. He looked at me strangely and answered, "You get plenty to eat, a place to sleep, and your mother buys or makes your clothes. What else do you need?"

Our outhouse—also known as a Chapel of Ease, Necessary House or Nessy, Comfort Station, Loo (for English visitors), Latrine (for the military), John, Sears Booth (for the catalogs used for emergency paper), Reading Room (with the Sears catalog handy for perusal), Throne Room (a royal room where one sits in state), and an Eleanor (from President Franklin Roosevelt's depression Works Project Administration of promoting rural sanitation by building outhouses), and other less acceptable names—a two-hole structure was about twenty frenetic steps from the house.

That may not sound like a long way but, in the depths of a North Idaho winter with freezing temperatures and blowing snow, it could be a long slippery trek, especially for the girls. They constantly complained that the boys didn't go all the way to the outhouse; the evidence was all the yellow snow alongside the path.

I did a lot of research on what frontier life in the 1800's was like for two of my books: *Return to the Bosque* and *Beware the Abyss*. In all the old photographs showing women from that era they looked worn and haggard, with a bit of fright gleaming in their eyes. Those only in their thirties and forties appeared much older.

My theory is the reason they looked old before their time was because they had to use an outhouse all their lives. During the heat of the summer they had to sit over a splintery dark hole above spiders, flies, ants, and even snakes and scorpions. And adding to the negative experiences was the smell of the droppings, which overwhelmed and nauseated them.

Any outhouse builder worth his salt wouldn't construct one that was air tight. They left gaps between the boards so the breezes could provide some relief from the odors. That left space for the fierce winter winds to whistle in, scatter the Sears and Roebuck catalog pages used for clean up, and cover the sitting boards with snow and ice.

I envision the poor women delaying their morning rituals until they couldn't wait any longer. Running through the freezing weather, they passed their husband's and male children's yellow marks on their way to plopping down on the icy outhouse hole. I'm not sure that made for matrimonial or motherly bliss.

We thought Dad's days as a sojourner were finally over when we settled in at Camp Nine, but that was proven wrong years later when Dad and Mom pulled up stakes and went to Arkansas for a time.

They might have stayed there but Mom became ill and she thought she was dying; and her skin had turned yellow. While Dad was out in the fields, she loaded up a few personal items in her car and headed back to North Idaho. That trip Mom made, while so sick she wasn't sure she would see the next sunrise, is one of the most awe inspiring treks anyone has ever made. Dad, my son Mike, and I followed her for days without word of her condition. I will tell the story in more detail later in this memoir.

The Kootenai Valley was surrounded by high mountains cleft by the omniscient river that clawed its way through the verdant lowlands, later to be called districts. A lofty peak named Clifty Mountain dominated the river valley like a Greek god overseeing his vast domain. Next to Clifty was a lower peak with the ominous name of Black Mountain, perched beside its better known companion like a smaller sibling that never received the recognition it deserved.

When I was a late teenager and working for the U.S. Forest Service, I spent several weeks in the Black Mountain observation tower overlooking the valleys reporting lightning strikes that might result in devastating forest fires that could consume thousands of acres of virgin timber.

My brother Dan was added to our family in 1950, and Clifford in 1951. I remember standing with Dad near a wood pile that was stacked high in the yard outside the house we lived in the night Mom was giving birth to Clifford. He would be the 17th and last child she would have. I felt a strange sadness at the thought someone else was coming into our family, and we would have to share with him. I asked Dad if he would love me less when the new baby came.

He put his hand on my shoulder, and I could smell the masculine aroma of chewing tobacco on his breath. "No," he said. "As our family grows, so does the love your mother and I feel. Some people have lots of money, your mother and I have more love than just about anyone."

I turned away so Dad wouldn't see the tears in my eyes.

Why were there only 17 of us children? I think Dad wanted a football team (which he got with 11 boys) and Mom wanted a volleyball team (which she got with 6 girls). I'm just glad they didn't decide to add a soccer team to their lineup; sharing a small room with another gaggle of brothers would have been difficult and the smell of so many feet over powering.

We had a 180-acre farm, which Dad called it a "Stump Ranch." He had to work out to help keep his large, voracious brood fed and clothed. We never had much spending money, but we were always well fed and had clean (often mended) clothes to wear. I used to tell people we were so poor Mom put me and my brother Floyd in the same diaper to make ends meet. Mom didn't appreciate the joke and told me not to tell it again.

I once asked Dad why he decided to stay in Idaho near the Canadian border. He thought about it for a moment, and then said, "I didn't want to go any further north and change my citizenship. I'll always be an American."

One of my early memories of Bonners Ferry was when Dad gathered us all up and took us to the railroad station in town to see Harry Truman on his 1948 whistle-stop election campaign. Truman gave a speech from the back of the train steps of the last car. I don't remember what he said, but I know Dad was excited, and he clapped heartily with the crowd supporting the presidential candidate.

Bonners Ferry in those days was a sleepy village that closed down with the sun on most days. It had one theater, which showed the latest movies in a double feature with cartoons on the weekends. Saturday was my mother's day to shop for groceries and sundries while we kids went to the movies.

We were given enough money for the movie and a drink or popcorn; but not enough for both of them. Since we had to choose, I and my siblings would trade goodies so we could share while the movies enraptured us with tales of western heroes like Jessie James, Roy Rogers, and the cartoons of Walt Disney, Looney Tunes, and others.

Back then, most of the movies were in black and white, but we didn't care. Television had not made its way into the mountains of North Idaho; that was still years away. The first TV signals were line of sight and couldn't penetrate into the deep valleys of the Kootenai

River basin from the nearest broadcast stations in Spokane, Washington. My parents did not even have a television until after I graduated from high school and moved away from home.

The movies provided me with an escape from the reality of the world, which I also found in books. The films lifted me up and made me feel like I could really be a knight of the round table, a false accused western hero, or the savior of an imprisoned heroine waiting for me to ride in on a white horse and snatch her away from the clutches of an evil, black hatted bandit.

The town theater (Rex) was not very big, but it did have an upper balcony. If someone stood up there, it blocked the film from showing on the screen, resulting in catcalls and whistles from the other viewers. The owner of the theater had a son who was, unfortunately, mentally impaired. The young man, however, did have a most unusual talent; before the movies started he would whistle like a bird, any of the birds that lived in the county. When the audience shouted a name at him, like a Robin or a Blue Bird, the idiot savant would whistle exactly like the bird.

Speaking of books, I have been a lifetime voracious reader, and I owe that trait to my Dad. His days, when he was home and not out working somewhere else to support our family, were long and demanding. We had cows that needed milking, chickens that scrabbled for edibles and must have their eggs gathered, wood that had to be cut down and sized for the furnace, and all the demands of a farm to support a large and rambunctious family. But whenever Dad had a spare moment, usually in the evening after dinner, he would sit in his arm chair in the living room and grab a paperback book from a box beside him and start reading. Perhaps it was his way to withdraw from the hectic environment of his day. If it was, I followed his example, even until today.

Dad's favorite books were the westerns written by Zane Grey, Max Brand, Ernest Haycox, William MacLeod Raine, J. Frank Dobie, Vardis Fisher, and others. I always waited until Dad finished a book before I snatched it up and started reading it. I noticed most of them had the front cover removed. I found out later Mom got them from a store in Bonners Ferry where the owner would remove the covers and then give the books to her for free. Apparently, he would send the covers back to the distributors so he wouldn't have to pay for the books.

We never had a television in our home when I lived with my parents. My older sister Eileen, was married to Pete Turner, and they lived near the Montana state border in Moyie Springs where Pete's mother had one of the first receivers that could snatch a TV signal out of the air from Spokane. Her set was a small black and white console with a rounded edge display that gathered more snow than picture from the ether.

Wow! It was so great. We would beg our parents to take us to Mrs. Turner's house on Friday evenings so we could watch the wrestling matches. I will never forget the images of Gorgeous George striding around the roped mat that faded in and out of the snow as he snatched gold pins from his flowing locks and threw them to his adoring audience.

In the back of the smoke filled room, Mrs. Turner would hack, cough, and spit as she smoked un-filtered cigarettes and laughed at the dim picture and us shouting kids. Back then, in the fifties, very few knew about the fatal complications that arose from smoking, which would impair the health of Mrs. Turner and so many others.

I have to thank Dad I did not get drawn into the smoking habit that probably shortened Mrs. Turner's life. One day when I was a young teenager, Dad and I were out in the snowy forest near our house cutting fire wood. Dad was dipping Copenhagen smokeless tobacco, which looked inviting to me. I asked him if I could have some. He looked at me and said, "I don't think your mother would like you to dip."

I kept pestering him and, finally, he gave in and said, "Okay." He pulled out his round container and told me to take a pinch. "Put it in your lower lip, and don't swallow it."

I stuck a bit of the finely ground tobacco in my mouth and immediately swallowed it. Then I vomited a dark, wet mass onto the white snow, the acrid taste of the tobacco staying with me for a long time. After that, the few times I put a cigarette in my mouth—and they were not filtered back then—I felt the urge to throw up again. Later in life I tried to smoke a pipe but, again, the horrible taste of the tobacco juice caused a rebellion in my mouth. So, today, when we know the negative effects of smoking, I have to look back and thank Dad for his wisdom in weaning me from cigarettes at a very early age.

Way up on the inside of the barn's inclined roof he had installed a pulley on a track for hoisting hay bales and stacking them. A rope hung down from the pulley almost to the floor. One day one of my sisters thought it would be fun to pull the rope up to a loft and then swing on it. It might have worked if she had held onto the rope, but it slipped through her hands and she fell and suffered bruises and a hurt ego.

Of course Dad heard about it. In his quiet way, he didn't say anything. He just went into his bedroom and returned to the barn with his Model 1873 Winchester lever action rifle. It was known widely as "The Gun That Won The West." He raised it to his shoulder and, with one shot, severed the rope up near the pulley. When it fell near his feet, he looked at us kids watching him in awe and said, "Well I guess that won't happen again."

That firearm was later to play a major role in one of my older brother Bob's hunting feats, and, unfortunately, in the tragic loss of the youngest member of our family: Clifford.

Dad was my first hero and that adoration has lasted a lifetime. The farm we lived on didn't produce enough income to support our large clan so Dad had to work outside jobs: road and building construction, forestry, vehicle and machinery operation and repair, and other employment opportunities. He was offered many jobs because he was so proficient at anything he worked at and had so many friends. He spent long days away and often had to travel to jobs far enough away that he couldn't return at night.

My brother, Charlie, told me Dad helped build the airport on the north hill above Bonners Ferry. He was given the task of clearing and grading the runway. The foreman told him he was going to get a surveyor to make sure the runway was laid out on a true line and compass heading. When the foreman left, Dad jumped on a grader and, without a map or compass, leveled out a landing strip. When the foreman and the surveyor finally showed up, he was finished. The foreman was upset at Dad, and was chewing him out, when the surveyor came back from measuring the runway and told him it was dead on for distance, smoothness, and direction.

Dad had an innate sense of time and direction that was amazing. It didn't matter where he was, he knew his exact location. We could be deep in the woods up a winding mountain road far from the nearest highway or habitation and he could tell me how far we were from home and what direction it was. He had a pocket watch but, without looking at it, and glancing up at the sun, could tell the time within a few minutes.

I inherited Dad's ability to sense directions. It has saved me from getting lost many times as I traveled through country sides and cities around the world, many of them in countries where I didn't know the language and couldn't read signs or ask for directions.

The first time I was aware of my directional ability was at an International Boy Scout Jamboree in the Rocky Mountains of Canada in 1953. There were hundreds of scouts and scout masters from around the world. Since Canada was a constitutional monarchy with Queen Elizabeth as its head of state, the event was in honor of her recent coronation. In addition to days of competitive events for group awards, the scoutmaster of our Bonners Ferry troop decided to take the 14 of us scouts out and try to get us lost in the heavy forest.

After leading us into the trees, he wove back and forth in a serpentine trail, even making a few loops, to get us disoriented. Finally, after a half hour of walking we came to a clearing where we could see far down a slope to a river below. He told us to sit down and he collected compasses from everyone who had them. Then he said we were to stay there for ten minutes. After that, if we made it back to camp within an hour he would award us a merit badge for path finding.

On the first day of our bivouac, I had noticed a high, snowcapped peak to the west of the camp in the direction of the setting sun. After the ten minutes were up, I climbed up a tree until I could see the peak. Shinnying down, I told the troop I knew where the camp was. When the overweight scoutmaster, huffing and puffing, finally arrived at our site, the rest of the troop and I were sitting around a campfire roasting marshmallows.

During the springs, the Kootenai River would become swollen with roiling, thrashing water from the melting of the heavy snows in the mountains of Idaho, Montana, and Canada. The Libby Dam built to control the annual floods was still years away. Bonners Ferry and the rich farmland of the valley was protected from the encroaching water by a massive dike system. Unfortunately, they weren't massive enough on some years and the river overflowed them and inundated the town and the farm districts.

In 1948, my family had to move from a house near the river in boats to escape the rising water. My senior year was cut short by another flood that forced the high school to terminate early.

One spring day Dad and I were walking along one of the dikes just a few feet above the raging river. I looked out across it and it seemed to be miles wide. "Dad," I asked, "How wide do you think the river is here?"

Dad always wore a narrow brimmed hat. When he took it off you could see the white skin of his forehead above his deeply tanned face. He pulled his hat brim down over his eyes and turned toward the rushing torrent. Squinting his eyes, he bowed his neck and stared at the far bank. Then he pivoted slowly, looked down the dike, and said, "Let's find out." He began pacing in increments that he said was exactly one yard, muttering numbers to himself.

Finally, we came to a spot on the dike just above a tree. Dad stopped and said, "The Kootenai is 875 yards wide here. How many feet is that?"

I knew a mile was 5,280 feet or 1,760 yards. Math was one of my favorite subjects in school. After a few moments thinking about it, I said, "A half mile is 880 yards, so it is about 2,600 feet wide."

Dad built many of the houses we lived in during his sojourner days, some of them even on the back of a truck. He did all the work himself, with the help of us boys. I recall one day when he had finished the framing of an outside wall on one of his constructions. We had taken a short break and were sitting on the ground. Dad looked up at the framework and, after gauging it, said, "There's something wrong with that wall."

I looked at it and couldn't see what he was talking about. "What is it?" I asked.

"That far corner is about an inch lower than this one," Dad said.

He took his measuring tape out of the chest pocket of his overalls and checked it. He was right, the corner was just under an inch off. How he could see that with his eyes, I could never understand, but Dad corrected the error.

Dad also had another rare talent, he was a dowser. He could use a water witch to find the location, flow direction, and amount of underground water. I saw him do it many times, and he was always right. He preferred to use the slingshot shaped branch from a cherry tree as he worked. He would grasp a fork tightly in each hand and hold it out in front of him as he walked. When he approached a subterranean deposit of water, the tip of the branch would start to go downward. As he stood over it, the tip would be pointing straight down. I've seen him hold the branch so tightly the bark would tear under the pressure bearing it downward. His dowsing talent gave Dad the location for digging wells on many of the places where we lived, including the farm on Camp Nine.

In today's high stress world of multi-media, video games, ear buds, violent movies, and high definition television, along with the demands of peer pressure and too little outdoors activities and exercise, many children have been diagnosed with Attention Deficit Disorder (ADD). Unfortunately, the parental solution to calm down the hyperactivity and to regain respect is to get doctors to prescribe medications that may have lasting side effects.

Dad believed us boys all must have ADD. Only in his case it meant Adult Daily Discipline. In a family as large as ours, thrust together in a small house, and often isolated by deep winter snows, arguments, scuffles, fights, and outright wars were nearly a daily event. Cliques developed where the boys, assisted by sisters occasionally, grouped together and ambushed each other. The winter was a favorite time for conflict since we could build snow forts and have stupendous snow ball fights. Although it was often colder than the inside of a freezer and the snow deeper than a tall cow's rear end, we loved to go to war with no quarters asked or given.

Mom tried to act as a referee but, with her gentle soul, she sometimes had to retreat into the sanctuary of her bedroom. But heaven help us when Dad came home from work. He would confer with Mom, and then grab the ringleaders from the day's altercations, take us to the woodshed, and administer ADD.

He would remove his belt, double it over and strap us boys across our buttocks. It hurt! I can remember many times when it was painful to sit down after Dad's whacks.

Once when Dad grabbed me for a suspected infraction, I told him I didn't do it; it was one of my brothers. He proceeded to warm my britches anyway. When he finished, tearfully, I continued my verbal defense. Dad looked at me with his eyes narrowed and said, "Well that might be true. So that whipping was for one time you did something wrong, and you didn't get caught."

I asked Dad why he never spanked the girls. He answered, "They don't need it like you boys do."

I understand his reasoning. I am a lifelong student of history and, looking back over thousands of years of conflicts that have often resulted in mass murder, some to the point of ethnic extinction, they were invariably led by men. I think if there was a world-wide mandate that every head of state had to be a woman there would be far fewer wars and less poverty.

Dad taught me many things that helped me later in life. One of them was to respect others and be kind to them. He told me to hold those older than me and the females in my life with respect. He always opened the car door for Mom when she got in her car or his pickup with him, and he called other women Mrs. Or Ma'am.

Christmas was a special time in our household. Usually there was deep snow covering the valley and the mountains overlooking it. It seemed like it was quieter in the winter as if the snow softened the noise of traffic and everyday life. We would go up on the hill above the house in the silence of the season and cut a Christmas tree for the house. Mom and we kids would decorate it with strings of popcorn, cut aluminum foil, colorful bulbs, and top it with an angel Mom kept through the years. She had the eye of an artist and the tree was always a thing of beauty.

I don't know where my parents got the money for presents for so many children, but every Christmas morning we were surprised and pleased with what we received.

But as special as Christmas was, Mom made our birthdays even more special. "Everyone has Christmas at the same time," she said. "But only you have a birthday on your own day." She would make that day pleasurable for each of us with a cake and a gift she had chosen just for us.

I recall several incidents when Mom's humor manifested itself under pressure. I think it was a trait I inherited from her, which helped me during times of stress in my life.

Saturday afternoon was the time when Mom went shopping for groceries and supplies while we children would go to the movies and let her shop alone. One clear fall day as we returned the nine miles to our house, the old car Mom was driving broke down. After repeated failed attempts to re-start it, she had us all get out. Handing each of us a package of groceries according to our size, we walked the last few miles home.

When we turned off the gravel road to our house, with Mom heading a trail of six or seven children, Dad was working in the garden. He looked up at us in surprise. I thought Mom was going to give Dad a hard time for not providing her with a car she could depend on. Instead, she returned his look with her secret smile, and said "If you have to walk, this is a good day for it."

During another Saturday shopping trip, this time during the winter just after a heavy storm piled up huge banks of snow at the highway edges from the plows, we were hurtling down the slippery slope of the North Hill like a bobsled on an Olympic run into Bonners Ferry. A car churning up the hill with snow chains biting into the ice covered road swerved over into our lane. Mom had to slide into the snow bank to keep us from getting hit. When she did, we were spun around and, suddenly, the car was pointed back up the hill. But we weren't through spinning, and went completely around, narrowly missing the car passing us, as we headed back down the hill.

All of us kids were screaming, even me. I looked over at Mom. "That was a close one," she said with a smile as we continued on down the hill to the town.

The barn where Dad shot down the overhanging rope was also the scene of one of the strangest things I have ever witnessed. I was milking one of our cows one evening when the door behind the stalls opened and a man entered with my brother, Bob, and stood watching me. I looked up and recognized him as a friend of one of our family members. I'll just call him Fred. He was dressed in shiny, pleated slacks and a long sleeved white shirt.

Fred watched me as I milked for a few moments, then he said, "That looks like fun. I've never milked a cow. Can I try it?"

I never thought it was fun to milk smelly cows that had a habit of kicking the bucket just when it became full, swatting flies with their huge tails, and urinating whenever the urge moved them. I looked up at Bob, who was leaning against the wall and smiling. He nodded at me to let Fred give it a try.

I let Fred replace me on the stool. I showed him how to put his fingers high up on the cow's teats, squeeze them, and then pull down to eject the milk. He picked up the knack of milking rather quickly, and he was smiling as the bucket began to fill.

Then the cow began swinging her tail at the flies that swarmed around her in a swirling cloud. It wasn't long before the tip of her tail swooped around and hit Fred in the back of his neck. I could see a red welt where he had been hit. He swung at the tail but the cow had flipped it around to her other side. As he continued to milk, I could see him keep watch on the swinging tail out of the corner of his eyes. It wasn't long before he got hit again, even though he anticipated it.

This time, he stood up from the stool and glared at the dumb animal in front of him. Looking around the milk room he spotted some concrete blocks Dad had stacked against a wall for one of his building projects. They weighed about five pounds and had several large holes through them.

I couldn't believe it when Fred picked up one of the blocks, tied a length of rope through it, and grabbed the cow's tail to cinch the block to it. I started to yell at him when I noticed Bob shaking his head at me, his grin widening. Fred dropped the block on the floor and, with a satisfied look on his face, sat down on the stool and began milking again, certain the cow didn't have enough strength to move the block.

But she did, and the block snapped through the air and stuck Fred in his lower back. The force knocked him sprawling under the cow and spilled the bucket of milk. I was just able to grab Fred by his ankles and pull him back before the cow began urinating all over the floor as she tried to shake the block loose.

Bob was one of my early heroes. Older than me, he had a kinship with the outdoors I always envied. He took a taxidermy class by correspondence and was soon mounting birds, fish, and small animals in the barn because Mom wouldn't let him do it in the house.

While still in high school Bob became a legend in Boundary County. One fall day, he was hunting deer around an abandoned orchard up the hill to the east of our house with Dad's Winchester 30-30. The rifle was old and had been fired many times over the years. Dad had killed lots of deer and a few elk with it. But the lever action had become worn and would usually jam up after one of two shells were put into the firing chamber, and you had to pry out the bullets with a knife or screwdriver. Fortunately, that didn't happen to Bob that day.

As he entered the orchard, he was attacked by three black bears, a mother and her two yearlings. Bob stood solid and fired three shots from Dad's rifle killing all three of the bears.

Bob had a ten-year-old Chevrolet, which had wide protruding fenders. He put the mother bear on the hood of the car and tied a yearling on each front fender and drove into Bonners Ferry.

I heard about it later; it was quite a spectacle. People in town for their Saturday shopping gathered around his car. The county game warden stopped him but, after talking to Bob, said he couldn't charge him with any offence because he was just protecting his own life. Bob made a rug, which included the head, of the largest bear. It lay on the floor of his Montana home for many years.

Our house wasn't very big, but fortunately some of my older brothers and sisters had married and moved out when I was growing up there. I shared a tiny bedroom with three of my brothers next to one where my sisters slept. The kitchen also served as our dining room. A long table stretched from the wood cook stove to the door that opened to the front yard. Dad sat at the head of the table with his back to the stove. Along each side of the table we children were seated by age, the younger you were, the closer to Dad you sat.

Mom never ate with us, she spent the meal times serving with Dad getting the plates of food and passing them down the lines. We called the chair at the end of the table the ejection seat.

Dad had a firm rule, when you finished high school or turned 18, you helped put food on the table or you went out the door. And out the door lurked strange unknowns including sub-zero temperatures and deep snow during the long Idaho winters.

I remember when Bob dropped out of high school and wasn't working. We were all afraid to tell Dad, because we knew his rules. After Dad passed the food plates out, he looked down the long table at Bob. "I understand you quit school. Have you found a job?"

Bob returned Dad's stare with a frightened look. Finally, he said, "No, I haven't."

"Okay," Dad said. "You have one week to find work and give your mom some money to help with the food, or I want you out that door."

Bob left the next day for Spokane and joined the U.S. Army. After his service, he went to work for the Forest Service where he had a long and very distinguished career in Montana.

I wasn't very far down the table from Bob that night when Dad told him to go to work or get out of the house. I can tell you, it had a tremendous impact on me, I didn't want to sit in the ejection seat.

During those days of the 1950's, we never locked our house or our vehicles. Crime in that rural part of the Northwest was almost non-existent. When one of our family was murdered thirty years later, Dad could not comprehend it, nor could he understand why the murderer was not immediately arrested.

One Sunday afternoon, when we sat down for our weekly fried chicken meal, I looked across the table to see a stranger, a disheveled young boy who looked to be about 12 years old. Mom, startled at first to see him, smiled and asked his name. He told her and the plates of food were passed to him. He didn't say much, but he seemed to really enjoy the meal. When we all got up from the table, the boy sought out Mom and thanked her for letting him share our food. Then he disappeared.

Mom looked around at us and asked, "Who was that boy? Is he a friend of one of you?" We all looked at each other, but none of us knew who he was, just a hungry stranger who wandered into the warmth of our house and companionship.

We didn't have much knowledge of the outside world in those years since we still didn't have a television. We did have a radio that pulled in faint, scratchy stations that faded in and out. Dad's favorite program was the Friday Night Gillette Cavalcade of Sports boxing matches. He could relate the accomplishments of Jack Dempsey, Joe Lewis, Rocky Marciano and other fighters that came into our living room.

When I started high school, he encouraged me to get on the boxing squad. However, after getting beat badly in the first two matches, I quit the sport and became a pole vaulter and broad jumper on the track team.

Many years later I was able to share an interesting boxing story with Dad. I saw the "Thrilla from Manila," in person in the Philippine Islands in 1975 when Mohammad Ali fought Joe Frazier. I was on temporary duty at Clark Air Base when the U.S. Air Force Special Services announced that free tickets and bus transportation to the fight was available at no cost for servicemen. Although it took place in

October, it was oppressively hot. Ali's doctor later said the arena was cooked by the sun and the atmosphere was boiling.

The uniform I wore was drenched with sweat, as if I had been sprayed by a fire hose, as I stood shoulder-to-shoulder with thousands of screaming locals and visiting fight aficionados. Ali won when the referee stopped the grueling bout after the 14th round. Ali reportedly said that was as close as he had ever come to dying.

Since we lived north of Bonners Ferry, I attended Mount Hall, a middle school near where we lived. Then I went to the high school down in the valley protected from the Kootenai River in town by high dikes that couldn't hold back the spring floods. It wasn't until the mid-seventies a dam in Montana was built to control the seasonal inundations.

My high school annual listed me as the most studious in my class. I'm not sure what that meant, it may have been because I wore glasses and was always carrying a book with me.

I think it was about that time I realized I would leave the comforting environment of the valley and become a sojourner like my father before me. I knew I was destined to search for a world that populated the movies and the books I devoured that promised so much more than the narrow valley where I lived.

In the late summer of 1957, Dwight Eisenhower was our president, Grace Metalious was the author of the most popular book *Peyton Place*, and Elvis Presley sang his big hit *Jailhouse Rock*. The average house cost $17,000, while the average income was only $2,000, milk was 36 cents a gallon, a stamp four cents, and gas 30 cents a gallon.

It was a good thing for me gas didn't cost more. I had a 1939 Chevrolet coupe that was the same age I was, but it had more miles on it. The sloping trunk wouldn't stay closed and bounced up and down as I drove the few highways and the many back roads of the county. The poor old thing leaked oil badly, so badly I would go to the corner Texaco gas station in town and get used oil out of barrels standing in the alley to pour in it. No one wanted me to park my car by their houses or businesses because of the messy leaks. Dad made me leave it outside our driveway by the road.

Even at that price, gas wasn't cheap for me. The second job I had, outside of the many chores on the farm, was stacking timber on night shift at the Bonners Ferry Lumber Company. They only paid me 70 cents an hour.

My prior job had lasted only briefly. I was hired to mow the graves at the Grand View Cemetery. I was wary about taking the job because

I didn't like the feeling of being around all the burial sites. I should have listened to my premonition. The first day there I was mowing some older plots on the slope of the hill with a view of the Kootenai River below. It was difficult to know exactly where the bodies were interred because the wood markers used years before were weather worn and, in some cases, completely missing.

As I stepped forward, my left foot broke through the earth up to my ankle. I screamed and let go of the mower, which crashed into the perimeter fence or it would have plunged over the cliff. When I finally extricated my foot, I ran to the cemetery office and, ignoring the caretaker's questions, called Mom to come pick me up. I didn't wait for her at the cemetery but ran down the hill to meet her.

When Mom stopped for me, she could see I was distraught, and she asked me, "Are you okay? Are you hurt?"

"No," I said. "I'm not hurt. I just don't want to work at the cemetery."

Mom smiled, "I don't blame you. I think it is a scary place, too."

I went to work at the lumber yard several days later. For months I had nightmares about the cemetery, people were coming up from their graves and grabbing my foot. I have always been blessed—or cursed perhaps—with having very vivid dreams.

I dream in color, smell, and sound like a high definition color movie with the added stimulus of odor. I also can recall my dreams in detail, some for years. My novel, *Return to the Bosque*, was born in a dream I had of a woman standing above a river talking to her departed father's empty grave at a small family cemetery. She was asking him why her husband had not come home from a trip to Fort Worth to sell horses to the army. She was in tears as she told her father's spirit that she might have to take her two children with her and search for her husband.

As the story developed from my waking reflection of the dream, I found the river on a map of Texas. It was the Bosque River near Waco. Why that river? I never knew, but I trusted my dream.

I believe dreams are developed by our imagination while we are sleeping. Void of outside stimuli like sounds, sights, odors, and wakeful thinking, our imaginations are free to run wild. I think if you have a dream about a two-headed baby it doesn't mean someone you know is going to give birth to a mutation. It just means you had a dream about a two-headed baby.

My dreams are like puffs of smoke, if I don't give them life by thinking about them while awake they rise and dissipate into the sky. Those I want to recall; I write down or put in my mind in a Dream

Room. That room is next to the New Word Room where I put new words I hear or read until I understand their meaning.

    I remember that summer standing beside our barn while the cows were stomping reluctantly into their milking stalls one evening as an airplane, high overhead, streaked through the pale sky leaving a thin contrail behind. I had heard that day in school the Russians had rocketed the first satellite into orbit: Sputnik. As I watched the silver streak of the aircraft disappear, I shivered as a thought overwhelmed me. Wherever that airplane was going, so would I. There was a world out there where I had to go. I had to follow that contrail. I had no choice, for I was my father's son, I was a sojourner.

Chapter 3
The Lights in the Sky Are Stars

I didn't go very far from Bonners Ferry after I graduated from High School in 1957. With so many children still at home, Dad couldn't afford to send me to college. Fortunately, I was awarded several scholarships at my graduation, which paid for my tuition and some of my books at the community college in Coeur d' Alene, Idaho. Dad did, however, rebuild an old Chevrolet car for me to drive.

The college was about 75 miles south of our home on the Camp Nine Road. I was fortunate to be able to rent an upstairs room with a friend of mine, Jim Morgan, from a family in a home near the campus.

Of all the scenic places I have seen around the world, in the USA, Canada, Germany, Scotland, South Africa, and so many other countries, I don't think there is a more beautiful place than Coeur d' Alene Lake. Framed by high forested mountains that drop down to the deep blue waters, the lake winds serpentine like among them for many miles. It is a place that haunts my memories and calls me back to its splendor and majesty over the years.

I was able to use a little of the money I had saved to buy a 12-inch reflector telescope kit from Edmunds Optics. I ground the main lens with fine metal sandpaper, silvered it, and produced an amazing instrument. I could read newspaper headlines from over a mile away. Studying astronomy on my own, I searched the night skies to view distant stars, the moon, and Cassin's Division, the large gap separating several of Saturn's rings.

I wrote my first short story that fall. This was before the Russians put Cosmonaut Yuri Gagarin into earth orbit in 1961 as the first man to go into space. It was about an American astronaut who would be the first one placed into an earth orbit. I titled it "Failed Retro-Rocket" because the capsule's rocket to enable a return to ground wouldn't operate. His capsule became his coffin, and he was seen from earth as a speeding dot of light as the metal surface reflected the sun. The astronaut was doomed to endlessly circle the world long after he died from lack of oxygen, a visible memorial to the dangers of space flight.

I mailed the story to John W. Campbell who was the editor of *Astounding Science-Fiction* magazine. First issued in 1929, the periodical exists until today under the title of *Analog Fact & Fiction*. Mr. Campbell sent me a hand scribed note that said he liked the story, if he used it he would send me a royalty check. For years after that, I bought the magazine when it came out but never saw my story published. I also never received a royalty check.

To make ends meet in college, and to have spending money, I worked after school and on weekends at a local department store. One of my jobs was to put up window displays of the store's products. Usually, I pulled a curtain across the window while I put up the displays, but one Saturday morning I forgot to draw the curtain while I was putting dresses on several female manikins.

I heard the laughter of voices outside the window and looked up at several girls pointing at me and laughing. I blushed as I recognized one of the girls from my freshman English class. I didn't know her name, but I did recall she was attractive, with a wide smile that lit up her face and gave it a special life that brightened her pale, blue eyes. I could hear her tittering through the window as I closed the drapes.

The next Monday morning, when I entered the English class I purposely avoided looking at the girl who had watched me through the store window. Sometime during the class, the student behind poked me on the shoulder. When I turned, he passed me a folded piece of paper.

I opened it and read, "Hello Ken. I am Sharon. I hope we didn't embarrass you Saturday. I would like to get to know you. Can we meet for lunch at the student union?"

I met Sharon for lunch and we developed a close relationship. I took her to several movies and dinners over the next few months. Then with the Christmas break coming up, I told her I had to return to Bonners Ferry to spend the holidays with my family. Sharon lived in Coeur d' Alene near the airport where her father was a pilot instructor and flew private company aircraft.

During the time I spent with my family, I often thought about Sharon. Mom, noticing my withdrawal, smiled wisely and asked me quietly if I had found a girl friend at college. I told her I had. The holidays passed slowly, and I called Sharon several times. We had one phone at home, it was on a wall mount near the front door. Calling long distance to Coeur d' Alene cost money and I didn't want to run up Dad's telephone bill. Several days before I left to return to school, I tried to call Sharon, but no one answered at her home.

When I drove into Coeur d' Alene, I stopped at Sharon's house north of downtown. There were a lot of cars parked in front of her parent's home, which I thought was a little strange. When I rang the doorbell her father answered. He was wearing a black suit and had tears in his eyes. "Hello Ken," he stammered. "I couldn't find your parents phone number or I would have called you."

"Called me, why?" I asked.

"Sharon came down with pneumonia several days ago," he said as he started crying. "We took her to the hospital, but she died yesterday."

I finished the school year at the college, but my heart wasn't in it. I returned to Bonners Ferry and went to work for the Forest Service for the summer. I volunteered for a crew that blazed trails through the national forest, often staying out overnight.

I tried to find solace among the massive trees during the days and under the brilliant stars and cyclic moon at night. I had discovered the library in Bonners Ferry when I first started high school. By the time I graduated, I had read most of the books on the shelves. One of them I reread that summer was Fredric Brown's *The Lights in the Sky Are Stars*. As I lay there, often awake, I thought about the brilliant stars and the bright moon above.

I couldn't see it, but I knew the Russian Sputnik satellite was somewhere up there, whirling around in an earth orbit. I realized there was something out there, far above that beckoned to me. I didn't know where those celestial bodies would lead me, but I had to follow them.

I couldn't foresee that one day I would play a part in putting the first man in history on the lonely beckoning moon above.

Chapter 4
From Basic to Sun Holidays

When the summer ended, I couldn't face going back to the campus in Coeur d' Alene. I didn't tell my parents, but I drove to Spokane one day and enlisted in the U.S. Air Force. After I was accepted, I told Dad what I had done as he was stacking wood in the yard in preparation for the coming winter.

He stopped what he was doing, spat tobacco on the ground, and then said to me, "Whatever you do is okay with your mom and me. We don't worry about you. You are smart, and you have a vision that will take you far in life."

Then he put his hand on my shoulder and added, "Just promise me that whatever you do and where ever you go you'll always be honest with yourself."

I wasn't sure what he meant by that then, but over the years the meaning came to me, and I tried to live up to his words. When I found out Dad had been dishonest with us children about his and Mom's life in Illinois, I thought about what he had said to me. It has been difficult to accept, but I believe Dad was honest to himself and to Mom. He wanted to protect her and himself and his growing family from a horrible situation during their first days together.

Basic training in San Antonio, Texas was not as difficult for me as it was for many of my comrades. Thanks to my good physical condition from tromping around the mountains and an innate ability to take tests that caused others to have brain cramps, I finished near the top of my class. While there, I met a young man who was to become a life-long friend, James Edward Brown from Epps, Louisiana.

In 1958 a new house cost $18,500, a gallon of gas only 25 cents a gallon, but the average wage was under $4,000. The National Aeronautics and Space Administration (NASA) was formed to lead America's role in space technology and exploration. The Japanese automobiles Toyota and Datsun were on sale in the U.S. for the first time. *The Bridge on the River Kwai*, *South Pacific*, and *Gigi* came out in theaters. Elvis Presley, Frank Sinatra, the Everly Brothers, and Jerry Lee Lewis topped the music charts. *Candid Camera*, the *Ed Sullivan Show*, and *Alfred Hitchcock Presents* aired on black and white television sets.

After basic, I was assigned to Keesler Air Force Base in Biloxi, Mississippi for electronics training. Mississippi in the late 1950's was still a bastion of black prejudice that had survived since before the Civil War. I had no knowledge of the deeply ingrained hatred the white citizens had toward the Negroes (today called Blacks to distance themselves from the negative connotation of the "N" word).

There were no black people in Boundary County when I lived there. I'm not sure there are any today. We did have a Kootenai Indian reservation nearby, but in our childish ignorance at that time, we didn't relate to the national problem that gave rise to the race riots that tore into the fabric of the entire United States.

I remember riding a local bus on the coastal highway between Biloxi and Gulfport. All the blacks were crowded into the back of the bus, and in front of them there were empty seats. I couldn't understand that. Then the bus stopped and a pregnant black woman got on. There was an empty seat beside me, but she continued past it to the back.

As the bus pulled away, I turned toward the woman standing in the aisle and holding on to a seat back to keep her balance. I stood up and asked her to sit beside me. Instantly, the bus driver hit his brakes and pitched everyone forward as he screeched to a stop.

He was a florid, white faced man with a drooping, tobacco stained mustache and an angry demeanor. He grabbed me by my shoulder and shouted at me, "What the hell you doing, you Yankee, son-of-a-bitch? The darkeys ride in the back of the bus."

When I started to say something in protest, the driver pulled me out of my seat and thrust me forward. Opening the door, he shouted "Get the hell off my bus."

I found myself on the side of the road as the bus thundered away with no idea what had just happened. That was my welcome to the South during the days before the Selma marches and Martin Luther King's "I have a dream" speech and his assassination by James Earl Ray in Memphis, Tennessee. It was a world I was not familiar with, and I felt helpless in.

After that incident, I stayed in the barracks on base or within in walking distance in Biloxi until I completed my electronics course. When I received my assignment to McCord Air Force Base near Tacoma, Washington as an aircraft electronics (avionics) technician, I felt like I was going back home and getting away from an environment I didn't understand, and I was not comfortable with.

McCord was part of the large North American Air Defense (NORAD) command. Established in 1938, the 17th Bombardment Group flew anti-submarine patrols from the base with the B-25 Mitchell Bomber during the Second World War in response to reports the Japanese were going to invade the U.S. Pacific Coast. They did, in fact, drop bombs on a Japanese submarine near the mouth of the Columbia River.

When I arrived at McCord AFB in 1959, it was a member of the Air Defense Command (ADC) protecting the Washington coast during the Cold War with the USSR. The base also supported scientific stations in the Arctic Ocean by airdropping supplies on the drifting ice and the building of the Distant Early Warning (DEW) Line in Northern Canada to detect incoming Soviet missiles and bombers flying over the short polar route.

I was assigned to the Avionics Squadron supporting the many aircraft that flew in and out of the air base. I repaired and installed radios, radars, and navigation equipment on airplanes and helicopters.

Tacoma, on the eastern shore of Puget Sound, was about four hundred miles from my North Idaho family. It rained a lot in that area. Very rarely, the skies would clear and I could see snowcapped Mount Rainier towering to the south east.

The first cloudy summer there, we had a rare day of clear sky without rain on a Wednesday. My commander declared a sun holiday and gave most of us the day off. I drove up to Mount Rainer Park and hiked up the slopes leading to the snowcapped peak. The next day it rained, and we returned to our normal work schedule.

I think the easiest and most boring job in the world would be as a TV weatherman at one of the Puget Sound cities like Tacoma or Seattle. You could just record a session where you say it will be cool, cloudy, and a high chance of rain today, tonight, tomorrow, and the rest of the week, the month, and the year. The station could then play it back daily while you went to the Bahamas for a long vacation.

The comedian Bill Cosby said he visited Seattle one time. While he was talking to a young woman, the sun broke through the clouds. She looked up and said, "What's that?" Then she dived into a sun shelter.

I met my first wife, Roberta in Tacoma. We dated for a short time before we married. Our son, Alan, was born in 1961.

Late that spring, tragedy struck our Miller family for the first time. My younger brother, Paul, was working with Dad on a logging job in Boundary County when he fell under a two tracked bulldozer that was skidding logs to a landing. The operator was unable to stop in time and Paul was crushed to death. I returned to Bonners Ferry for Paul's burial in the Grand View Cemetery above the Kootenai River. I didn't know it then, but that quiet, windswept burial ground was to take many more of my siblings and both of my parents into its bosom.

My second son, Michael (Mike) was born early in 1962. About that time, I was honored as the McCord Air Force Base Airman of the Year. This was followed by my selection as one of the first airmen to be sent to a university to get a college degree followed by commissioning as an officer through the Officer Training System (OTS). I was fortunate to be sent to Washington State University (WSU) in Pullman, Washington in the Palouse Region south of Spokane, which was even closer to my Idaho family than Tacoma.

The Air Force promoted me to staff sergeant and paid for my tuition, books, and living expenses, which included a house on campus, while I was in college at WSU. I enrolled as an electrical engineering major, which revealed the magnificent world of science to me. In addition to the engineering courses, I was able to take nuclear physics, astronomy, spherical geometry, and other courses that opened my mind to the wonders of the universe.

Several events of historical significance occurred while I was at WSU. The Cuban Missile Crisis occurred in October of 1962. The confrontation between the United States and the Soviet Union over Soviet missiles deployed in Cuba played out on television worldwide and was the closest the Cold War came to escalating into a full scale nuclear war.

Then just over a year later, President John Kennedy was assassinated in Dallas, Texas. The rush to judgment Warren Commission concluded that Kennedy was killed by Lee Harvey Oswald acting alone, and Jack Ruby also acted alone when he killed Oswald before he could stand trial.

Through those momentous events, I attended classes year round, including special August sessions, which allowed me to finish my degree in less than three years. I graduated in the summer of 1964.

San Antonio, Texas was my next stop where I completed OTS. Thanks to my prior service and innate ability to score high on tests, I finished second in my graduating class of several hundred cadets. A few years later in my career, that high finish was a factor in my selection as a regular officer in a force at the time largely reserve.

My test scores were so high in avionics and electronics that the Air Force sent me back to Keesler Air Force Base in Mississippi for their electronics officer school. Since I had already been through the airman electronics training and had an engineering degree, I finished the six months course in less than four weeks by test challenging most of the curriculum.

While I was in Biloxi, I enjoyed eating out at some of the local restaurants instead of picking at the bland food served in the base mess hall. Fresh shrimp was a major source of income on that part of the Gulf Coast, as was oysters and salt water fish. Mary Mahoney became a favorite dining place of mine I visited many times over the ensuing years.

After Hurricane Katrina, one of the deadliest and costliest storms to hit the U.S. mainland, decimated the coast in 2005, Mary Mahoney was one of the first restaurants to open for business in Biloxi. I would visit the town just after Katrina with my son, Brian, and his wife, Laura, whose family survived the devastation but lost their cars and home with all their belongings.

Chapter 5
Deadly Old Cape Cod

The assignments office at USAF headquarters wasn't sure what to do with me since I had previous service, an engineering degree, and finished the electronics officer school so rapidly, so they sent me to one of the bastions of Cold War surveillance, Otis Air Force Base on Cape Cod, Massachusetts. I arrived there early in 1965.

The cost of a new home was $14,000 then, although I had no intention of buying one. My military pay as a second lieutenant was about equal to that of a beginning elementary school teacher. A first class stamp was still only 5 cents and a gallon of gas was 31 cents. A new Chevrolet Impala sold for about $3,000, which was above my means, so I was driving a ten-year-old Ford.

Looking back, I realize the only financial instruments I had were a bank checking and savings account. A few credit cards were available, but I didn't have any. Debit cards, personal computers, and the internet were far in the future; a future imagined at that time by the great science fiction writer Arthur C. Clarke, but not yet a reality.

In 1965 the Watts Race Riots broke out in Los Angeles, California resulting in the deaths of 34 people and the onset of racial tensions that persist up to today. President Lyndon Johnson announced the creation of Medicare, the federally funded health program. The Voting Rights Act, guaranteeing African Americans the right to vote became law. The "Bloody Sunday" march in Selma, Alabama, led by Martin Luther King, Jr. resulted in the civil rights marchers being attacked by state and local police with nightsticks and tear gas. *Mary Poppins*, *The Sound of Music*, and *Goldfinger* debuted in theaters. The Beatles, the Rolling Stones, and Tom Jones lit up the music charts.

I didn't know anything about Cape Cod before moving there. I did remember the song Patti Page made famous a decade before:

> *If you're fond of sand dunes and salty air,*
> *Quaint little villages here and there,*
> *You're sure to fall in love with old Cape Cod.*

I fell in love with Cape Cod immediately. Otis AFB was one of the largest bases in the United States at that time. But the waiting list to get into base housing was lengthy, so I rented a house nearby in Buzzards Bay for my family. The cape was the summer home for a lot of North Easterners and the permanent residence for the Kennedy family in Hyannis Port, where they still mourned the loss of John and Robert to assassin's bullets.

I remember going to the seaport of Woods Hole and waiting for the lobster boats to come in. For a dollar I could put on a glove, select a cold water lobster, and drop it in a vat of boiling water. Eating it off a paper plate while the sun set to the west was a gourmet's delight and my first time to really enjoy fresh ocean seafood, which was almost non-existent in Idaho then.

My favorite time on the cape was in the winter when snow covered the ground and whitened the landscape, creating a wonderland of silent beauty. The crowds of noisy tourists that frequented the summer beaches and caused traffic jams on all the roads had withdrawn to their work and family responsibilities elsewhere, and they left the gentle seaside scenery to us local inhabitants.

We were within an hour's drive of Boston, and I quickly fell in love with that city also. Walking its historic streets and visiting its old buildings and museums made me aware of the special place Boston holds in the development of our country: from the harbor where the insurrectional "Tea Party" took place, to the streets where Paul Revere alerted the Continental Forces about the approach of the English army, to Bunker Hill where the "Shot heard round the world" was fired.

The base Special Services gave us free tickets to the Boston Celtics basketball games. I remember going to Boston Garden one night when the Celtics and their Hall of Fame center, Bill Russell, played the Philadelphia team led by the prodigious scorer Wilt Chamberlain. My seat was high up in the nose bleed section, and I had to lean around a pillar to see the game.

Wilt scored 46 points that night and Russell only 19, but he was clearly the better team player, as the Celtics won by 20 points. Late in the fourth quarter, I watched the Celtic coach, Red Auerbach, light up a victory cigar and blow the smoke upward to the applauding crowd.

As the junior officer on the base at Otis, I inherited two dubious assignments: I was the officer who proposed formal toast's for dining-ins, and I was designated as the reporting officer for Project Blue Book, the official reporting, analysis, and evaluation agency for the U.S. government for all Unidentified Flying Objects (UFO'S).

I was assigned to the Avionics Squadron with nearly eighty technicians and support personnel. My commander, Major R, was not a people oriented person. He was very aloof as if communicating with enlisted men was beneath him. The son of a prominent New York City attorney, he went into the Air Force after college as a rebellious act against his father. As a result of his disinterest, I became the intermediary between him and his men.

I related well with the squadron because I had spent time in the enlisted ranks. Officers like me with prior service were called "Mustangs."

The first day at the squadron, First Sergeant K, a grizzled veteran of over twenty years' service, which included several tours in Korea during the war, came by my desk and told me we had a Commander's Call meeting that afternoon. He smiled at the gold bars of a Second Lieutenant on my shoulders and added, "It's at fourteen hundred hours, that's two o'clock for you, Lieutenant."

I smiled back at him, "Thanks Sergeant. And thanks for giving me the time in civilian hours."

K wore the rank of a Master Sergeant on his sleeves, which was five rocker stripes framing a star. Since he was also the squadron first sergeant, his insignia included a square turned on one corner. I looked at his rank and asked him, "What does that square mean?"

K snorted, "I am the First Sergeant."

When he walked away, I heard him whisper to an office clerk, "I always wanted to own a brown bar. Looks like I have one now."

That afternoon, the commander introduced me to the squadron. He told them, "Don't be fooled by the gold bar on his uniform, Lieutenant Miller was enlisted for six years."

Sergeant K, who was sitting beside me, looked at me and shook his head. With pursed lips he muttered, "You son-of-a-bitch, Lieutenant. You put it on me."

"I did," I whispered to him as I looked into his eyes. "And don't you ever call me that again. That's an insult to my mother. Once more and I'll rip some of those stripes off your arm."

"I won't, Sir," he said as he dropped his gaze. "You can count on it."

One Saturday night, I was awakened near midnight by a phone call. When I sleepily picked up the receiver, I heard a husky voice say, "Lieutenant Miller. This is Sergeant Hanson of the Falmouth Police Department."

"Yes," I responded, wondering what he wanted with me.

"We are holding one of your airmen in our jail, Lieutenant." Hanson said. "He was drunk and disorderly."

"Okay," I said. "Who is it and what do you want me to do?"

"His name is Kowalski. We don't want to charge him with anything. We like to maintain good relations with you folks out at Otis. If you'll come down here, I'll release him into your custody."

"Why did you call me?" I asked.

"Well, we have a list of squadron commanders. I called your's and he gave me your phone number. He said he wasn't going to get out of bed for a drunk airman."

There was a cold wind blowing out of the darkness from the northeast and about two inches of snow covered the ground and swirled around my legs when I got out of my car and entered the Falmouth Police Department. Sergeant Hanson escorted me back to the holding cells with a ring of keys in one hand.

As we approached his cell. Airman Jack Kowalski, a short, thin youngster with shaggy black hair, stood up from the narrow bed on the far wall. I recognized him as one of our communications technicians who was on flying duty.

Staggering to the bars, Kowalski shouted at me, "Hurry up and get me out of here, Lieutenant. I got another party to go to."

I turned to Sergeant Hanson. "How long can you keep him?" I asked.

"Well, until nine in the morning," he said. "After that I either have to turn him loose or charge him with something."

"Keep him here and let him sober up," I said as I turned to leave. "I'll be back in the morning."

Monday morning, I gave Airman Kowalski an Article 15, which is a squadron level punishment. My commander signed it without looking at the charges. I didn't fine Kowalski because I knew he didn't make much money and just tried to survive from payday to payday. But I did restrict him to base for a month, and I assigned him to kitchen police (KP) duty for four hours a day for two weeks to be served after his regular duty hours. I also ordered him to get a haircut.

Kowalski was very contrite when I gave him a lecture about making a public nuisance of himself and bringing dishonor to the air base and his squadron. He apologized with tears in his eyes, and my estimate of him increased. He turned out to be one of our best airborne technicians, often volunteering for the two o'clock in the morning block times.

The takeoffs after midnight were the most difficult for the back end equipment operators. It was like they were in a cave during an earthquake with no outside light for orientation while the aircraft pitched and rolled as it struggled to remain on the proper heading and altitude. The airborne technicians had to maintain communications with the aircrew and ground control through all the bouncing around while they stared at blips on the radar scopes to identify airborne threats to the east coast of the U.S. For their hazardous duty, in all kinds of weather and at any time of the day or night, they received just $50 a month flight pay in addition to the normal pay for whatever rank they held.

This was during the height of the Cold War that existed between the USA and its NATO allies versus the Soviet Union and its allies in the Warsaw Pact. Historians commonly refer to the Cold War as existing between 1947 (just after the Second World War) and until 1991 (the demise of the Communist Party in the Soviet Union and the formal dissolution of the USSR under the leadership of Premier Gorbachev).

The two superpowers never engaged in full scale armed combat, but each were heavily armed, which included nuclear capable Intercontinental Ballistic Missiles (ICBM's), bombers, aircraft carriers, submarines, and battle ready armies.

Those of us who were in the military during the Cold War had the around the clock task of monitoring Soviet threats that might result in the exchange of nuclear missiles and the invasion of the United States by foreign air force, naval, and ground forces.

Otis AFB, which was established in 1938, was named in honor of the pilot and prominent Boston surgeon, Lt. Frank Otis. President John Kennedy used Otis many times when he visited the Kennedy Compound in Hyannis. His wife, Jacqueline, gave birth at the base hospital to their son, Patrick Kennedy, who died two days later.

The base was a key Air Defense Command (ADC) base. The major unit, the 551st Airborne Early Warning and Control Wing, had Lockheed EC-121H Warning Star aircraft (the military equivalent of the civilian Super Constellation), which were modified with heavy radio and radar equipment for monitoring airborne threats. Beneath the fuselage, a long oval cover extended several feet down into the wind stream and contained the antenna for the search radar system. Powered by four large engines, the aircraft had to fly at a three degrees nose up attitude just to maintain the altitude of its assigned race track patterns up and down the coast as its radars scanned for airborne threats.

The Russians would fly their M-4 Bison and TU-95 Bear bombers across the North Atlantic and then turn south toward the United States taunting our air defense warning systems. When their radar picked up our reconnaissance aircraft and accompanying armed jet fighters, they would turn around and fly back toward the north and over the polar route to their home bases in the USSR.

I went on a number of the sorties so I would understand the demands put on the technicians and get a sense of the difficulties of the flights. Major R said I shouldn't go onboard, although he didn't order me not to participate. During the entire time he was in charge of the squadron, he never flew a single time.

I got to know many of the air crews personally, and was able to spend some time in a jump seat in the cockpits. That gave me the opportunity to observe the pilots, co-pilots, and navigators as they drove the heavy, clumsy aircraft through the sky.

At times, during takeoffs and landings, and while on the western leg of the racetrack pattern we flew, I could see Cape Cod and the Massachusetts coast.

My favorite time was at night when it was clear; the stars shone brightly overhead and the black surface of the ocean beckoned ominously below. When storms moved into the area, the aircraft became a pitching, rolling nightmare. But we had to fly our missions in good and bad weather. If we cancelled, it left a big gap in the security surveillance protecting the mainland.

Using my training and experience as a technician and an engineer, I gained the respect of the airmen in the back of the plane. I was able to assist them in the operation and maintenance of their electronic equipment. They soon accepted me as their friend and mentor, rather than as an officer who would order them to perform duties the officer wouldn't or couldn't perform himself. Throughout my career, I maintained such a relationship with those who worked for me.

Unfortunately, all the extra weight and the air drag from the antenna radomes made the EC-121 a flying coffin. During the time I was there, three aircraft crashed into the ocean, killing fifty airmen.

The first one fell out of the sky in July 1965 due to a fire in the number three (starboard) engine. Sixteen crewmen died and only three survived. One of the survivors was a navigator who was sucked out of the bottom of the fuselage when the radar dome was torn off by the impact with the water. Somehow, he was able to fight his way to the surface of the ocean and, with two of his plane mates, keep afloat until a sea rescue helicopter could reach them.

When the second plane crashed during its night mission on November 11 (ironically on Veterans Day) of the following year, the young airman I had gone to see at the Falmouth Police Station, Jack Kowalski, was killed along with all eighteen other crew members. None of the bodies were ever recovered from the cold waters of the North Atlantic. Eighteen of the flyers were married and they left behind 40 children and three pregnant wives.

Looking at the schedule, I discovered Kowalski had volunteered

Tales of a Sojourner

for that flight to replace a friend of his who went to sick call. His family, who lived in Worcester, Massachusetts, was notified of their loss by a casualty reporting officer from the base. I followed up a few days later to give them information to file for insurance and benefits for the son they lost.

Stopping at a gas station in the middle of the state, I asked the attendant for the closest route to get me to Worcester. I had been raised in Idaho where I didn't think I had a unique regional speech inflection. Then I went to Mississippi where the locals elocute their vowels; even one syllable words were often turned into two or more syllables. As Mark Twain said, "The educated Southerner has no use for an 'r', except at the beginning of a sentence."

But now I was in Massachusetts where extra syllables in words were dropped for expediency. When I said I wanted to go to Worcester, the young man looked at me as if he couldn't understand what I had said. I pointed the town out to him on my map.

He smiled and said, "Oh, you mean Woosta."

When I knocked on the door of the parents of my lost airman, a thin, dark haired woman wearing a brown calico dress opened it. Her eyes, stained and saddened from crying, looked at me briefly before she dropped her gaze. I was wearing my dark blue Class A Uniform with a black, shiny brimmed cap and carrying a folder of papers in one hand. My appearance seemed to startle her.

"I am Lieutenant Miller, Mrs. Kowalski," I said. "I am so sorry for your loss. Your son, Jack, worked for me. He was a fine young man. I brought some papers for you to apply for his insurance and benefits."

A large, beefy hand grasped the woman by her shoulder and pulled her rudely back away from the open doorway. A short and very wide man wearing dungarees and a white t-shirt thrust his unshaven jaw out at me. "What the hell you doing here?" he demanded. "You killed my son. Leave us alone."

Then he stepped onto the porch and hit me in the jaw with his huge fist. The blow staggered me, and I fell back down the steps, just able to catch my balance on the icy sidewalk before I fell. As I reached down to retrieve my cap from the ground, Mrs. Kowalski hurried down to me.

"I'm sorry," she said. "Our son's death has hit him so hard."

I handed her the folder I was carrying. "I understand," I said, tasting blood on the inside of my lip. "Please fill these forms out and send them to us in the envelope. You are entitled to insurance and benefits."

"We will," she said. "He will calm down after you leave."

Several months later, the air base erected a monument to those brave airmen who had died in that second aircraft crash. Their family members were invited to the ceremony.

I went there that Saturday morning, not sure what to expect. As I stood up while the base band played the National Anthem, I noticed Mrs. Kowalski coming in to the seating area. She was wearing a long, black dress and was accompanied by the heavy-set man who had slugged me at their house. He was wearing a dark suit with a black tie struggling to close the white collar of his shirt around his protruding throat.

The Wing Commander, Colonel James Lyle, gave an inspired speech about the importance of the wing's missions. He said those who died while performing their duty paid the ultimate sacrifice for a grateful country. He then presented each of the next of kin with a United States flag after a lone bugler played Taps; the sad, tearful tune played at the end of each day on U.S. military installations and at funerals of active duty and retired soldiers, sailors, and airmen.

Mr. Kowalski approached me after the service still holding the flag honoring his son. He held out his hand and said, "I am sorry about what happened, Lieutenant. I know you meant well."

Tears stained his eyes as he grasped my hand in a hearty shake. "I know my son died protecting our country."

The last of the EC-121 aircraft to crash was piloted by that Wing Commander, Colonel Lyle, on April 25, 1967. Shortly after attaining their assigned altitude, the crew reported the number three engine was on fire, and they declared an emergency. Later, they reported the loss of the number two engine and were preparing to ditch near Nantucket Island.

At the last moment, realizing they were about to crash on the island, Colonel Lyle turned the aircraft on one wing and cartwheeled it into the ocean preventing carnage on the residents and visitors to the tourist island. Fifteen crew members were killed, but one survived the crash to attest to the heroism of the pilot.

Ten of the bodies from the accident were recovered, including Colonel Lyle's. He was to be buried with full military honors in the Arlington National Cemetery near Washington D.C. Our Base Operations scheduled a C-47 (military version of the Douglas DC-3) to fly his casket to Washington. Passenger seats were assigned to key personnel, including my squadron commander, to accompany Lyle's body and attend the ceremony. Major R told me he had a golf tournament that day and I could go in his place.

We took off Saturday morning in a driving rainstorm. Towering cumulus clouds thrust out flashes of lightning and booms of thunder. I envisioned that the Norse God of storms and lightning, Thor, was angered by us puny humans daring to encroach into his heavenly regime, and he was punishing us by hurling his hammer, *Mjolnir*, through the heavens creating the thunder.

As the airplane gathered itself and bounced off the runway, I looked out the window beside me at the maelstrom thrashing outside. I have to admit I hoped it would cancel Major R's golf tournament.

The twin engine Douglas C-47 was a military transport aircraft developed during World War II. Nicknamed Sky Train, Dakota, and Gooney Bird, it remained in service for many years and became a legend for its airworthiness, especially when it flew "The Hump" from India into China.

Some years later in Thailand, I would personally attest to the indestructible nature of the plane. But on this day I was to witness something I could never imagine in my wildest dreams.

As we climbed up through the storm, flashes of lightning lit up the cabin, the sound of thunder was so incessant it was impossible to talk above it, and driving rain swept across the windows and blanked out the world going mad outside.

All of us passengers were secured with seat and shoulder harnesses, and we were thrown violently against them as the aircraft clawed its way through the tempest. I remember thinking I hoped the Colonel's casket was tied down in the cargo compartment behind us.

Then a brilliant bolt of lightning lit up the interior with a blinding white light followed almost immediately by a deafening explosion from the cockpit area. The interior lights flickered for a moment and then went out. Flashes of lightning created an eerie kaleidoscope of light in the cabin. The aircraft pitched forward and we started losing altitude rapidly.

"We've been hit by lightning," one of the passengers yelled above the reduced noise as the sound of the engines suddenly quit, replaced by the howl of wind rushing past the fuselage and flexing wings.

As we hurtled downward, I was sure we were going to crash. Even though only a few seconds had transpired since the lightning strike, it seemed like an eternity. I was aware of that phenomenon many times over my life; during times of severe mental or physical stress, time seemed to march by at a slower pace.

Then the pilot pulled the nose up and threw us back into our seats as he regained control over the plane. With a sputter, the sound of the engines running again came to my awareness.

"Oh, my God," someone shouted as he pointed toward the front.

I looked up to see a ball of fire roll out of the cockpit's open door toward me. About the size of a volleyball, its bright red center supported a blue halo, which threw off white sparks. It crackled and popped as it spun down the aisle. The strange, whirling object, accompanied by lightning flashes from outside, turned the cabin into a demonic world beyond belief. I stared at the incandescent ball as it passed by me and exploded in a shower of sparks at the rear door housing Colonel Lyle's casket. It disappeared so suddenly it left a void, a vacuum where it had once existed.

"That's Saint Elmo's Fire from the lightning strike," a Colonel sitting across the aisle from me said.

"What is Saint Elmo's Fire?" someone asked.

"Saint Elmo is a patron saint of sailors and aviators," the Colonel responded. "The ball of fire is formed when lightning strikes and builds up a tremendous charge of static electricity. I have only seen it one other time when it hit the metal mast of a sailboat I was on."

"Gentlemen," the overhead speakers blared. "This is the pilot. As you know, we've been hit by lightning. We have regained control of the aircraft. Both engines are operational. Radar shows clear weather ahead, and we will continue on to our destination. Have a pleasant rest of the flight."

The trip to honor and bury Colonel Lyle was the first of several visits I made to the Arlington National Cemetery over the coming years. While there, I viewed the *Tomb of the Unknown Soldier* and watched the changing of the guards, a formal and very impressive event. I also went to John Kennedy's grave and saw the eternal flame that will honor him for time immemorial.

As the wind soughed through the trees and whispered over the graves of thousands of departed military personnel, many of whom died in battles or while performing their country's cold war duties like Colonel Lyle, I thought I could hear their voices wafting in the air as they called out to their comrades and loved ones.

I heard that sound once again years later when I visited the Punchbowl National Cemetery in the extinct Diamond Head volcano in Hawaii where many of the soldiers, sailors, and airmen who died during the Second World War were buried. Although it was a warm summer day on Oahu, I felt a cold breeze that caused me to shiver as I remembered Arlington and those brave men and women who were also interred there.

In addition to my many squadron duties, thanks to being the junior officer on the large base, I had to lead drinking toasts at the formal dining-ins. Wearing a black mess dress uniform with a white cummerbund (sash), I took cues from the base commander and proposed toasts to everyone from the Chief of Staff of the Air Force, to President Lyndon Johnson, to the Queen of England, when we had Royal Air Force (RAF) visitors.

At first, I was nervous and apprehensive about standing up in front of so many dignitaries, but I soon got into the spirit of things—after a few drinks of bubbly spirit. I threw in homages to Walt Disney, Bob Hope, Raquel Welch, and others to the humorous approval of the senior officers, most of whom were heavy drinkers.

My other interesting job was as the base reporting officer for Project Blue Book, the official government reporting agency for Unidentified Flying Objects (UFO's). From 1947 until 1969, the Air Force investigated UFO's from Blue Book's headquarters at Wright-Patterson AFB, Ohio. Over 12,000 reports were received and evaluated.

The first of the modern era of UFO's was reported by a private pilot, Kenneth Arnold, on June 24, 1947, when he claimed he saw nine shiny unidentified flying objects flying near Mount Rainier in Washington State. He estimated they were traveling over 1,200 miles an hour. His description of the objects led the national press to coin the term "Flying Saucer" as a popular term for a UFO.

As I became involved as the Blue Book officer, I was entranced by the concept of extra-terrestrial visitors to our planet. From my incessant readings of science fiction novels since my early teens, and my subsequent science and engineering studies, I was certain interstellar travel was plausible, but probably in the far future. I was to start a life-long study of UFO's that continues today as a member of the Mutual UFO Network (MUFON), which is an American based organization that investigates alleged UFO sightings.

During my extensive research, I discovered that UFO sightings go back many centuries. In 214 BCE (Before the Common Era), the Roman author, Livy, recorded in his writing, *Republic*, that a number of portents were reported as "an appearance of ships had shone from the sky."

In 74 BCE, another Roman author, Plutarch, wrote, "...a huge, body fell between two warring armies. It was like molten silver." According to Plutarch, the silvery object was reported by both armies.

Many other reports of UFO's were recorded by countries all over the world in the ensuing years. In 1897, a tale of a UFO crash near Aurora, Texas and the burial of its alien pilot in the local cemetery was reported by newspapers in Dallas and Fort Worth. I included the occurrence in my novel, *Beware the Abyss*, which was set in that time period.

By the time I became the reporting officer at Otis AFB, Major Hector Quintanilla, had taken over the Blue Book office in Ohio. He was highly skeptical of the thousands of reports that flooded into his office, and he tried to debunk their veracity. Possibly at the direction of his superiors, he claimed they were not a threat to national security.

UFO researchers wrote that Blue Book had lost all credibility with him in charge. Quintanilla's explanations of UFO reports were not universally accepted, and critics—including some scientists—thought Blue Book was engaged in questionable research or, worse, was perpetrating cover ups. This criticism grew strong and was widespread in the 1960's when I took over the base reporting.

During that decade, many UFO reports were forwarded to the Blue Book office. They came from credible witnesses, meteorologist, pilots, and other professionals. Although they received wide publicity, Major Quintanilla determined the witnesses had mistaken Jupiter or bright stars like Rigel or Betelgeuse for UFO's, even though scientists attested the planet and the stars were on the opposite side of the world from many of the sightings.

Most of the UFO sightings in the Massachusetts area were called into the Base Operators at Otis AFB and then forwarded to the Public Information Office (PIO). After I was appointed the Blue Book Reporting Officer, the POI gave me some blank form letters for evaluating and reporting UFO sightings called in to the base. They were then to be signed by the Base Commander before forwarding to the Blue Book office in Wright Patterson AFB.

I was excited to take on the new challenge. I remember during the mid-1950's when our family was sitting at the dining table and were talking about Flying Saucers. Dad got our attention when he said, "If I see one of those, I'll shoot it down with my rifle."

"Oh, Dad," one of my sisters said. "There might be a little Martian in it. You don't want to kill him, do you?"

Dad just smiled and passed another platter of food around the table.

During my first year as the Otis AFB Blue Book Project Officer in 1965 there were many hundreds of UFO sightings reported in the newspapers and on television from countries around the world.

In September numerous reports came from sightings over Exeter, New Hampshire. It would gain notoriety as "The Incident at Exeter." Eighteen-year-old Norman Muscarello was hitchhiking home when he saw strange lights in the woods in nearby Kensington. The lights moved toward him. He panicked, dove into a ditch and, when the lights moved back into the woods, he bolted for a nearby farmhouse for help.

The house was empty so he flagged down a motorist who took him to the Exeter Police Department. An officer went back to the farmhouse with Muscarello and later said he had also seen a flying object he couldn't explain. Sightings came in from others in the area, too.

I would find out later the incident was initially reported to the Project Blue Book office by military investigators from Pease AFB. But before Major Quintanilla could send an evaluation to the Pentagon, Air Force headquarters had already released an explanation to the national press that the Exeter civilian and military observers had seen "nothing more than a temperature inversion or one of five B-47 planes in the area at the time." A definitive answer was never given.

In that climate of official disinterest and high level debunking efforts, and the derision from my own commander, I didn't get very far in trying to evaluate and report UFO sightings. When I spoke to the Base Public Information Officer in his office about contacts from the public, he laughed at me.

"Lieutenant," Captain H said with a wave of his slender hand. "Being a Blue Book Reporting Officer is a bottom of the barrel, dumb shit, don't waste your time assignment. Every base has to have one; that's why we give it to new gold bars like you."

H had a thin, sallow face with skin the color of white parchment. He dipped his head and peered up at me through glasses as thick as the bottom of a Coke bottle that magnified his dark eyes.

"My office gets lots of calls from drunks and publicity seeking idiots," he said. "Most of them...well, really all of them lately, have been so far out in left field I haven't passed them on. If I were to have you fill out a report, the Base Commander has to review it, and he thinks UFO's are a crock of shit. He wouldn't send it on to Wright Patterson; it might come back to bite his ass. The first thing he would do is call me and chew me out for wasting his time. Then he would throw it in his trash can."

So much for me being the first official investigator in history to produce concrete evidence UFO's were real and actually from another planet or solar system. During the next two and a half years, I did not receive a single UFO report from Captain H, although dozens of sightings and alien abductions were given coverage in the local and Boston newspapers.

Project Blue Book would end in January 1970 when the Secretary of the Air Force, Robert Seamans, announced further funding "cannot be justified either on the grounds of national security or in the interest of science." Of a total of 12,618 sightings reported to Blue Book, only 701 were left as unidentified. Those were explained in the final report with the statement, "There has been no evidence indicating the sightings categorized as 'unidentified' are extraterrestrial vehicles."

Do I think there might be intelligent life elsewhere in the universe? I think it is highly probable. Is their IQ higher than a West Virginia coal miner? That's hard to predict. Since our universe began with the Big Bang from a singularity point, smaller than the dot over the 'i' in this sentence just under 14 billion years ago, it has expanded (or inflated as the scientists like to call it) into hundreds of billions of galaxies like (or bigger than) our Milky Way. Each of those far flung galaxies contain hundreds of billions of stars.

The piece of rock with a molten center and snowcapped mountains we call earth took about the last 4.6 billion years, give or take a few nano-seconds, to transition from primordial gases into a semi-solid oblate ball with water in the oceans and oxygen in the air to support the life that evolved from one celled micro-organisms under water to walking, talking human beings wearing computers on our wrists and listening to hip-hop music beamed digitally through the air. So that gives several billion years for other planetary systems to develop before ours. I surmise there are planets out there about the age of earth, some older, and some younger.

A Cornell professor name Frank Drake developed an equation to estimate the number of planetary systems that might support life. (Astronomers and scientists think in equations due to hereditary imperfections in their cerebral cortex, I believe. That way they can communicate with each other and keep the non-Mensa public in the dark and thinking they are smarter than the average bear.)

Just within our Milky Way, Drake came up with a number in the millions. Multiply that by the billions and billions of other galaxies, and the possibility of life elsewhere is truly staggering. Carl Sagan, scientist and host of the popular public television series *Nova*, and the author of *Contact* a novel about earth's first communication with an alien civilization, calculated the number of probable life supporting planets in our universe as large as 10 billion trillion.

With so many out of our world cousins whirling around stars on planets uncountable, why haven't we seen one of the creatures? There have been a lot of people over the millenniums who believe we have been visited by extra-terrestrials, but those reports have been officially placed in unsolved mystery files like Project Blue Book; along with sightings of Big Foot, the Loch Ness Monster, and an adult Billy the Kid.

The answer is so simple we tend to minimize it. The reason why we aren't inviting inhabitants of the Crab Nebulae to our daughter's wedding is it would take so long for them to get the *Save the Date* invitation, figure out which of a billion trillion remote planets it came from, respond with a *RSVP*, and then get their butts (assuming they have butts as a part of their alimentary canals) down here to the church on time.

You see, the universe is so large (and it is getting larger all the time as inflation continues) even the nearest planets that might support life are many light years away. A light year is the distance a beam of light will travel in a calendar year: that's about 6 trillion miles. Most of the universe is empty space, oodles of it, space that would take many thousands of years for a Star Wars type ship carrying a solid entity like extraterrestrial bodies to cross (just think of the frequent flyer miles you could rack up). By the time they got here in response to our invitation, our daughter's 100th great grand-daughter might be of age to marry.

Chapter 6
Land of Fire and Ice

Keflavik, Iceland was my next assignment after Otis AFB in the late summer of 1967. I was moving farther north and deeper into the Soviet Cold War threat zone.

Before I left Otis, the Base Commander, Colonel Robert Helton, called me into his office and swore me in as an officer in the Regular USAF. Until then, I had been a Reserve Officer. He told me it was an honor to give me the rank, and it was based on my service as an enlisted airman, my high placing in Officer Training School, and my performance as an officer since then.

Leaving Massachusetts for Iceland was quite a shock. A large island between the North Atlantic and the Arctic Ocean, Iceland had about 250,000 inhabitants spread around the perimeter of the country, which was over 40,000 square miles. It was the most sparsely populated country in Europe because over 80 percent of the land was covered by deep snow and glaciers the year round. The main industry was salt water fishing, the harvesting of wool from hardy, long haired sheep, and it suffered under freezing temperatures most of the year.

Iceland was settled in 874 AD when Norway explorers, driven by fierce North Atlantic storms, took sanctuary on the land. It was ruled by Norway and Denmark until it became independent in 1918 and a republic in 1944.

Most Icelander's are descendants of Norwegian forefathers, and they inherited the Scandinavian way of family names. Sven's daughters last names were Svensdottirs, and his sons became Svensens. Curiously, when the women married they retained their birth names and did not take their husbands last names, a practice almost unheard of in the United States at that time.

Iceland prospered during and after the Second World War because of their fishing industry. The frigid waters of the North Atlantic and the modernization of refrigeration allowed them to export cod, haddock, lobster, and other fresh seafood to many countries around the world, especially to the voracious market to the south, the United States.

As part of the Atlantic Ocean area of the North American Air Defense (NORAD), the U.S. Navy and Air Force established a dual usage base near the sleepy fishing village of Keflavik about 50 miles from the capital city of Reykjavik.

The Navy flew P-3 Orion sub-chasing aircraft looking for Soviet underwater threats, and the USAF unit I was assigned to as the Assistant Avionics Officer operated F-102 Delta Dagger interceptor jet airplanes, which flew interdiction missions on enemy reported aircraft.

Our unit, the 57th Fighter Interceptor Squadron, also known as the "Black Knights of Keflavik," had a long and illustrious history dating back to the start of World War II. Initially flying P-40 Warhawks, the unit served in combat against Japanese forces that invaded the Aleutian Islands early in the war. The 57th moved to Keflavik in the mid-1950's, transitioning from propeller airplanes to the F-102's, which they operated while I was there.

The base was established during the Second World War by the U.S. Army to defend Iceland and secure north Atlantic air and shipping lanes. During the Cold War era, the F-102 and other fighter aircraft made over 1,000 intercepts of Soviet aircraft in the northern sector of the Atlantic Ocean. Those intercepts, with armed fighters, were credited by government leaders for deterring the Soviet air fleets from continuing further on south, over the Atlantic seacoast, where the aircraft from my previous assignment at Otis AFB prowled in wait.

The Navy managed the base with the assistance of the Iceland Defense Force (IDF). It made for strange bedfellows since we Air Force men (and a few women) were considered tenants: a status expressed by the airmen as "red-headed step children."

I often thought over the next year if the Navy ran their ships the way they did Keflavik Naval Air Station (NAS), I was glad I joined the Air Force. Icelandic Customs officials manned the entrance security gates, which made for some difficult and, at times, hilarious entries and exits for American servicemen and the few dependents who accompanied them.

The year I was there, we had to wear uniforms off base and there was a ten o'clock curfew in Keflavik and the larger capital city of Reykjavik. But, like many soldiers, sailors, and airmen around the world, those in Iceland found ways to avoid arrest after curfew. Private clubs, with liberal late hours, and hotel lobbies and rooms catered to the big spenders from the south, the majority of whom were on unaccompanied assignments without dependents including wives and children.

That meant they were, in the vernacular, Class B Bachelors, which caused Icelandic parents to keep a close eye on their unattached daughters, who sometimes presented them with nearly disastrous consequences: unwanted babies with disinterested fathers who were transferred back to the U.S. on short notice.

The Icelandic women were certainly tantalizing and alluring to the high testosterone military males from the south. Many of them carried the most attractive genes from their Norwegian descendants: long blonde hair, blue eyes, tall statuesque figures, independent natures, and lenient sexual attitudes.

The agreement the U.S. forces had with the Icelandic government then included the requirement that no Black, Hispanic, Asian, or Native American servicemen would be stationed at Keflavik NAS. The Icelandic's were proud of their pure racial background and they wanted to preserve it if they could. Occasionally, minority flyers and sailors touched down at the base, but they quickly continued on to other locations.

As I did at Otis, I requested flight training so I could fly in the TF-102, which was a dual seat trainer version, as an observer. I had to attend a short survival course, which included learning how to eject from an aircraft mockup and how to survive in the frigid waters in the ocean. I was fitted for a "poopy suit," which was a heavy and cumbersome waterproof outer coverage that fit over a flight suit. The frigid ocean temperature almost year around afforded downed pilots only about eight minutes of treading water, even with the suit, before hypothermia shut down their internal organs and interrupted blood flow to their brains, which resulted in unconsciousness.

During one of the first intercepts I went on, I was flying with a young captain with the call sign "Wedge." When I asked him how he had picked up that name, he smiled at me with a twinkle in his eyes and said, "It's the simplest tool known to man. I was last in my pilot training class."

During my assignment to the NASA Apollo Program a few years later, I was given the call sign "Padre" because of an event that would occur on Mauritius Island in the Indian Ocean. I don't think I truly understood the appreciation of peer identification by fellow aircrew members by bestowing call signs until then.

I immediately took a liking to Wedge and his self-deprecating humor. We played together on our squadron softball team. I stumbled around first base and he was the catcher. In the first game I played with him against a navy team, he tagged out a runner storming down the line from third base. The impact knocked Wedge out. As he lay on the ground, our flight surgeon, Doc Rich, brought him to consciousness with smelling salts.

When Wedge came to, he looked up at us standing over him and, as he spit out a bloody, broken tooth, asked with a painful smile, "Is he out?"

Tales of a Sojourner

On my first flight with Wedge, using the aircraft call sign Black Knight 6, we were supposed to fly a routine training mission out of Keflavik over the ocean and then south before turning on a heading that would take us back to the base. Suddenly, our radio traffic was interrupted by ground control.

"Black Knight 6. Acknowledge. Black Knight 6."

Wedge responded as I listened in. "Black Knight 6."

"Black Knight 6. Be advised. Black Knight 3 and 4 responding to ADIZ (Air Defense Identification Zone) threat in sector 72."

"Copy," Wedge responded.

"Black Knight 4 returning to base with engine malfunction. Can you accompany Black Knight 3 on bogie intercept?"

"Roger," Wedge replied. "Intercept coordinates?"

When we received the coordinates, Wedge pulled the stick over and swooped the TF-102 around and thundered back toward the northeast. Off in the distance, I could see a buildup of strata-cumulus and cumulus clouds foreboding a weather front moving down toward Iceland.

As we flew at 20,000 feet just short of afterburner, which would have burned our fuel at a tremendous rate, we closed in on Black Knight 3 and the bogie from the Russian interlopers.

When we approached, I could see a huge lumbering Soviet Bear Aircraft off to our starboard side; contrails churning behind the propellers. The Tupolev Tu-95 was a four engine turboprop strategic bomber. The aircraft had contra-rotating propellers, which made it one of the noisiest military planes ever built. It also had distinctive swept back wings making it easily identifiable by ground and air observers.

Although we didn't know it then, the Bear was so heavy the piston engines were not fuel efficient enough to reach the northeast coast of the United States. We did know their weapons platforms could carry atomic weapons, so we had to be ready to identify, intercept and, if needed, shoot them down short of our country's shores.

Wedge handed me his Leica camera as he increased speed and closed in on the underside of the Russian bomber. I could see the huge enemy aircraft growing larger above us.

"I'm going to swing up on his port side," Wedge said as he flipped his microphone from the Intercommunication System (ICS) to the radio position. "Knight 3, Knight 6 here."

"Roger Knight 6," the response crackled in our earphones. "The bogie has identified me. They will be turning back to Roosky."

"Let's get some close-ups," Wedge said as Knight 3 dropped under the Bear and then accelerated until he was directly underneath.

"Get as many pictures as you can," Wedge said laughing. He added, "We need some new Christmas cards."

I didn't know what Wedge was talking about since I was new to the arena, but I lifted the camera and began clicking. As I looked up from the lens, I could see the Bear looming larger and Knight 3 climbing up until I couldn't see any separation between the two aircraft.

"Wedge," I said. "I thought the international rules of confrontation said we have to stay over four hundred feet from the Russian aircraft." We were swooping up past the Bear at a distance that seemed very close.

"True," Wedge said. "Not to worry. They're used to us buzzing them."

Grabbing the camera, I clicked picture after picture from off the Bear's wingtip of our sister F-102 nestled up against the under belly of the leviathan.

When I looked up from the eyepiece, I saw a strange sight. The Bear had a bubble window just aft of the wings. I could see a man dressed in an olive drab flight suit looking out at me. While I stared at him, he lifted one hand and gave me the international sign of ill will. The Russian had given me "the finger."

I had no idea the photos I took on that interceptor flight would cause repercussions that would echo from Iceland, through our Air Force headquarters in Plattsburg, New York, all the way to the Pentagon and the U.S Senate, and possibly as far as President Lyndon Johnson.

When we landed at Keflavik, Wedge took the camera from me. "I'll get them developed," he said with a smile. "I think we'll have some great Christmas cards this year. I'll meet you at the Whiff. First round is on me."

The Whiff was the Air Force officer's bar. An end room with an outside door at the Bachelor's Officers Quarters (BOQ), where I stayed, had been turned into a saloon with an African motif, which included drums, crossed spears over a dart board, and pictures of lions, tigers, and other animals from the African continent. On a place of honor above the bar was a large framed photograph of Adam Clayton Powell, the black congressman from New York. In a strange twist of irony, Powell looked sternly down over the milling, carousing, and often inebriated Whiff customers. It was ironic because no black servicemen were authorized to be assigned to the Keflavik NAS by the Icelandic government.

In the center of the Whiff sat a low, square table famous far and wide in the Air Force as the "Table of Tits." Under a thick plate of glass covering the table were photos of beautiful women from the *Playbook* magazine. Many of them were centerfolds, but they all had one thing in common: bare breasts with conspicuous nipples displayed tantalizingly under the glass. Visitors who didn't know better would put beer cans and liquor containers on the surface creating moisture circles until they were admonished by elder Whiff members to maintain clear views of the Sistine Chapel of photographs of the luscious flesh below.

Alcohol was plentiful and cheap across the Whiff bar. American beer and Heineken from Holland was a quarter and shots of premium whiskey and scotch was a half dollar. The booze was airlifted in by Navy and Air Force cargo planes from all over the world at a fraction of the cost at the Whiff. Excess profits went into a fund for special dinners and fund raisings.

One of the time honored traditions of the 57th Fighter Interceptor Squadron, as in many Air Force units around the world from the inception of flying squadrons and their unique camaraderie, was an initiation ceremony into the Black Knight fraternity. As a newly assigned officer, I was invited to take part in the rite. Actually, I was ordered to be present soon after I arrived in Iceland by the squadron commander, Colonel Joe Joiner.

Colonel Joiner was a living legend in fighter pilot history. Born in Plainview, Texas in 1921, he graduated from flight school in 1943 and was assigned to the Eagle Squadron in England. Joiner completed his World War II tour credited with shooting down four German aircraft in aerial combat. He had logged over 10,000 flight hours in jet fighter aircraft.

I met him when he called me into his office the day after I arrived in Iceland. When I came to attention in front of his office desk and saluted, he waved at me and smiled as he opened a sealed Mason jar in front of him.

"Sit down, Lieutenant," he said in a thin, reedy voice. "I don't like salutes, do you?"

I didn't know how to respond. I knew of his reputation and was awed by it.

Joiner, a thin man with a large nose that emphasized his pale, blue penetrating eyes, pulled a long, thin pepper out of the jar he had opened, and stuck it in his mouth. Chewing rapidly, he held the jar out to me.

"Jalapeno peppers," he said. "My wife sends them to me from Texas. Can't buy them in this land of ice and fish."

Hesitantly, I declined his offer. I didn't know what a jalapeno pepper was, but it didn't look appetizing.

"I've been looking at your service record, Lieutenant Miller," he said as he pulled out another pepper and chewed on it before he continued. "I see you are a Mustang, and you have an engineering degree. Robert Helton from Otis was a classmate of mine. He put a letter of recommendation in your folder. We are expecting good things of you here at the 57th. You'll be working for Major C in the Avionics Unit. Unfortunately, he is ill with a blood disorder. We sent him to Brooks Hospital in San Antonio for treatment. Until he returns, you'll report to Colonel Mailon Gillis, the Chief of Maintenance. You'll like him, he has a crusty, grouchy manner but, inside, he's just a big teddy bear."

Joiner raised his gaze from the folder in front of him and added with a penetrating look, "You may have to run Avionics for some time. Can you handle that?"

"Yes sir," I responded.

"I'm sure you can," Joiner said as he grabbed another pepper out of the jar and stuck it in his mouth. "Get the hell out of here and go to work."

I stood up and started to salute when I remembered Joiner's aversion to the gesture.

"Oh, Lieutenant," Joiner said as I turned to leave. "We want to welcome you as a member of the 57th at the Whiff. Be in your room at six tomorrow evening. Wear civvies you don't mind getting dirty."

I thought, "Uh, Oh," as I left the colonel's office.

The initiation into the Iceland officer corps of the 57th Fighter Interceptor Squadron took place in the Whiff accompanied by a taped recording of African drums and the sing song ululations of natives. The bar was dark except for a roaring fireplace along one wall casting ominous shadows of the assembled officers chugging drinks and chanting along with the music emanating from large speakers driven by a reel to reel Akai recorder.

When I first entered, I was wearing a blindfold and guided by two officers who had fetched me from my room down the hall.

The acrid aroma of beer, liquor, cigarette smoke, and fireplace fumes overwhelmed me. My escorts held my elbows as they led me into the crazy maelstrom whirling about me. Then they turned me around and sat me down in some kind of metal contraption.

Suddenly, the raucous music stopped and my blindfold was removed, and I stared into Colonel Joiner's pale, penetrating eyes. Wearing his flight suit with a black scarf tied around his neck, he reached above me and pulled down a shoulder harness and fastened it at my waist. Looking down, I realized I was sitting in an old fighter aircraft ejection seat. Beyond the colonel I could see a swaying mass of men, each of them holding a beer bottle or liquor glass high in the air as they chanted meaningless phrases.

"Lieutenant Ken Miller," Joiner thundered at me as he put an ancient leather flying helmet on me. "You have come before this august body of warriors of the 57th Fighter Interceptor Squadron. Are you ready to join them and become a Black Knight?"

"Yes, Sir," I whispered.

Joiner turned to the assembly behind him and yelled, "Do you Black Knights accept this miserable, lowly lieutenant as a member of the greatest fighter squadron in the world."

"No…No…No" thundered from every throat in the dark room.

Joiner waited until the noise abated, then he shouted, "What does this worthless piece of garbage have to do to join this majestic group?"

As if scripted, the men stared at me with eyes widened by alcohol and gleaming in the flickering fireplace flames and screamed in answer, "The Black Glass…the Black Glass."

I tried to remain calm, but I had no idea what they were talking about. All of a sudden, I remembered an article I had read about the Black Hand organization that existed in Eastern Europe prior to World War I. They were responsible for the assassination of the Archduke Ferdinand of Austria and started the war to end all wars World War I (which it didn't of course). I don't know why that thought came to me, but it did. Surely I wasn't going to be killed by a group of fellow American officers because they didn't want me in their elite assemblage.

Colonel Joiner loomed over me and demanded, "Are you ready for the Black Glass?"

I'm wasn't sure, but I think I squeaked, "Yes, Sir."

Joiner held out his hand and someone placed a very large, empty water glass in it. Several officers in flight suits with black scarfs began pouring liquor into it. The first bottle contained vodka, followed by gin, whiskey, scotch, and tequila, until the glass was filled to over flowing. Then Joiner handed the tumbler to a tall, heavy-set colonel wearing glasses who stood beside him. I wasn't familiar with him, but I could read his nametag: Mailon Gillis.

Colonel Gillis passed the glass to another officer who grasped it with a large pair of metal tongs.

The African music began again, and I watched the man with the tongs go to the fireplace and hold the glass of alcohol over the roaring flames. I couldn't believe my eyes as I watched the outside of the glass blacken from the smoke.

Then I heard a voice whisper in my ear, "You have to drink all of it without taking it from your lips. Do it! Then go outside and put your finger down your throat and throw it up. Trust me."

I looked up into the intense blue eyes of a thin, blonde, shaggy haired officer with the two bars of a captain on one of his lapels and the traditional Greek symbol of medicine, a caduceus, on the other.

"Trust me," he said again. "I'm Doc Rich, the flight surgeon."

Colonel Joiner handed me a cloth napkin, and then he took the tongs from the officer who had heated the glass over the fireplace, and thrust the blackened glass into my hands.

I covered my hands with the napkin and put the hot glass of alcohol up to my mouth. As I gulped it, the heat and the smothering odor made me gag, but I finished it and coughed violently. The black smoke discoloring the glass smudged my lips and nose as tears ran down my face.

Turning to the swaying crowd, Colonel Joiner shouted, "Do you now welcome Lieutenant Miller to the Black Knights?"

"Yes...Yes...Yes," came the response.

As soon as I could escape from the welcoming embraces of the squadron, of which I was now an official member, I staggered outside, and with Doc Rich's assistance threw up into a light skiff of snow swirling around and covering the ground.

I don't remember much about the next day after the ceremony. I met the Chief of Maintenance, Colonel Gillis, in his office for his welcoming speech, but I don't recall what he said. I couldn't wait to get back to my BOQ room and crash on my bed.

The snow I had vomited into the night of my squadron initiation was normal for the early fall season in Iceland. Although the sun was still below the vernal equinox, the northeast winds blowing down over the North Atlantic, tinged with frigid Artic air, chilled the island and promised it a long, cold, wet, and icy winter.

Under the surface of Iceland was a churning mass of intensively hot, molten lava from underground volcanoes. In places it bubbled up through raised up-thrust hillocks spewing fire, smoke, and ash into the sky. In other locations it super heated the aquifer water deep beneath the porous earth and provided heat and hot water for the inhabitants to warm their homes and businesses and provide individual showers and community bathing facilities.

The capital city of Reykjavik had several municipal bath houses heated by the underground thermal activity. Covered by glass enclosures like giant hot houses, the steaming units were packed by individuals and families seeking relief from the frigid weather outside.

During my 12-month tour in Iceland, the highest recorded temperature at Keflavik NAS was only 57 degrees Fahrenheit. On the 4th of July, the next summer after my arrival, my squadron played a softball game against a Navy squad. I hit a long, high drive over the outfielders. It was so cold I ran by our bench on the way to first base to get my fur-lined parka. By the time I could get it on and return to the base line, an outfielder retrieved the ball and threw me out.

In addition to the underground heat from the subterranean volcanic activity, the island shook constantly from earth quakes. Many nights I was awakened by the rattle of my bed in the BOQ. The tremors often lasted for several minutes before they quieted with an ominous lapse that promised further agitation.

Several years before I arrived at Keflavik, a tremendous explosion had thrust up thousands of tons of volcanic rock above the surface of the ocean to create the new island of Surtsey just off the main island of Iceland. Named after a fire giant from Norse mythology, the volcano was part of the fissure in the ocean floor called the Mid-Atlantic Ridge.

I was driving my flight line pickup truck on a taxiway one day when Surtsey, now over a square mile in area, exploded with tremendous force. I could see the macadam in front of me begin to roll and pitch from the ensuing earthquake. As I slammed on the brakes, a rift appeared just in front of me. At first it was just a thin line across the taxiway, then it expanded into a gaping maw extending for over ten feet wide. If I had continued, my truck would have dropped into the new crevice.

There has been a lot of debate over the years about Columbus being the first European to set foot in the American continent. Icelandic sagas attribute the historical event to an ancient Norwegian, Eric the Red, and his son, Leif Ericson, who was born in Iceland. Eric's father was banished from Norway for manslaughter and sailed across the Atlantic around the year 970 AD.

Later Eric and Leif journeyed to Greenland, south by southwest of Iceland. Traditional tales related later they went all the way to the modern day country of Newfoundland, which is part of today's Canada.

The oldest seat of democracy in the Americas was established in Iceland at Tingvellir. The parliament was set up in 930 AD and remained there until 1798. Now a national park, it is one of the main tourist attractions in Iceland.

The country didn't have a lot to offer visitors. Over 80 percent of the island is covered year round by snow and glaciers. The shaggy haired local sheep, raised for meat and wool, and the plentiful cold ocean fish and crustaceans provided most of the income for the country during my tour. I remember a debate in the legislature about either paving one of the main island roads or building a battery factory; there wasn't enough money in government funds to do both.

Early in December during a heavy snow storm I received an order to report to Colonel Joiner's office. When I entered, Wedge and another officer, Lieutenant J, the pilot who flew his F-102 beneath the Russian Bear aircraft while I took photographs, were already seated in front of the commander.

Joiner, normally laid back and calm, was red faced and livid. He picked up some cards from his desk and threw them down forcefully. "What the hell were you thinking?" he shouted. "You stupid assholes violated every rule of international air space. Then you made it a national issue by putting the photo on Christmas cards."

Wedge leaned forward over the colonel's desk and picked up several of the cards. He handed me one. It was a color picture of an F-102 nestled up against the belly of a Russian Bear. The inscription in bold script read, "Merry Christmas from the 57th Fighter Interceptor Squadron, Keflavik, Iceland."

"Do you know where I got these cards?" Colonel Joiner demanded.

After glancing at J, Wedge nervously responded, "No, Sir."

"General Smither from Plattsburg," Joiner snapped. "In case you have forgotten, he is the commander of 10th Air Force. He got them from the Air Force Chief of Staff at the Pentagon. Someone sent them to him anonymously. How many copies have you idiots sent out?"

Wedge took a deep breath and replied, "Quite a few, sir. We didn't know it would be so negative."

"Negative!" Joiner stormed. "Negative! I'll be lucky if it doesn't cost me my career. Smither has asked me to retire."

Then turning to me, Joiner said, "What the hell were you doing, Lieutenant Miller. I know you were using the camera. J's tail number is readable. I looked at the scrambles that day. You were in the right seat with Wedge, weren't you?"

"Yes sir," I said. "I was."

"So you took the picture?"

Before I could reply, Joiner stood up and turned his back to us. He looked out his floor to ceiling window at the driving snow outside. Silence descended on the office for a long moment before the colonel turned to face us.

"Okay," he said, his face softened but his eyes narrowed. "We can't undo what's been done. I want every card that hasn't been sent out on my desk this afternoon. You are on my shit list. From this day on, every drink I have at the Whiff will be on your account. I hope you all have wealthy uncles, because it is going to cost you. Now get the hell out of my office."

Colonel Joiner continued as our commander; it was hard to fire a fighter pilot who was also a war hero. As the year wound down, the fervor over the infamous Christmas card died down. Unfortunately, every month when I got my bill from the Whiff, there was an added charge for liquor I hadn't consumed.

When I first checked into the BOQ, I was given a room with a hallway that abutted at my entrance door. My windows were covered with heavy papers taped down. When I asked the reason, I was told that during summer, the long days of light had to be dimmed so the room was dark at night for sleeping.

The building was about a hundred yards from the mess hall. When I checked in, I noticed there were several ropes strung at shoulder level from the quarters to the dining room. I didn't think much of it at the time. Then, when the heavy snows of the Iceland winter set in, I realized the ropes had a purpose. It was hard to see into the black swirling maelstrom of a North Atlantic blizzard and get your bearings. You had to grab one of the ropes to stagger to and from the mess hall.

One night, about three o'clock in the morning, I was awakened by a thunderous crash. As I tried to understand what was happening, it came again; a loud bang. I thought someone was throwing a hand grenade against the wall.

I opened the door and stared out at a strange sight. Arrayed against the wall of my room were bowling pins. Looking up, I could see two men holding bowling balls. As I watched, one of them drunkenly rolled his ball down the hall missing most of the pins as it impacted into my wall.

I later found out the two had stolen the pins and the balls from the bowling alley next to the mess hall and set them up in the hall by my room. It was one way the members of the squadron fought off the cabin fever depression brought on by the long, dark nights and weather so bad the aircraft were often grounded for days at a time.

Fortunately, the Russians also avoiding flying into the treacherous winds and inclement weather. The Arctic Circle ran through Iceland not far from Keflavik. During the depth of the winter, the sun had to fight its way upward to bring three or four hours of twilight to the base before it sank below the horizon again in defeat.

The Whiff stayed open 24 hours a day. If a volunteer bartender wasn't available, everyone just helped themselves and jotted down their purchases in a notebook. Loud music fed by reel tapes blared from the floor speakers around the clock.

The music library selections were reflective of the diverse backgrounds of the officers: Peter, Paul and Mary, Johnny Mathis, The Beach Boys, and The Rolling Stones came from the West Coasters; Frank Sinatra, Barbra Streisand, and Tom Jones from the East Coasters; James Brown, Aretha Franklin, and Ella Fitzgerald from the upper Mid-Westerners; Elvis Presley, Willie Nelson, Johnny Cash, and Merle Haggard from the Southerners and Westerners; and The Beatles represented those embracing the English music invasion.

My room was just far enough away from the cacophony blaring from the bar so I could sleep at night, although it was difficult to know the hour of the day without a clock. I stayed in my room reading many evenings. I think I went through every book in the Whiff library and most of those from the Naval Station library.

I tried to maintain a normal schedule at the Avionics Unit during the many non-flying days due to the horrendous winter weather. Major C. reported in briefly from his hospitalization in Texas, but had to return because of recurring headaches.

I had all the airmen (we didn't have any women assigned to the unit) who worked for me report for duty every weekday in proper uniform. We cleaned up the maintenance areas until they shined, and I kept them busy studying for their proficiency exams. After reviewing their records, I told each one who was near to a promotion I would ensure they received it if they maintained good work habits and a positive morale.

Wedge was a frequent Whiff visitor that winter. Like the other pilots, he was chaffing like a fish out of water to get his aircraft into the air and swoop to the North and intercept the Russian bombers.

I walked in the bar one morning to get some coffee before reporting to the Avionics Unit and found Wedge passed out on the floor. When I lifted him up and deposited him on a sofa, I could smell liquor on his breath and clothes.

Wedge woke up and stared up at me, "You know," he said weakly. "I used to think an alcoholic was someone who had a drink before lunch."

He hiccupped and went on, "Now I think it's someone who has a drink before breakfast."

Finally, the dark nights began to diminish as the sun crawled higher seeking to fulfil its annual domination of the southern sky. Although it didn't warm up much, the increased light brought with it a surge in the attitude and energy of the members of the 57th Fighter Interceptor Squadron. Colonel Joiner returned from leave in his home state of Texas and immediately took charge.

The Whiff was put on restricted hours: noon to midnight. The pilots and support officers were called into daily planning meetings to meet the anticipated increase in activity of the Russian Bear and Bison incursions into the North Atlantic area. As our fighter aircraft leaped into the air on their spring interceptor missions, an electric attitude infused the squadron officers and enlisted men. It was like being released from prison after a long sentence.

As daylight came up earlier and earlier each day and blasted light into my room's windows, I appreciated the foresight of the man who preceded me in taping the windows with heavy paper to dim the glare.

In addition to the work load picking up in response to the Russian bomber incursions, the longer days afforded opportunities to see some of the interesting places on the small island. I was able to rent an apartment on the base for a few weeks and brought my wife, Roberta, and my young sons, Alan and Mike, for a visit. We toured the adjacent fishing village the base was named for and the ancient site of Parliament, Tingvellir, and viewed some of the massive glaciers that dominated the landscape.

Thanks to the squadron's first sergeant, Williams, I also discovered a golf course north of Keflavik near a radar station named Rockville. The course was rather crude with fairways often encroached on by old lava flows and the rough putting surfaces by shaggy, slow moving sheep. One of the holes was a dogleg around large fish drying racks. Huge Cod and Haddock hung from overhead poles, twisting in the constant winds. As the weather warmed up, getting above freezing on most days, the stench from the fish, many of them rotting from neglect, was overwhelming at the tee area.

Sergeant Williams had played the course several times, and he told me long hitters could carry their balls over the racks and cut the par five distance down to make it an easy birdie hole. Of course I had to try it. I never saw my ball again. It came down somewhere in the middle of the fish. I didn't even try to go into the smelly racks to find it.

A few months later at the summer solstice on the 21st of June, the 57th FIS had a midnight golf tournament at Rockville. The midnight sun is a natural phenomenon that occurs when the sun is visible at all times. We had a shotgun start where each threesome teed off at different holes exactly at midnight, with the sun peeking over the horizon as a red glowing orb.

As it turned out, Sergeant Williams and I started out at the fish drying racks. I didn't try to carry them this time, turning and hitting down the fairway to the left side. Williams took the hero route and lost his ball forever to the fish gods protecting their departed progeny rotting in the wind.

The long hours of daylight during the summer made it difficult to sleep, even when my room was darkened, because it was so bright outside. Doc Rich said the perpetual light caused hypomania, which is characterized by irritable moods. The interminable winter darkness causing bad moods seemed to have a devil for a companion during the summer; incessant light.

Wedge's infectious devil-may-care attitude got him into serious trouble one Saturday afternoon. A visiting soccer (called football in every country but the United States) team from Norway was playing the national Icelandic team near Reykjavik. Air space around the capital was off limits to our military flights because of the busy commercial airplane traffic.

Wedge was certainly aware of the restriction that day when he launched into the sky for a test flight on one of the F-102's that had just undergone periodic maintenance and an engine change. His flight plan called for him to turn east as he gained altitude and then fly several racetrack patterns over the ocean while he checked out the engine, fire control, and avionics systems using a standard checklist.

The weather was rare for a late spring day with bright sunlight dimmed only slightly by high cirrus clouds. Wedge told me later, after he finished the checklist, he didn't want to return to base because of the beautiful weather. After the long, dreary winter, he said he was feeling his oats.

Whatever his reason, he increased the distances on his circling turns and flew higher and higher. During one of the legs going south, he looked out to the right and saw the tiny football field near Reykjavik far below.

In addition to AIM-4 Falcon air-to-air missiles, the F-102 carried an ADM-20 chaff dispenser pod. If threatened by enemy radar guided rockets, the pilot could eject tiny strips of aluminum foil from the chaff pod into the trailing airstream to camouflage the radar signature of the aircraft and, hopefully, divert the rockets fired at it.

On that fateful Saturday, Wedge carried a full load of chaff and, as he looked down at the international arena and the packed spectator stands, he decided to test the pod's capability. The next time he made a turn and headed south, he checked the wind direction and reduced his altitude. At the appropriate time he pressed the chaff dispenser eject button and filled the sky with thousands of tiny pieces of metal that glittered in the sun.

I later read an English translation from the Reykjavik newspaper account of the "Attack From Heavens Cancels International Match." As the chaff, twisting and roiling in the air, and reflecting the light of the sun, descended upon the players and spectators at the football match, pandemonium reigned. By that time, Wedge's aircraft was far from the area as he darted back to Keflavik Air Station and no one could hear or see the source of the foreign objects covering them.

Other than a few military spectators who knew what chaff was, the tiny objects frightened everyone because they didn't know if they had been covered by some strange contamination from outer space. Women, children, and even several men fainted and had to be revived by medical personnel.

It didn't take very long for the chaff to be identified by Icelandic authorities and the probable source identified. I was in the debriefing room with Wedge while he reviewed his flight test results when Colonel Joiner stormed in and threw everyone out but Wedge.

As Wedge said a few hours later with his B-4 bag over his shoulder as he stopped by the packed Whiff to say goodbye, "The shit hit the fan, and I was the fan."

Before he left, Wedge handed me a rolled up magazine. After he left in a jeep heading at high speed toward an aircraft waiting with engines idling impatiently to take him to 10th Air Force Headquarters in New York, I opened the magazine. Surprisingly, it was the latest *Playboy* issue.

Playboy was the holy grail of magazines to the men at Keflavik isolated so far from their wives and woman friends. Unfortunately, a subscription was mostly a waste of money. To get to their post office box and into their hands, *Playboy* had to swim through the shark invested waters of the magazine's distribution sites, then into the U.S. Postal Service system, which dumped it into the Fleet Post Office (FPO) military mail system. From there it went into the world-wide Navy distribution system and eventually would be put on a Navy ship or aircraft headed to Iceland.

If it arrived at the remote island, *Playboy*, with its colorful and obviously tantalizing cover, would be handled by numerous sorters before being put into a small numbered mail box. The chance of it ever arriving at the subscriber was infinitely small; it had to pass through too many greedy, sexually stimulated hands. During the year I spent in Iceland, I never heard of a single copy arriving as ordered.

How, I wondered did Wedge get a copy; not only a copy, but the latest one? Then I recalled him telling me his wife, a high school teacher in North Carolina, sent him magazines she pasted inside the cover of *Life Magazine* to make sure he received them.

As I looked through the *Playboy*, I realized it was time to replace some of the old pictures on the Table of Tits. I sure had some great candidates.

A few days later one of the married pilots who rented an apartment off base in the town of Keflavik so his wife could join him, Major W, came into the Whiff with a concerned look on his face. Doc Rich, who frequented the BOQ bar but rarely drank, called W over and asked him what was upsetting him.

"Well, today Alice and I have been married for five years," he said.

"Great," Doc Rich responded. "You should be happy, an anniversary and a beautiful wife waiting for you outside the gates."

"That's the problem; the gates," W said.

"The gates? Why are the gates a problem?"

"Alice wants a steak for dinner tonight," W said. "I'm over my quota for meat."

"Ah, I see," Doc Rich said.

The station gates were manned by a combination of Icelandic locals, Navy, and Air Force security personnel. As part of the status of forces agreement between the United States and the host country, there was a restriction on certain items that could be taken off the base into the local area. Liquor was very controlled because it was so cheap on the station compared to buying it on the economy. Another highly limited item was beef. Iceland's sole four-foot animal was the long haired sheep. Beef had to be brought in from other countries and was very expensive for the locals. Also, the Icelandics wanted the Americans to buy the products they harvested from the surrounding ocean: fish and lobster.

To control the egress of the limited items, every serviceman who lived off base was assigned a monthly quota. Once that was exhausted, and detailed lists were kept, the guards would confiscate the forbidden items. Untold number of bottles of liquor and pounds of beef were taken by the guards and disappeared into their private homes.

By this time, everyone in the Whiff had gathered around Doc Rich and W. "Anyone have a card for beef?" Doc Rich asked.

None of us did. Since we all resided on the base, we were not authorized to take out quarantined items.

"She wouldn't be satisfied with a cold water lobster?" someone asked. "They are really good here."

"No," W said. "She has seafood allergies."

"Okay," Doc Rich said. "We'll have to come up with some way to smuggle a couple of steaks out. Anyone have any ideas?"

A number of proposals were offered and rejected as unsuitable. One was to load the steaks in a cannon and shoot them over the perimeter fence to W as he waited outside. Another was for W to wrap them in leak proof paper and sit on them as he went out the gate. But he said he had tried that and it didn't work.

Finally, Doc Rich spoke up, "I have an idea."

Turning to me, he said, "Ken. Take some money out of the kitty. Go to the commissary and buy two of the best steaks they have and bring them back here."

"Okay," I said. "What are you going to do?"

"Just get the steaks," Doc Rich said. "Leave the rest up to me."

When I returned with the meat wrapped in butcher paper, Doc Rich was sitting next to W with his medical bag on his lap.

W was a husky man with wide shoulders and an unusually large head for a pilot. His helmets had to be custom made to fit him even though he kept his hair sheared into a crewcut.

Doc Rich reached into his bag and removed a bandage roll. He told W to lean over, and then he put the butcher paper covered steaks on the top of his head and wrapped them around and around with the bandage. When he finished, W looked like a Hindu Swami with a white turban, the steaks camouflaged under the strips of cloth.

"What do I tell them at the gate?" W asked uncertainly.

Doc Rich handed him a slip of paper. "Give this to them," he said. "It's a prescription for headache medicine. I wrote you suffered an injury when you got out of your airplane, slipped, and hit your head on the wing."

W left with all our best wishes lingering after him. He walked awkwardly as he tried to keep his head from moving and dislodging the steaks.

Did W make it out the gate unimpeded? No, he didn't. By the time he reached the gate, the steaks had begun to warm up from the heat from his head and blood seeped down over his eyes. Aghast at the sight, the Iceland guard panicked and called the station hospital.

Fortunately, Doc Rich had anticipated the call and was in the hospital when it arrived. He jumped in an ambulance and, after swearing the technicians aboard to secrecy, sped to the gate with sirens blaring. He took W out of his car and put him in the ambulance.

With sirens still wailing, W arrived at his off-base apartment and, after a comforting word to Alice, proudly snatched the steaks off his head and strode inside.

Colonel Joiner, in addition to being a World War II Ace, was one of the early pilots selected for an Air Force aerial performance team, the forerunner to the present day Thunderbirds. When the Navy scheduled an annual station open house day for the Icelandics, he volunteered to put on an air show with the F-102's.

I was standing outside the Avionics building with several technicians on the day before the open house was to take place. Joiner had selected six of his best pilots to perform in the show, and they were practicing their maneuvers over the main runway. One of the highlights of the show was the low altitude scenario of two aircraft hurtling at each other at a high speed. At the last split second each pilot would put his plane on one wing and they would narrowly miss each other.

Unfortunately, on that practice maneuver one of the pilots, a young captain who I played with on the squadron softball team, was flying a few hundred feet above the runway when, suddenly, his plane nosed down and impacted the macadam runway in a horrendous explosion, killing him instantaneously.

I watched in horror as the Navy and Air Force emergency vehicles sounded their sirens and sped toward the accident site. A board of inquiry would later find pilot error as the probable cause of the fatal mishap. That finding was difficult for us to accept because the pilot, who was only 28 years old, was one of the most skillful aviators in the squadron.

Over a year later, after I left Keflavik, I heard that pathologists who examined the pilot's remains reported the young man had a myocardial infarction (a medical term for a heart attack). They said it may have been brought on by the tremendous gravitational forces from the air show maneuvers, but they couldn't determine that for sure.

As my tour of duty in Iceland came to an end, I anxiously awaited transfer orders to my next assignment station. When I received them, I couldn't believe what I read. It was a dream come true: I was to be assigned to an Air Training Command (ATC) unit at Patrick Air Force Base, Florida near the Kennedy Space Center in support of NASA's Apollo Program. The day the first human stepped foot on the moon was drawing near, and I would be a part of it.

Chapter 7
Giant Leap For Mankind

Patrick AFB was located near Satellite Beach and Cocoa Beach, Florida with the Atlantic Ocean to the east and the Banana River to the northwest. Just to the northeast Cape Canaveral housed the operational sites for NASA's Apollo Program Saturn 5 rockets at the Kennedy Space Center (KSC).

Cocoa Beach was famous as a filming site for the 1960's TV sitcom, *I Dream of Jeannie*, starring Barbara Eden and Larry Hagman. They used the space program as a key background element in the series. It was also noted as a favorite motel and saloon hangout for servicemen and civilians supporting the Apollo Program and newsmen and women covering the event as well as space groupies and tourists hoping to catch sight of one of the astronauts.

The Apollo Program was the third NASA spaceflight program. It was preceded by Project Mercury, which put the first American, Alan Shepard, in space less than one month after Russian cosmonaut, Yuri Gagarin became the first human to rocket into space in April of 1961. The second program Project Gemini, which carried a two-astronaut crew, flew low Earth orbit missions between 1965 and 1966. It put the United States in the lead during the Cold War Space Race with the Soviet Union.

Apollo gained impetus after President John Kennedy announced a national goal of "landing a man on the Moon and returning him safely to the Earth" by the end of the 1960's.

I arrived at Patrick AFB in the fall of 1968 assigned to Field Training Detachment (FTD) 326K. The "K" denoted Keesler AFB, Mississippi the headquarters for the FTD unit of two officers and ten enlisted personnel. The unit commander, Major Nathan (Blackie) Blackwell became my mentor and good friend. Since we were such a small unit, we became a close-knit team as we worked long hours and traveled worldwide in support of Apollo.

After a year in Iceland I had to buy an automobile. A new car cost over $5,000 so I bought a six-year-old Dodge Dart. Gas sold for 34 cents a gallon. The median house was about $26,000, but I was able to move into the Patrick AFB housing right away. We had a comfortable and roomy two-bedroom unit about two miles from my FTD building.

In the 1960's we didn't have satellites overhead to provide data and voice communication for the Apollo Program. NASA developed a global ground system with sites in many countries and territories. However, since most of the world is covered by oceans, there were large gaps in coverage. NASA in partnership with the USAF developed a fleet of aircraft to cover those limitations. Twelve EC-135N's (Modified Boing 707's) were built and assigned to Patrick AFB. The Apollo Range Instrumented Aircraft (ARIA) could receive both voice and data information and record it for transmission to the ground systems.

My FTD had the task of training the ARIA technicians who operated and maintained the avionics systems in flight and an airborne mission coordinator with the task of coordinating between the technicians, the pilots and navigators, and the ground stations. Using simulators and aircraft our instructors trained twelve Air Force crews for their flight duties. Our FTD group became the thirteenth crew, available to assist the regular crews as advisors if needed, which required us to travel to the orbital launch areas and on around the globe.

After the Apollo capsule, consisting of the Command/Service Module and the Lunar Module, was launched into a 110-mile earth orbit, it then had to be propelled into a trans-lunar path to take it to the moon. Unfortunately, the minimum energy trajectory point was over the Indian Ocean. Like a rock from a slingshot, the capsule had to be launched at precisely the correct point to take advantage of its orbital speed to head toward the moon.

The ARIA would launch from Patrick AFB and fly racetrack patterns over the ocean below the Apollo capsule to gather voice and data at the exact instance it left the grip of Earth's gravity. Once the Apollo capsule left for its journey to the moon, the ARIA would travel on around the world to assist in the Apollo Command Module recovery near the Hawaiian Islands. The sorties were long, very demanding on the crews, and absolutely essential to the success of the manned lunar program.

My first trip was in support of Apollo 8 where the astronauts Frank Borman, Jim Lovell, and Bill Anders spent Christmas Eve in 1968 circling the moon with no intention of landing. To celebrate the holiday season the astronauts read from the Bible's *Book of Genesis*. They ended the message by wishing everyone a Merry Christmas.

It was on that ARIA support mission I was given the call sign "Padre."

Our Indian Ocean departure point the day Apollo left the earth's orbit was on Mauritius Island. The island, an area resort location for Africans and Australians, had a tropical climate with clear warm sea waters, attractive beaches, and tropical fauna and flora. A former British Territory about 1,200 miles off the African coast, Mauritius had declared their independence a few months before our two ARIA crews arrived, and the locals, English and French speaking, were still in a festive mood. They welcomed us American visitors with open arms, open bars, and Christmas celebrations featuring their sega music and fresh ocean seafood.

We stayed for three nights in the finest resort on the island. It was managed by a very personable Englishman, named Howard, who made sure we had a great stay. "You certainly must beat those rascals the Russians to the moon," he told us when we arrived.

His comment reflected the attitude of most people in the countries and territories we visited during the Apollo days. Everyone thought we were in a race with Russia to be the first to set foot on the lunar surface. It was understandable because of the success Russia had with the Sputnik and Yuri Gagarin's orbital flight.

However, the truth wouldn't be known until after our successful Apollo 11 flight. The Russians did not have the technical capability to put a man on the moon and return him to earth. They had rockets with tremendous lift capability, but they lacked the avionics, computer technology, and mission management and support to successfully complete the project.

That's where NASA and its many military and civilian support groups succeeded where the Soviet Union failed. We had the "Right Stuff" as depicted in Tom Wolfe's book about the development of our space program.

The night before we were to depart, Howard threw us a party, which included dinner, a stage show, and music and dancing. I wore black slacks, a white mock turtle neck sweater, and a black Nehru jacket. The jacket, popularized by the Prime Minister of India was a hip length tailored coat with a mandarin collar. It was a popular fad during the 1960's, and one I liked to wear because it was so comfortable and did not require a tie, which I've always felt was too restrictive.

Howard, spotting me with the Americans as I entered the dining room, came up to me and grasped my hand in a warm embrace. "I did not realize you Yanks had an Anglican Padre as part of your crew."

I suddenly realized I must resemble a man of the cloth, and I tried to blend into the crowd. But it was too late, all the ARIA officers and airmen had heard Howard's welcome. The rest of the evening I tried to downplay it, but whenever they came up to me, they addressed me as Padre.

After we launched into the Indian Ocean the next day, I put the previous evening's festivity behind and concentrated on the mission. We had about a three-hour flight to get into position to contact the Apollo astronauts. I was talking to one of the technicians who was working on a defective radio when I heard the overhead speaker call my name.

"Lieutenant Miller, this is the captain."

I picked up the intercom and responded to the pilot's request. My words were broadcast on the cabin speakers.

"Padre," the pilot said. "ARIA 3 and our crew would like you to lead us in a Christmas prayer."

I realized that not only was I on our aircraft's speakers, but I was on our sister ARIA's speakers. I hesitated a moment, then recalling the many times I had given impromptu dining-in toasts at Otis AFB, I offered a prayer for the success of the crucial Apollo lunar orbital mission and for the safety of the ARIA aircraft and their crews.

From that day on, my call sign was "Padre" and I would have to say a prayer every time I flew. The acceptance into the ARIA brotherhood was certainly easier than my initiation into the Black Knights of Iceland.

We were scheduled to spend several days in Hawaii supporting the recovery of the Apollo 8 Command Module after it came back from the moon's orbit. However, as we cruised over the mid-Pacific we had engine trouble. The captain alerted us to the problem and, after repeated attempts to correct it, announced we would have to make an emergency landing on Wake Island about 2,300 miles from Hawaii.

An unincorporated territory of the United States, the coral atoll, which was shaped like a crab, had a coastline of only 12 miles. The day after the Japanese attacked Pearl Harbor on December 7, 1941, they struck a small Marine aircraft squadron based on Wake and destroyed eight of their twelve F4F Wildcat fighters. Several Japanese landing attempts were repelled.

When the American commander on Wake was asked by his superiors if he needed anything, he replied in a famous World War II aphorism, "Send us more Japs."

When our ARIA landed with its malfunctioning engine, there were only a few hundred people on the island who supported the airstrip, which was used by the U.S. military and some commercial cargo planes without long range fuel capability. From one of the crab legs, you could see all the way across the inlet to the other leg.

There was a small commissary near the control tower, which carried a meager supply of consumables. We landed about ten in the morning; by sundown, we had exhausted all the store's supply of beer, liquor, and foodstuffs that didn't require cooking.

We weren't sure how long we would have to stay on Wake since a replacement engine had to be flown in from Hickam AFB in Hawaii. We were hoping it would only take a day or so.

Unfortunately, four long days filled with fitfully sleepless nights and frayed nerves on the island passed before a C-130 aircraft arrived with the new engine. By the time it was installed and we were able to take off for Hawaii, Wake was on short rations, desperately awaiting re-supply. The regular inhabitants plus our ARIA group had depleted all the alcohol, most of the consumables, and a large part of the fresh water available. As we boarded our aircraft for departure I looked back to see a group of the island regulars lift their hands and give us the international sign of ill will, their middle fingers.

Ill fortune also plagued one of our ARIA flights when we were supporting the Apollo 11 launch. After leaving Patrick AFB in Florida, we were scheduled to fly to Johannesburg, South Africa for a stopover before continuing to the rendezvous with the capsule's trans-lunar firing over the Indian Ocean.

As we neared the west coast of Africa, we had an engine malfunction that forced us to make an emergency landing at the Luanda, Angola airport. We didn't realize it until after we touched down, but Angola was in the throes of a civil war.

A Portuguese territory at that time, Angola was in the middle of its "Colonial War" where insurgent groups threatened to overthrow the Caetano regime and force independence from Portugal. The day we landed, a heavily armed rebel army stormed the national airport. Just as we taxied up to the control tower, it was taken over by the insurgents and small arms and mortars impacted all around us. The ARIA captain frantically called on his radio for assistance from the local American embassy when he realized the dilemma we were in.

I think the only thing that saved our aircraft from being damaged during the firefight was the United States flag prominently displayed on the vertical tail surfaces. As we waited for a response from the embassy, the pilot had to shut down the engines to conserve fuel. In a matter of minutes, the cabin temperature climbed to unbearable levels. We opened all the outside doors, but didn't want to put down the egress stairs because we could still hear small arms fire.

Over an hour went by with no response from the embassy. The ground war still raged outside, although we couldn't see much through the small fuselage windows. It was so hot in the aircraft we had to strip down to our shorts. Even then, sweat poured off us from the enclosed heat and the fear of being targeted by the rebel armed force.

Finally, the captain came on the speaker, "The hell with this," he said. "We're going to get out of here. We'll have to do it on three engines. Let's dump everything we can get by without out the door."

Then he added, "Padre, we will need a special prayer from you."

As we taxied away from the war-torn terminal with the air conditioning finally lowering the temperature, the pilot accelerated with one dead engine. After we lumbered up into the humid, heavy air, I uttered a prayer into the intercom system. The aircraft shuddered, banged, and creaked from the overload on the remaining engines as it barely cleared the high rise buildings at the end of the runway.

After we were able to reach a cruising altitude over the African continent, the captain came back on the speakers, "We can maintain this altitude and heading. Johannesburg has a high runway, over 5,700 feet. We don't have any alternate landing sites. We're going for Jo Burg. I can't guarantee a smooth landing, so hang on folks. But what the hell, it's not Angola."

"It's not Angola," became the mantra for our ARIA crew. No matter how difficult things got after that, "It's not Angola" lessened the tension.

Many years later, I talked to one of the technicians who was on that flight. Now retired, he told me he was facing a cancer operation, and he was frightened about the consequences. "But, what the hell," he said. "It's not Angola."

Johannesburg originally inhabited by the ancient San people, was eventually taken over by the Dutch Boers early in the 19th century. After gold was discovered in 1884 nearby, the population exploded. When our ARIA arrived in 1969, laboring with three engines toward the high altitude landing, the city was the largest in South Africa. Thanks to the consummate skill of the aircrew, we were able to land safely and taxi to the terminal.

When we arrived at the Hillbrow Hilton Hotel in our sweaty, reeking flight suits we received a warm welcome from the manager and his staff, all of whom spoke English. Like the residents in Mauritius, they thought we were in a race with the Russians to the moon.

That evening, after we had a few hours to shower, change clothes, and rest, the manager hosted us with a dinner attended by city dignitaries including the mayor and some of the city's civic and business leaders. I wore a shirt with a tie and a sport coat instead of my Nehru jacket. I didn't want to have to bestow any blessings on sinners or christen any new born babies.

During an informal cocktail hour after the dinner, which included impromptu speeches from the visitors and the ARIA pilot, a young woman came up to me. She said she was on the mayor's staff. She had come from England for a vacation ten years before and stayed to marry a local businessman in the banking industry. She was very knowledgeable about the Apollo Program. When I asked her how she knew so much about it, she told me her father was a professor at a university in England and he wrote science articles for the London Times.

Before I could respond, she looked at her watch and said, "My, I must get home. My husband and little girl are awaiting me."

I asked her where she lived, and she pointed out the window down the hill and said, "Oh. Only a few kilometers."

When I asked her how she was going to get home, she smiled and said, "Why I will walk of course. It is not far. Walking is something we Africans do."

"It's dark out," I said. "Aren't you worried about your safety?"

"Oh no," she said. "Why would I worry? We have apartheid. No black would dare to touch me."

That was my introduction to the apartheid system of racial segregation that existed in South Africa then. Apartheid was an Afrikaans word meaning "the state of being apart," literally "apart-hood." It was a system of racial segregation in South Africa enforced through legislation by the National Party (NP), the governing party from 1948 to 1994.

Under apartheid, the rights, associations, and movements of the majority black inhabitants and other ethnic groups were curtailed and Afrikaner minority rule was maintained The majority of the residents were black but their human rights were curtailed by the white minority.

I found out that if a black was to accost that woman as she walked home authorities would round up and arrest numerous suspects and their families, including children, and jail them. They could be held in squalid prisons for years without formal charges. The court system wouldn't even be aware of them, since they didn't recognize the protection of habeas corpus, which existed in the United States and many other countries of the world.

It wasn't until 1990 that the president of South Africa started efforts to prohibit apartheid, which culminated in the multi-racial election that elevated long time prisoner Nelson Mandela to the presidency.

As I walked the streets of Johannesburg the days after our arrival, I saw evidence of the demeaning aspects of apartheid. When a black man or woman approached me on the sidewalk, they would not look at me, and they would turn and walk out in the street rather than pass close by me.

One afternoon, I was having lunch at a café while reading a pocket book when I met the woman who told me I ate like a Yankee. That chance meeting with her and her husband, because of a fork and a book, resulted in me making new friends in South Africa. Their son was a guide with a safari company, and I was able to go with him on a safari near Krueger National Park. While I didn't have a license for large game, I was able to shoot ducks and pheasants for the camp larder. After two days I had to cut my trip short to return to my Apollo duties for our takeoff from Johannesburg.

We were about to take part in one of the most momentous events in human history: the landing of the first men, Neil Armstrong and Buzz Aldrin on the moon. Our ARIA was flying further into the Indian Ocean to provide airborne voice and data support for the mission.

We made our rendezvous with the astronauts, whose call sign was *Columbia*, high overhead. They had been launched by the powerful Saturn V rocket from Kennedy Space Center on July 16. As they fired the onboard rockets to send them on their three-day journey to the moon, we successfully recorded crucial voice communications and data. Then we flew on to Australia where we dumped the information to one of NASA's world-wide ground stations for analysis at the Houston Space Center.

The astronauts included Michael Collins who would remain in lunar orbit while Armstrong and Aldrin, using the call sign *Eagle*, sat down in the Sea of Tranquility in the Lunar Module on July 20, 1969.

President Kennedy's challenge to the American space program was finally realized the next day when Neil Armstrong radioed his famous saying, "One small step for man, one giant leap for mankind," as he exited the Lunar Module and stepped into the dust of the moon. After staying on the surface for just over 21 hours, Armstrong and Aldrin lifted off and rendezvoused with Collins for the return voyage to earth.

After a short stay in Perth, Australia, our ARIA continued on around the world to assist in the recovery of the astronauts near the Hawaiian Islands. When we finally returned to Patrick AFB, our weariness was replaced by euphoria as we realized what had been accomplished. The world, except for the Russian federation, was acclaiming the historic event of Americans traveling over 280,000 miles into space, setting foot on the moon, and returning safely to earth.

But there was little rest for the fatigued because Apollo 12 loomed in November. The second lunar landing with Pete Conrad, Richard Gordon, and Alan Bean, was scheduled for an Ocean of Storms touchdown.

I didn't think I would be involved, but the ARIA commander requested I fly with them. I had established a good relationship with the aircrews, the technicians, and the mission coordinators. They all wanted me to accompany them. I'm not sure if it was because of my technical expertise, or because they wanted the "Anglian Padre" aboard for impromptu prayers. Whatever the reason, I packed up and boarded the EC-135 when it left Patrick AFB.

When we returned from the successful mission, we had a brief respite before the ill-fated Apollo 13 with James Lovell, Jack Swigert, and Fred Haise blasted off toward the moon in April of 1970. Our ARIA was soaring toward Hawaii after our rendezvous with them over the Indian Ocean when we heard the lunar landing was aborted when an oxygen tank exploded, which crippled the Service Module.

Despite great hardship caused by limited power, loss of cabin heat, shortage of potable water, and the failure of the carbon dioxide removal system, the crew, thanks to their own ingenuity and the rapid response from the ground engineers, returned safely to earth.

Their heroic and near fatal mission was memorialized in the major Hollywood film, *Apollo 13*, directed by Ron Howard and starring Tom Hanks, Bill Paxton, and Kevin Bacon.

There had been a lot of consideration given by NASA to skip the number 13 for that mission because of the negative connotation of the number, but they decided to go with it. Judas was the 13th participant with Jesus at the Last Supper, and he was the one who betrayed Jesus.

Years later, I would learn the Chinese also had a number they avoided: four. Their explanation was that four in their pronunciation sounded similar to the word for death. Many hotels in the Far East skipped the 4th floor and airplane seats and rows jumped from three to five.

I also supported the third lunar landing of Apollo 14 in January 1971. By then, I had spent precious little time at home with my family. When I wasn't flying around the world on the ARIA missions, I was training mission coordinators and assisting with the airborne technician's preparation. The long hours and the travel took a toll on my marriage and resulted in separating from my wife. Unfortunately, my sons Alan and Mike were caught up in the maelstrom, something I have regretted ever since.

Apollo 15 was scheduled for launch in July 1971, but I received orders to report to our FTD headquarters in Keesler AFB, Mississippi that spring, where I met Carolyn Wetzel who was to become my second wife. She was the daughter of a legend in Biloxi, Percy Wetzel.

Percy was a large, very strong man who back in the 1930's hit five home runs in a coastal league baseball game. He turned down an offer from the New York Yankees to join one of their minor league teams during the depression because they wouldn't pay him enough to get him to leave his home and family. Percy became a career city employee and a story teller of the first order.

After a short tour at Keesler AFB, I was transferred to Lowry AFB, Colorado where I was assigned to teach a mid-level officer management course. Before I went into the classroom, I received promotion to captain and was sent to Montgomery, Alabama for a six-week Squadron Officer School (SOS).

I remember looking up at a large sign above the airport when I landed that read, "Cradle of the Confederacy." The lingering effects of the Civil War died hard in the south.

At SOS, Colonel Robin Olds, a "triple ace" with a combined total of 16 aircraft shot down during World War II and the Vietnam War, was the graduation speaker. A bigger than life hero with a large dark mustache, Olds had been a college football All American and a Hollywood celebrity after he married actress Ella Raines. He was regarded by his peers as the best wing commander in Vietnam for his air-fighting skills and his reputation as a combat leader.

The conflict in Vietnam—it was never congressionally declared a war—had been in the daily news for the past few years. But I had been so involved in the Apollo Program, I hadn't paid it a lot of attention. I did know fellow servicemen who had been sent to the small Southeast Asian country. When they returned, they seemed distant and disillusioned.

One B-52 bomber pilot who was assigned to the ARIA wing told me over drinks at the officer's club, "It was like fighting a ghost. We dropped bombs on suspected Viet Cong cells, but they disappeared into the jungle, and all we killed were women and children working in rice paddies."

Colonel Olds, who was on his way to become the Commandant of Cadets at the United States Air Force Academy in Colorado, said something at the SOS graduation that had a lasting impact on me,

"Never once, during my tour in Vietnam was I ever told by my superiors that we were there to win the war."

I couldn't believe what he said. How can you go to a war half-way around the world against Communist aggressors with no intention of winning it? I was about to find out, up close and personal.

When I returned to Lowry AFB in Colorado after the Squadron Officer School, I taught a systems management course to officers from throughout the Air Force. The syllabus I was given to teach from was about ten years old, and the practice examples were extracted from old Cold War scenarios, which involved NATO (North Atlantic Treaty Organization) forces in opposition to Soviet incursions into Europe and the Americas.

After several days of following the trite lesson plans, I deviated from them. The haunting memory of Colonel Olds' statement about the lack of clear goals from high ranking officers and politicians and the ominous echoes of daily Vietnam reports, mostly about battle losses to both American and ARVN (Armed Forces of Viet Nam) forces, bothered me. Instead of using the prepared syllabus, I offered some of my own. In one of them, I asked the class to address the reason why America was involved in the conflict in Vietnam.

The consensus replies supported the "Domino Theory" espoused by President Lyndon Johnson and his advisors: if we didn't stop the communist threat by the North Vietnamese, who vowed to unite the country, other nations in Southeast Asia might fall under their influence; perhaps even Indonesia and Australia. After that, the far country of the United States could be vulnerable.

Needless to say, my classroom discussions became very animated and vocal as the students were caught up in the furor of the day's events. Many of them, after returning to their units, were expecting assignments to Vietnam, so they had a personal interest in the dialogs.

Several days later, I received a summons to report to the school commander before my class started. I had anticipated the request, since several times during the loud responses from the students in my class, the hallway door had opened and one of the commander's assistants stuck his head in to see what was causing the uproar.

The colonel lectured me on sticking to the tried and true course syllabus. "They have served us well," he said. "We don't have the budget to change them every time a new instructor comes in with wild ideas that causes disruption."

"My ideas aren't wild, Sir," I said.

The colonel cocked his head to one side as I spoke to him. His secretary had told me he was nearly deaf in one ear, but he was too vain to wear a hearing aid. I'm not sure why he was so sensitive about his appearance, his long swarthy face reminded me of the horse who played in the television series *Mr. Ed*.

"We are in the middle of an unpopular war in Vietnam, and many of the students are facing assignments there," I continued. "I know the Cold War against the Russians is a concern, but we should encourage discussions about a war that is going on right now. We should bring in guest speakers who have been over there to share their experiences with the students."

Then I repeated what Colonel Robin Olds had said in his speech at the SOS graduation about the lack of clear goals for American forces involved in the Vietnam War.

The colonel turned his head straight and stared down his nose at me. "I won't tell you again, Captain," he stormed. "We have a very limited budget, and I intend to adhere to it. We certainly don't have funds to fly in and put up guest speakers. Your classes have become loud and unruly. Get back to the approved course prospectus."

I thought for a moment, and then I said, "And if I don't, Sir?"

"Young man, you either follow my orders or I will have you transferred immediately."

"I'll take the transfer then, Sir," I responded. "I would like to go to Vietnam."

"I can't believe you want to leave a cushy training assignment in Colorado to go to that God forsaken country," the colonel said. "If that's what you want, you got it."

The colonel buzzed his secretary and had her place a call to officer assignments at Randolph AFB in Texas. Before I left his office, I had verbal orders to prepare for immediate transfer to the 377th Air Base Wing at Tan Son Nhut Air Base in Saigon, Vietnam.

Chapter 8
Evening of Pale Sunshine

The Vietnam War, as we Americans called it, was known in that country as the Resistance War against America. It actually began back in the 1950's when Dwight Eisenhower was president. American military advisors were sent to what was then French Indochina. U.S. involvement escalated the following decade, under Presidents John Kennedy and Lyndon Johnson, with increasing army boots on the ground and the introduction of massive air power.

The country was renamed Vietnam and partitioned into opposing forces from the North, supported by the Soviet Union, China and other communist allies, and the South supported by the United States and other allied countries. The armed forces from the North consisted of the Viet Cong (a guerrilla group) and the North Vietnamese Army (NVA), a regular army force.

The U.S. government viewed our involvement as a way to prevent a Communist takeover of South Vietnam and the further spread of communism throughout Asia and possibly into the Americas. In retrospect, that was never the intent of the North Vietnamese government. When they toppled the U.S. backed South regime in the fateful spring of 1975 and unified the country under the communist flag, they never ventured outside the country, content to be a single nation after generations of warfare against foreigners. But we didn't know that in the late fall of 1971 when I reported for duty at the huge Tan Son Nhut Air Base.

Disillusionment with the war by U.S. military and political leaders due to rising death tolls and violent protests at home had led to a gradual withdrawal of American forces as part of a policy known as "Vietnamization." The vast superiority of American weapons, including high performance fighter aircraft that ruled the skies, and B-52 saturation bombing was unable to stem the incursion into the South by the Viet Cong and the NVA.

Tan Son Nhut stayed awake 24 hours a day. As the outlying United States air bases closed or were transferred to the South Vietnamese, the aircraft retained by our Air Force and Army relocated to the Saigon base where they continued to fly bombing and air cover missions over the Ho Chi Minh Trail, Cambodia, Laos, and throughout South Vietnam. Sorties north of the DMZ (Demilitarized Zone) separating the two countries had been curtailed during ongoing peace talks.

The U.S. Secretary of State, Henry Kissinger, brought his secret Paris discussions with the North Vietnamese out of the closet and into the open with his ill-timed comment, "Peace is at hand." That statement further divided Kissinger and South Vietnamese President Thieu, who violently opposed the unilateral peace efforts. In an attempt to placate Thieu and ensure the continuance of the Paris negotiations, the Pentagon accelerated the transfer of arms to the South Vietnamese weapons arsenal under a newly titled Vietnamization program called Project Enhance. In addition to aircraft and helicopters, they turned over tanks, artillery pieces, trucks, and armored personnel carriers.

The sky over Tan Son Nhut thundered day and night with the sounds of aircraft arriving and departing at 30 second intervals. The ground below hummed and throbbed with the sounds of vehicles, radios, phonographs, tape machines, and thousands of voices babbling in English, Vietnamese, French, and Korean.

Rotating beacons and searchlights flashed through the sky and mixed with the lights of the hundreds of airborne aircraft to form a kaleidoscope of color that dominated the hours of darkness. At ground level, the florescent and incandescent lights flooding the streets, runways, taxiways, perimeter fences, and security areas and pouring out of the restaurants, stores, bars, clubs, libraries, living quarters, hangers, and other work areas turned the night into livid brightness. The energy produced by the giant air base stayed at a frantic level regardless of the clock or the calendar.

I was assigned a small Bachelor Officer's Quarters (BOQ) room with a narrow cot, a small desk and chair, and an open closet. Two of the walls faced the outside and were made of horizontal wooden slats running from the ceiling to the floor. Set at an angle, they provided an opening between each board. Screen wire nailed to the outside of the slats acted as a minor deterrent to mosquitos and the many other flying and crawling creatures that infested the tropical location.

While the slats provided some ventilation for the room, they let in more sound and light than fresh air. Bright street lights next to the building bathed the room in narrow yellow bands, diffused by the dirty screen and the particles of dust swirling in the air. A pulsating roar from the noise outside buffeted the screens and clawed its way through the openings.

The noise, the lights, and the oppressive humidity made it almost impossible to sleep. I could see why many of the officers assigned these quarters spent what little non-work time they had at the Officer's Club, which never closed, or downtown in Saigon, which offered black market goods, loud music, air-conditioned sleeping rooms, cheap liquor and drugs, and even cheaper sex.

I had several pair of camouflaged fatigues and some civilian clothes the mamasan assigned to my room kept washed and ironed. For ten dollars a month she also kept the room clean and shined my boots and shoes. She was the only benefit I could see for staying at the BOQ.

We never communicated verbally because I couldn't speak Vietnamese and she didn't speak English. That was okay with me because I didn't want to look at her rotting teeth, stained dark red by the betel nuts so many of the older Vietnamese were addicted to.

The Avionics Squadron I was assigned to was about a half mile walk from the BOQ with the Officer's Club on the route. I would stop there in the mornings for breakfast and, on the way home in the evenings—often late at night—for dinner.

Avionics was a large, single story building with offices along one wall and a vast open space in the center for maintenance consoles, repair benches, and equipment storage. Facing one of the bases main runways, the noise level from aircraft outside and the whine and hum of the maintenance equipment was extremely high throughout the day and night.

We had a complement of over a hundred enlisted technicians and their supervisors, and four officers. There were two lieutenants assigned plus the major who commanded the squadron when I reported for duty.

One of the lieutenants, Ken Brown, became a good friend. After he left Vietnam, he separated from the Air Force and moved to Denver, Colorado to work with his father in real estate. "I thought I'd make a career out of the military," he told me before he departed just a few months after I arrived. "But a year in this hell hole has burned me out. The first thing I'm going to do in Colorado is sleep for a week."

It didn't take me long to discover what Ken was talking about. We operated on two 12 hour shifts a day at a frantic pace. Before Project Enhance began, all the aircraft based at Tan Son Nhut could have been parked in the revetments or hangers for security from air and ground assaults. Now, over 500 planes occupied the space previously used by less than a hundred. F-4 Phantoms, OV-10 Broncos, AC-47 gunships, A-12 Avengers, C-7A Caribous, and C-130 Hercules crouched impatiently on the open macadam, momentarily resting before leaping skyward again on missions around the clock supporting the beleaguered ARVN and U.S. forces under attack from the expanding NVA and Viet Cong forces pouring down the Ho Chi Minh Trail.

The war was coming ever closer to Saigon, and I could sense a growing desperation in the American and Vietnamese men and women I worked with.

The avionics building was a cool sanctuary compared to the flightline where we had to trouble shoot systems and remove and replace failed units. Most of the outside work was done with external power, which meant there was no air conditioning inside the aircraft and temperatures often climbed over 120 degrees in the sweltering heat.

My shift often stretched far beyond twelve hours as our workload skyrocketed with the expanding aircraft fleet when more outlying bases were closed as the draw-down for Project Enhance accelerated. Maintaining communications, radar, and aircraft guidance systems that failed at rapid rates in the hot, humid country sapped the men's energy and morale. I found myself at times falling back on my technician experience from my enlisted days, and I pitched in to help repair malfunctioning aircraft and units.

The major in charge of the Avionics Squadron spent most of his time in his office, rarely leaving it during the day shift he worked. Rumors circulated around the work area that he kept liquor in his desk and spent most of his time drinking. As soon as I reported in, he told me he wanted me to attend the daily Chief of Maintenance meetings held at eight o'clock each morning.

"I would go," the major said, not looking at me. "But I'm a short-timer."

Short-timer, I thought. What the hell does that mean? Do short-timers not have to do their job?

One of the strange developments in assignments for American servicemen to Vietnam was the one-year required tours. Everyone was given 12 month deployments and then returned stateside. As a result, hardly anyone came and left at the same time. As I walked around the work area, I saw many pictures posted on cubicles, work benches, and walls. Some of them were pictures from Playboy or family photos. But most of them were an outline of an attractive, and noticeable naked, woman.

The drawings (Called DEROS calendars for Date Effective Return Overseas) were divided into pieces like a jigsaw puzzle: 365 of them. As each day passed, the owner would color or shade in one of the days. Some of them were nearly clean while others were almost colored in. Whoever the talented artist was who came up with the calendars, he also had a sense of humor. Days 363 and 364 were the model's nipples and 365 was her pubic area. I realized the airmen were all obsessed with one thing: reaching the calendar model's vagina meant they could return home.

The Chief of Maintenance, Colonel L, was in charge of all the logistics support in the air base wing reporting to the Wing Commander. The maintenance and supply squadron commanders reported to him. I had not met him before going to his first daily meeting. He had a large conference room that was crowded and noisy when I walked in with charts provided to me by the Avionics senior supervisors. A large padded chair with armrests sat open at the head of the long table with an overhead transparency projector on the other end. I found an open chair along one wall.

Suddenly a side door opened and a tall, heavy set colonel wearing wire rimmed glasses strode in. The room instantly silenced as everyone came to their feet, the sound of chairs scraping on the floor.

"Take your seats," the colonel rumbled in a voice that sounded like a bull frog in a swamp at night calling for his mate.

The meeting started with the various commanders giving status reports on their activities using the projector, which flashed the charts on a wall screen. After each presentation, Colonel L asked sharp questions, often deriding the presenter with caustic comments. The Supply Squadron commander, a major with graying hair, came under special fire from the colonel.

When the major finished his report on shortages and requisitions status, Colonel L did something that shocked me. He stood up and threw the pen he had been making notes with on the table and berated the major with some of the worst language I had ever heard. In essence he said we were fighting a war we could lose because of diminishing supply support and he wouldn't stand for it. He expressed himself in negative epithets about the supply commander's heritage that would start a fight in any officer's club in the world.

I was scheduled to follow the supply officer with the avionics report, and I wasn't looking forward to it. We had many repeat malfunctions on aircraft avionics systems that had caused aborted flights. I wasn't familiar enough with the reporting system to defend it.

Then, before I could walk to the projector, the side door opened again and a thin, elderly woman with a narrow pale face and neatly styled gray hair glided into the room. Her feet were covered by a dark blue full length dress.

Colonel L stopped ranting and sat down as the woman whispered something in his ear. Then she turned and glided out through the open door, closing it behind her.

I found out later the woman was L's secretary. She had been with him for over ten years and seemed to be able to quiet him down with her gentle voice.

The colonel picked up his notepad and pen, and as he stood up, rumbled in a lowered voice, "Meeting is adjourned. We just lost a C-130 and a chopper over An Loc. The wing commander wants to see me."

For the next Chief of Maintenance meeting, I was better prepared and was able to weather Colonel L's caustic and filth laden comments.

A few days later I met the colonel in the hallway of his building. As I approached him, I smiled and said, "Good morning, Sir."

Colonel L stopped abruptly and, staring through his glasses at me, said "What the hell do you mean, good morning, Captain. This is not a God damn good morning. Never again say that to me."

The days went by in an exhausting blur. It was hard to rest in my noisy and bright BOQ room. Some nights I was lucky to get three or four hours of restless sleep. Our workload only increased with time while our manpower decreased. It seemed like every day several technicians and supervisors were derosing, as they called it, and many of them were not replaced. Our petitions for additional personnel fell on deaf ears at the Chief of Maintenance and Wing Commander's offices. Project Enhance meant we had to do more with less.

Meanwhile the North Vietnamese were increasing their forces south of the DMZ. One of the reasons for the incursions was that support for the war waned in the U.S. congress and from President Johnson who would refuse to run for a second term because of his frustration with Vietnam. As a result, B-52 bombing sorties of the Ho Chi Minh Trail decreased drastically.

This was the first war in American history where the president micro-managed the armed forces. Johnson had models of Vietnam battle scenarios built in the White House, and he would move miniature aircraft, tanks, and soldiers around like a child playing war. Then he would tell his Chief of Staff of the Armed Forces how he wanted the forces in Vietnam to proceed.

We received so many conflicting orders from halfway around the globe it felt like "Catch 22." If we followed the president's orders, which didn't fit the local scenario, it seemed as if we were crazy. But if we didn't, we would be disobeying the president, which would certainly label us as crazy. The local air and ground commanders didn't know if they were coming or going, and they were afraid to question the ridiculous orders coming from the Pentagon. They were damned if they did, and damned if they didn't.

Almost two months after I arrived, I went to the Chief of Maintenance meeting and was briefing repeat avionics write-ups to Colonel L. One F-4 had failures of its UHF (Ultra High Frequency) radios used for air to air and air to ground communications four flights in a row.

"God damn it, Captain," Colonel L stormed, his voice rising like the sound of an approaching typhoon. "I have a Magnavox television at home. Every day for the past three years it worked when I turned it on. How the hell can a fucking radio fail four days in a row?"

I turned around from the wall projection and stared at the colonel. I was weary from the daily work pressures and the lack of sleep. I should have heeded Mark Twain's advice when he said, "It is better to keep your mouth closed and be thought a fool than open it and remove all doubt."

All of a sudden, I removed all doubt about me being a fool. "God damn it, Colonel," I shouted back at him.

Every eye in the crowded room turned toward me in astonishment. No one had ever spoken to the colonel like that.

"Give me your Magnavox TV," I continued through my clenched teeth. "I'll put it in the nose of an aircraft that rolls over rough taxiways in 110-degree heat, then takes off with 4 G's as it climbs up to freezing weather while juking around to avoid ground fired rockets. It will throw that TV of yours around as it dives down to drop bombs before pulling up with 5 G's. Then it will return for a hard landing to avoid getting hit from behind by other airplanes low on fuel or battle damaged wanting the runway at the same time. When it taxis up to me, I'll remove your damn TV and take it into your office and see if it still works."

When I finished ranting, all eyes turned toward the colonel, expecting the wrath of God to strike me.

Colonel L stared at me silently for a moment, then he took his glasses off and wiped them with a tissue. Finally, he said quietly, "Who's the next briefer?"

After the meeting was over, Colonel L said he wanted to see me in his office. As the other officers exited, I could hear them snicker at me as they looked away. I thought about what I had said, and I was sure my military career was over.

"Captain Miller, sit down," Colonel L said to me from behind his desk. He waved at a chair across from him.

"When was the last time you had a day off?" he asked, his voice lowered almost to a whisper.

I hesitated for a moment, and then answered, "I took a week leave before I came over here."

"That's what I thought," the colonel said as he removed his glasses and massaged his nose. "Today is Friday. Go to the BOQ, shower, and get out of those miserable fatigues. I don't want to see you until Monday."

He smiled, the first time I had ever seen him do that, and continued, "Get off Tan Son Nhut and go into Saigon. It used to be called the 'Pearl of the Orient.' Only three hundred thousand people lived here in the early sixties before we got involved in this ridiculous war. Now there are over three million. Most are country folk from all over Vietnam and Cambodia. You have to understand these people are not the same as us Americans. They have never known anything besides war, which has made them a nation of refugees, beggars, and thieves. Plus, their religion takes care of them. I once asked a Vietnamese reporter, who worked for our public relations department, why he drove his motorcycle out into traffic without looking. His response was, 'Buddha take care of me.' When I told him I had seen people run over and killed, he just said, 'Buddha take care if I die.' Either way they are covered."

"I heard on the radio," I said. "The North Vietnamese and the Viet Cong have surrounded Hue."

"Yes," Colonel L responded. "It's like being in the eye of a cyclone here in Saigon."

"I thought we were winning this war," I said. "Just before I left the states, Henry Kissinger told the press the Paris peace talks were going well and a settlement would be signed in a few weeks."

"Since this non-war started," the colonel said, "the State department and the military have painted rosy pictures about what is really happening over here. The papers have reported the South is 98 percent pacified. Jesus, it isn't safe to walk a kilometer during the day or one hundred meters at night outside any city or village perimeter."

Colonel L paused and wiped his glasses with a tissue before going on, "Saigon hasn't had a major attack since Tet '68, but our time is coming. We wonder why General Giap is striking now when he could wait another year or two when most of the Americans will be gone, thanks to the assholes in Washington, but he always does the unexpected. He's a great military strategist, much better than either the French or the Americans have ever had over here. He fooled the

French at Dien Bien Phu in 1954. They scoffed at reports his troops were hand carrying cannons over the mountains until the shells started raining down on their outposts and command center. Then they took down their flag and surrendered in traditional French fashion, with dry powder and much pomp and circumstance."

I looked at Colonel L with renewed respect. He was talking to me as an equal, not as a colonel to a captain who had just disrupted his morning meeting.

"Vietnamization, balderdash," the colonel continued. "We can equip their soldiers through Project Enhance, but we can't give them or their leaders the will to fight. The generals stay here in Saigon so they can profit from the black market and curry favors from President Thieu's family. We can't train them in our sophisticated ways of killing. Oh, we can use Pavlovian rewards to get them to push color coded buttons, but these gentle people are first generation technicians and pilots. They haven't progressed past the cognitive stage of learning. They can mimic, but they can't originate or improvise actions. Jesus Christ! Vietnamization be damned. It is an exercise in futility, like Don Quixote jousting with windmills."

He looked at me and added, "This war can destroy even us, if we let it. Captain Miller, don't let it destroy you."

"I don't think it will, Sir," I said.

"No, I don't think it will," Colonel L said quietly. "Get the hell out of here for a while and recharge your batteries. You are too valuable to us to lose. I've read your record and heard from your senior NCO's and airmen. I know you are a mustang. You're doing a great job. I wish we had more like you."

The colonel smiled and added, "All I ask is take it easy on me at the morning meetings. You are right, my fucking Magnavox TV wouldn't last one sortie on our aircraft."

After I left the colonel's office, I met Dick Castle who was a civilian tech rep for General Electric engines installed on many of our aircraft. Dick was in his third year in Vietnam, and he lived off base with a Vietnamese woman. A short, broad man with sandy hair, shiny white teeth, and a wry smile on his face most of the time, Dick and I had become casual friends.

When he saw me, Dick, who had been in the morning meeting, came up to me and said, "Well, is it Mr. Miller now, Ken. I really enjoyed seeing you throw the spear back to the Chief of Maintenance. You've got the biggest balls on the base."

When I assured him I was still employed by the Air Force, and the colonel had told me to get off the base for a few days, Dick smiled and said, "Wonderful. I'm having dinner tonight at eight with a few friends at the La Cigale. It's the best French restaurant in the country. Come join us."

When I agreed to meet him, Dick gave me a business card from the restaurant printed in French, English, and Vietnamese.

On the way to the BOQ I saw Lieutenant Willis, who was the pilot of the F-4 I had to brief the four-time radio repeat write-ups on, walking up to the Officer's Club. I stopped and talked to him. When he told me he was flying again late on Sunday, I asked him to not put an entry into the aircraft forms if the radio failed again. I told him I would meet him when he landed and he could tell me of any problems.

After I promised Willis two drinks at the club he agreed to hip pocket any discrepancies. At least I wouldn't have to face Colonel L with a five-time repeat on Monday morning. I knew we were going to have to ground the aircraft and checkout the wiring system, but I was hoping to delay that until it was due periodic maintenance in about ten flight hours.

I dressed in a tan short-sleeve uniform with the two silver bars of a captain clipped on each lapel and a dark blue overseas cap. My transportation to downtown Saigon was a three-wheeled Lambretta cyclo. The driver was an old man with skinny, bare legs browned by hereditary and darkened by years of labor under the hot Southeast Asia sun. He wore only dirty leather slippers, loose black shorts, and a conical straw hat, which he tied under his chin with a string. His blackened teeth unconsciously chewed betel nuts as he stared straight ahead oblivious to any danger as we weaved in and out of the heavy traffic.

I sat in front of the driver on a wide seat mounted between the two front tires. My feet rested on a narrow step only a few inches above the pavement rushing by. There were no seatbelts to secure me. If the motorcycle had to stop quickly it would eject me forcefully forward. I was a human bumper in front of the hurtling machine.

A huge ARVN truck, crowded with camouflaged soldiers, cut closely in front of us. The heavy mass of steel scraped the side rail of my seat and would have hit my arm if I hadn't pulled it back.

I arrived at the patio bar of the Continental Palace Hotel just after the noon hour. The four story concrete building sat on the corner of Saigon's Boulevard Lei Loi and Rue Tu Do. Over the tables, long wooden ceiling fans barely stirred the hot, humid air. Wide archways opened onto the sidewalks intersecting at the street corner. A wooden propeller from an ancient French aircraft hung over the long bamboo bar at the rear of the room.

The customers included U.S. service men and women, French businessmen, American Red Cross workers, and Vietnamese prostitutes—wearing traditional ao dai silk dresses split to the hips and worn over pantaloons—trolling for an early catch to start a lucrative weekend. Beggars and peddlers of all ages and both sexes hawking black market items and locally produced goods milled the tables.

A young girl with dark, piercing eyes walked up to my table and handed me a hand scribed card with the words, "I am blind. Have no father. Please help me. Give me money,"

That was my introduction to Phu who was to become my friend. Of course she wasn't blind, but that was okay. She was a needy child of the streets scrabbling for survival. A few months later, I would hold her hand as we watched her mother die with terrible agony from the ravages of heroin. Phu became one of the main characters in two of my novels, *Evening of Pale Sunshine* and *Weep Without Tears*.

After Phu left, I watched with horror as a Buddhist monk, doused with gas by an assistant, lit himself on fire on the steps of the National Assembly Building across the way to protest the persecution of Buddhists by the present Thieu regime. Surrounded by protesters shouting mantras, soldiers and policemen had a difficult time gathering up the charred body and getting things under control.

I thought about returning to Tan Son Nhut Air Base, but I decided to meet Dick at the French restaurant. I hadn't eaten anywhere outside of the mess hall and the officer's club since I arrived in Vietnam.

The La Cigale Restaurant was an unimposing wooden two-story building. Iron lattice work installed ten years before when throwing bombs from passing motorcycles was in vogue protected the doors and windows. The dining room was illuminated by diffused light from a large chandelier hanging from the center of the high ceiling. Dark red floor length curtains covered the windows and isolated the room from outside lights. A short bar ran along the interior wall. Across from it, on a raised platform, a piano player and a string quartet of elderly Vietnamese men played quietly.

The room only contained one large and eight smaller tables, each covered with a white tablecloth and elegantly set with candles, white china dishes, and fine silverware. At the far end of the room a doorway, covered in a curtain of full length beads, led to the rear.

Dick Castle welcomed me to his table where I was to meet his three companions: Richard Carpenter, a huge and rotund newspaper correspondent, Colonel Tho Hang, an ARVN officer of such small stature he appeared to be a child, and Bill Jamerson, an area supervisor for the large engineering consortium of Brown and Root.

I described this momentous evening in *Evening of Pale Sunshine*. In addition to the wonderful Provencal French dinner presented by the owner of the La Cigale, Monsieur Andre Ramade, I enjoyed the stimulating conversation with Dick, Richard, Tho Hang, and Bill.

I witnessed something that evening that appalled me. To this day, it seems beyond the realm of possibility, but it actually happened. The new Saigon area ARVN commander, General Khang, was seated at the large table with his party. During the meal, a shot sounded from outside. One of Khang's escort soldiers had accidently fired his rifle. Khang went out, made the soldier kneel, and he shot him in the head for disturbing his dinner.

I was introduced to the sisters who provided the evening's singing entertainment, Linh Thu and Anh Thu, that night. Anh, who was slightly heavier, wore a dark red silk ao dai over white pantaloons. Linh, several inches shorter, had on a light blue ao dai over black. Her high cheekbones and a thin nose beneath piercing black eyes gave her a mysterious look that seemed to be a blend of the Orient and the West. Both had black hair so long it fell down over their shoulders. They were beautiful women, the daughters of a French business man and a Vietnamese woman. They sang a number of songs, most of them in Vietnamese with a few in French.

One of the songs, Linh sang alone. The Vietnamese language normally sounded harsh, guttural, and staccato to me, using inflections to evoke emotion and emphasis. But on this song, Linh softened the edges of the words and caressed each syllable as she held the audience spellbound.

At the conclusion of the song, everyone in the dining room stood and applauded, many of the Vietnamese with tears in their eyes.

I turned to Colonel Hang and asked him about the song, which affected everyone.

"The literal translation is 'Evening of Pale Sunshine,'" he answered, his eyes still misting. "It is about a Vietnamese soldier leaving his family to go off to war. His wife is telling the story. When I hear that song, I think of my three sons who left their families to go to war against the communists...and did not return. They were young officers like you Captain Miller. They had much to live for. Now I am father to their children."

Turning to Richard, Hang continued, "That is the story you American reporters fail to tell. The United States has lost fifty thousand men and women in this war. Our losses exceed two million."

Over the next few months, I was to become friends with Monsieur Ramade and the Thu sisters. Anh was eagerly looking forward to joining her American officer fiancé in the United States as soon as she could get a visa to travel out of the country.

Linh, who had a five-year-old daughter, had lost her husband several years before during a battle between the ARVN and the NVR north of the city of Hue. She was very withdrawn and private. Her eyes reflected the pain she felt for her lost mate and the uncertainty the future held for her and her child. Her singing voice was tinged with the haunting memories she carried in her mind every day.

Each time I went to the restaurant, Linh sang the haunting ballad that brought tears to the Vietnamese audience. One evening I asked Anh, who was engaged to an American army major and understood English, if I could get a translation of the song.

The next time I went to the La Cigale Anh was waiting outside. As I approached her I could see tears flowing from her eyes and streaming down her face, discoloring her eye shadow and makeup.

"I am so sorry to tell you, Ken," she sobbed. "Linh was killed early today."

"Oh, no!" I said. "What happened?"

"She was going to the market on her motor scooter to buy food for her daughter," Anh said. "There was an ARVN blockade. One of them shot her for no reason."

I couldn't say anything. I was so overcome with the negative emotions this horrible war evoked in me. Why would anyone think a young woman like Linh was a threat?

"She asked me to give this to you," Anh said as she handed me a sheet of paper.

I was so upset I couldn't read it until later after I returned to my BOQ room at Tan Son Nhut. When I unfolded the paper, I realized it was an English translation of the song Linh sang with such feeling at the restaurant. It was a haunting rendition of the effects the long and disastrous war had on the Vietnamese who were caught between the communists of the north, who wanted to unite the ancient country, and the Americans from halfway around the globe, who didn't really understand nor care about the losses the elongated war brought upon the local population.

As Richard Carpenter had said at the first dinner I went to at the La Cigale Restaurant, "The Americans back home don't care about the Vietnamese from the north and the south who die. All they think about is the high school sports hero who is being buried at the local cemetery and the anguished parents who are presented with the U.S.

flag."

The song title became the name for my first novel *Evening of Pale Sunshine*. I wrote it after returning from Vietnam to a hostile American public who didn't accept the war in Southeast Asia or the brave servicemen and women who sacrificed their limbs, their psyches, or their lives for that foreign conflagration. When I tried to get a mainstream publisher to accept the manuscript, I met resistance. One New York publisher wrote that he liked the writing but novels about the Vietnam War were not acceptable. He asked me if I could re-write it with a different setting.

But I believe every story has a sense of time and place. I couldn't change that to please the publishing world. Eventually, I started my own publishing company and had it printed myself. I distributed it through many outlets and, even today, it is available from Amazon and directly from me. It has received positive reviews from throughout the world, including Vietnamese readers.

I am including the lyrics from *Evening of Pale Sunshine* here because it capsulizes the horrible effect the long conflict had on the Vietnamese, a gentle people who hadn't known peace in many generations.

> *I gave you my love my love of thirty springs,*
> *and you packed it into your battle bag.*
> *You bid farewell to the capital city,*
> *on a cold evening of pale sunshine.*
>
> *I will love only you all my life,*
> *although we are separated far apart.*
> *It is raining on the deserted streets,*
> *under the glimmer of midnight lights.*
>
> *The feelings I have for you will not change,*
> *as time steals our youth and bows our backs.*
> *The quiet moon above witnessed our pledge,*
> *and stays with me through the lonely nights.*
>
> *I pray for you on your difficult journey,*
> *and wait in hope and sorrow for your step.*
> *The time of war has been so long and hard,*
> *and the sun no longer shines through the rain.*
>
> *I think of you with your rifle at ready,*

as you fight for your family and country.
The struggle is still very long and sad,
and the road of life has many pains.

I call out your name in love each night,
as the flowers drop down with the leaves.
I dream of the time we will be as one,
on a warm evening of pale sunshine.

Several months later, in early March, an interesting and humorous event happened that involved my mother. I received a call from our base mail service. A very concerned voice said, "Captain Miller, this is Airman Howell. Can you come to the post office right away?"

When I arrived at the office, a young airman led me past the mailboxes where I received my mail, through the area where incoming and outgoing mail was sorted, and outside the back into an alley with several garbage dumpsters. A misshapen pile, exuding a putrid smell, lay on the ground.

Howell pointed to it and said, "I am sorry, Captain. We couldn't put that inside. It smells too bad. We could just make out your name on the address label."

"What is it?" I asked.

"We don't know, Sir," Howell said as he handed me a long stick.

I probed the horrible mess for a moment before realizing what it was. My mother, who had lived through the Second World War and the Korean War, was always sending me care packages. They included things I certainly didn't need or could buy cheaply at the base-exchange like razors, combs, and other toilet articles. But this was something different.

Sometime in early December, Mom had baked a fruit cake, put it in a tin container, and mailed it to me. Apparently it was delayed in transit and, now almost three months later it was delivered. The top had come off under the paper wrapping, and the hot, humid weather in Southeast Asia had turned the cake into a soggy, smelly mess. I gave Airman Howell permission to toss the rotten cake into dumpster.

After I returned from Vietnam, I went to visit my family in North Idaho. Mom asked me how I enjoyed the Christmas fruit cake. I told her it about the late and messy delivery, and we had a good laugh together.

Shortly after the mail incident, I received a summons to see Colonel L in his office. When I walked in, it was crowded with officers and enlisted personnel. I had no idea why we were summoned.

Colonel L stomped in from his adjoining office and stood at the head of the table. "Gentlemen," he said glaring through his glasses, "we have a challenging problem we need to overcome. As you know, Project Enhance had accelerated withdrawal of ground and air forces to satisfy the assholes in Washington. What you may not realize, is that we are also losing all our airborne warning and control systems. In their infinite wisdom they've pulled out AWAC's. The EC-47's and EC-135's have been withdrawn to Hickam."

Colonel L took off his glasses and wiped them with a tissue as he often did when he needed to compose himself.

"That means we don't have airborne control over the few U.S. fighters we still have or the ARVIN planes," the colonel resumed. "The commies are about to kick our asses unless we can come up with some way to manage the fighters from the air. Gentlemen, I need your ideas. How do we do that with the resources we have at hand?"

There was a furious round table discussion as ideas were thrown onto the table. Most of them involved modifying some of the C-7 Caribou aircraft still in the theater with airborne communications and control equipment.

Colonel L interrupted. "We only have 12 C-7's left and we need them for munitions and cargo transport and to evacuate our forces and the locals when they are overrun by this new offensive from the north."

During the silence after the colonel's remarks, I blurted out something that was in my mind. I didn't mean to say it out loud, but I did, and it came during a lull in the group conversation, so everyone heard it. I said, "Occam's Razor."

"What the hell are you saying, Captain Miller?" Colonel L barked. "If you need a shave, go to the BX and buy a razor."

"Sir," I responded from a chair back against the far wall. "Occam's Razor is a problem solving principle developed by an English Franciscan monk in the 13th century. It states that among competing hypotheses, the simplest one with the fewest assumptions is normally the best solution."

"Okay, oh wise one," Colonel L drawled as everyone in the room stared at me. "What the hell do you propose is the best solution?"

"Don't modify the aircraft and take them out of their normal missions," I said. "We can build a pallet with AWAC's capability and with interfaces to the C-7 communications and radar systems, then install it in any aircraft to support the battlefield scenarios. The pallet could be rolled in and operational in a few minutes on available aircraft."

After Colonel L cleared the room, I was assigned to put together a crew to build and check out the new AWAC's pallet. When he asked me what I wanted to call the new undertaking, I responded, "Our aircraft can fly around the enemy air and ground forces like Joshua did around the walls of Jericho until they fell down."

And so Project Jericho was born. I selected a sergeant and six avionics technicians, and we worked around the clock in a secure hangar to build a mobile communications pallet. We finished the project in less than two weeks, and it proved very successful in coordinating U.S. and ARVIN air strikes against enemy forces surging into South Vietnam. If a host aircraft was not available, we could roll the pallet into an operational one in less than half hour and continue the mission.

I would be awarded the Air Force Commendation Medal (Second Oak Leaf Cluster) for my work on the C-7 Jericho Project.

About a month later, I received another summons to see Colonel L in his office. This time he was waiting for me seated at his chair at the head of the table. After taking off his glasses and cleaning them, he pursed his lips and said to me, "Captain, I have a problem I need you to help me with."

"Of course, Sir," I responded. "What can I do?"

"I've had to remove Lieutenant Colonel Massey as the commander of the Aircraft Maintenance Squadron. He's on his way back to Iowa. I want you to take over the squadron."

I was flabbergasted, and it took me a moment to respond. "Sir, I am an Avionics Officer."

"You are," Colonel L said. "You are also an innovative leader of men. That's what I need right now. That squadron is royally fucked up. We're losing many sorties every day because routine aircraft maintenance isn't being done."

He reached down on his desk and picked up a thick stack of papers as he continued, "I have over 50 reports of falsifying repair records and another dozen from the security police for drug usage on and off duty. If the men don't want to show up for work, they don't."

"But, Sir," I said. "That is a large squadron, over three hundred men. It calls for a lieutenant colonel as commander. I'm just a captain."

As I walked out of his office in a daze, Colonel L said, "I am going to send you some help Captain. Get the hell out of here and go to work."

And so I became the commander of a large aircraft maintenance squadron with massive morale and discipline problems facing the demanding support of an air fleet increasing daily in the approaching eye of the cyclonic activity of the North Vietnamese armies invading the South.

When I walked into the orderly room of the aircraft maintenance squadron, the first thing I noticed was the dirty, disheveled appearance of the office and the slovenly dress of the airmen and sergeants slouched behind the desks. Although they recognized me as an officer, not one of them stood up to acknowledge me.

On one of the desks, where a broad faced man with curly black hair showing through an open collar shirt sat with his feet propped up on the desk top staring at me, I saw an ornate carved wooden name tag that read, "MSgt J, First Sergeant."

Although I could relate to enlisted men since I was one of them for several years, I recognized the importance of the chain of command. In a time of crisis, especially during wartime, I knew that discipline was important.

"Sergeant J," I said forcefully. "Get your feet off the desk. I am an officer. Show me some respect if you want to keep those stripes."

J came to his feet and flashed me a casual salute, a sly grin sneaking over his face.

After a session in the commander's office, which was now mine by Colonel L's order, I decided Sergeant J was part of the problem. He was sloppily dressed, needed a shave, and was disrespectful to me for being only a captain and replacing a lieutenant colonel.

When I told Colonel L I would have to court martial Sergeant J if he stayed, he said, "Don't worry. He's out of here. His replacement will be there tomorrow."

It took me several hours early the next morning to clean up the previous commander's mess and get a handle on his filing system. I was sitting at the desk reading through a stack of negative personnel reports, which included open squadron punishment Article 15's that should have been implemented, when the door opened and the largest black man I had ever seen strode into my office.

He stood at least six and a half feet tall and was broad as an ox. Dressed in a blue uniform, he was wearing the stripes of a Chief Master Sergeant, the highest Non Commissioned Officer (NCO) rank, and a chest full of award ribbons from as far back as the Second World War.

The mountainous man took off his visored hat revealing a head of closely cropped, steely gray hair. He snapped to attention and saluted me. His deep, rumbling bass voice filled the room, "Captain Miller. Chief Underwood reporting for duty. I understand you need some help to straighten out this squadron."

That was my introduction to the finest NCO I ever had the pleasure to work with. By the end of that first day, word spread like wildfire through the squadron that the "Right Hand of God," as one airman described Chief Underwood, had arrived. Suddenly work areas were cleaned up, personnel showed up for work in proper attire, and a fresh breath of morale swept through the squadron.

A strange ritual had arisen among the black servicemen in Vietnam at that time. It was a black power greeting called the *Dap*. It consisted of a series of mutual touches on the hands, wrists, elbows, and arms when meeting. It had grown out of the black power movement of the 1960's and was nurtured by the Vietnam conflict.

Minority cliques used it to solidify their identity in the face of perceived persecutions by the white race as a whole and, in particular, the white military hierarchy in Washington D.C. that sent them to fight and die in a tropical country halfway around the world. It had become so rampant at Tan Son Nhut Air Base that it interfered with normal activities. People quit going to the movies or the mess halls because they didn't want to have to put up with blacks making a big show out of dapping each other and holding up the waiting lines.

Chief Underwood decided he had enough of the Dap, and he set out to stop it. It was interesting how he went about it. Whenever he saw anyone doing it, he got up close and personal in their face, and with his massive physical presence, they paid attention.

"Gentlemen," he would rumble in their faces. "You don't have to do this silly shit to impress anyone. Be proud of who you are and what you are. You are Americans, and you represent your country by wearing your uniform. Be proud of that."

Thanks to Chief Underwood's efforts, the Dap began to die out on the base. Unfortunately, the NCO in charge of the tire shop in my aircraft maintenance squadron, Staff Sergeant W, was a vocal spokesman for the black power movement, and he sat out to oppose Chief Underwood.

The tire shop was one of the most important units in our squadron, and one of the most dangerous to work in. High pressure aircraft tires were crucial for take offs and landings in the hot humid conditions that often raised the tarmac temperatures over a hundred and thirty degrees. Changing tires for excessive wear or damage required special equipment and skilled technicians aware of the dangers involved.

In the two months before I was assigned to the squadron, there were three accidents in the tire shop. In two of them workers had tires blow up while removing them from rims and suffered broken arms. Unfortunately, the third incident was a fatality. A tire ring was ejected into an airman's face and he was killed.

Sergeant W decided the tire shop was going on strike to oppose Chief Underwood's efforts to curtail the Dap. When I heard about it, I ordered W to report to me.

I looked up as the door to my office exploded open. Chief Underwood stormed in, dragging Sergeant W, who was at least a hundred pounds lighter, by one arm.

The chief threw W into a chair and told him to shut up. The young black sergeant stared at me with a sullen, defiant glare.

Chief Underwood rumbled at him, "The commander has given me the authority to wall to wall counsel you. Isn't that right, Captain?"

I had no idea what he was talking about. What was wall to wall counseling? I nodded in agreement as the chief snatched W out of his chair and stormed out of the office.

Behind my office was a small room that housed power distribution and heating and air-conditioning units for our building. A few minutes later I heard the muffled sounds of impacts against the power room walls. They went on for several minutes, then there was quiet.

After Sergeant W was released from the base hospital recovering from broken limbs and facial injuries, he was sent stateside immediately. His replacement as the tire shop supervisor was a pleasant young sergeant of Puerto Rican descent who was personally selected by Chief Underwood.

Shortly after that, I was able to personally attest to the amazing airworthiness of the C-47 Goony Bird. One of the aircraft from Scatback Operations in Tan Son Nhut Air Base, used to fly personnel and goods to and from Bangkok, Thailand, was struck by a T-33 jet trainer aircraft piloted by the nephew of the King of Thailand while it was on final approach to the Bangkok airport. I was assigned to be on the official investigation team as the maintenance advisor and went with the team to Bangkok.

When we arrived in Thailand, the damaged C-47 was stored in an airport hangar. I could not believe it when I saw the plane. The T-33 had come up from behind the Gooney Bird as it was descending about four miles from touchdown. At the last moment the jet veered to the right to avoid a direct impact, but the left wing sheared off over a third of the right wing of the C-47. Somehow, the cargo aircraft pilot was able to maintain control and land at the airport without even blowing a tire. Later he was awarded the Air Force Flying Cross for extraordinary airmanship.

Tales of a Sojourner

After reviewing the aircraft records, air traffic control reports, and aircrew and eyewitness accounts, our investigation board came to an obvious conclusion: it was pilot error from the Thai T-33 pilot because he had violated the air space of the landing aircraft.

The next morning, after we arrived at our team conference room from the local hotel, we were informed the colonel originally in charge of the investigation board had been relieved and sent back to the United States. A new colonel stood at the head of the table, and he announced the official report would state that local air traffic control was at fault not the pilot.

As I would find out a few years later during an assignment to Thailand, the King and his family were sacrosanct. They were above reproach, as they had been for centuries.

I had several months to go on my Vietnam tour when I received orders to see Colonel L. He had already exceeded his twelve-month requirement in country (I don't think his secretary let him keep a short timer calendar!), but he had asked the Pentagon for an extension. His intention was to return to the United States in retirement status.

"Captain," he barked at me when I sat down across from his desk. "I have a problem I need you to help me with."

"Of course, Sir, what can I do," I responded.

An F-4D Phantom fighter aircraft, flying out of Takhli, Thailand, after a mission ran low on fuel and attempted to land at a small South Vietnamese airfield near a hamlet named Cu Chi located about 60 miles northwest of Tan Son Nhut Air Base. The pilot and co-pilot survived the crash landing and were rescued by friendly forces, but the airplane was not flyable and was still in territory held by Viet Cong forces after dark.

"We need that F-4 back," Colonel L said. "We don't have enough now. I want you to take a crew and a flatbed truck with a heavy hoist to Cu Chi, remove the engine, and put it on the truck. We'll have a CH-54 sky crane copter lift the body out and bring it back here. Think you can handle that, Captain?"

I looked at the colonel and nodded my head.

"Oh," he said as he opened one of his drawers and withdrew a bottle and sat it on his desk. "This is Johnny Walker Black Label Scotch. My wife made me swear off liquor. It's yours if you can get that plane back."

When we got to Cu Chi, it was early in the afternoon. The temperature was pushing a hundred degrees and the humidity close to that. Steam rose from the rice paddies surrounding the tiny hamlet as we approached. We could see the deep slash in the wet earth where the heavy F-4 had plowed into the ground on impact.

A Quonset hut housing U.S. Marines nearby had been narrowly missed by the crash. We were able to have a cool beer and some lunch there before we started the salvage operation.

As I stood at the makeshift bar, I read a note pinned on a bulletin board from an anonymous writer, *"For those who fight for it, life has a flavor the sheltered few never know."*

The afternoon was sweltering hot. Just touching the surface skin of the downed aircraft caused blisters. All of us in the crew pitched in to remove the large engine from the fuselage. Stripped down to our trousers, we sweated gallons of perspiration even though we drank massive amounts of water. My knuckles were bloody and I had a large gash in one finger by the time we finished late in the afternoon.

The CH-54 helicopter was well named, *Cyclone*. When it picked up the F-4 fuselage, we had to step back out of the furious ground wash from the rotors.

I was on a hand held radio with the pilot. "Captain," he squawked. "We can't lift this very high in this heat. If we get any ground fire, I'm going to pickle it. Understand."

Pickle meant the pilot would drop the aircraft at any sign of enemy fire. On the long trip in the truck back to Tan Son Nhut with the engine, while watching for Viet Cong and NVN forces, I worried about the helicopter soaring low above the jungle canopies with an F-4 body tangling tantalizingly below it.

When we pulled up in the dark of the evening to the aircraft maintenance hangar at Tan Son Nhut with the engine, Colonel L was waiting for us. As I stepped down from the truck, he handed me the bottle of Johnny Walker.

"The chopper brought in the F-4 without a scratch, Captain Miller," he said shaking my hand. "You and your crew have saved us several million dollars."

I gave the sergeant who was in charge of the crew from the engine shop all the money I had in my billfold and told him to buy everyone drinks at their club. I was so exhausted I headed for my BOQ, a shower, and a few drinks from the bottle of scotch Colonel L gave me.

The next morning, I awoke to the ranting and banging of my Vietnamese mamasan. She was holding my filthy fatigues up with a broom handle and muttering, "Dinky dau, GI."

A few months later, after I had left Vietnam, I was awarded the Bronze Star Medal for meritorious service by the Secretary of the Air Force. Although his name wasn't on the award, I knew it was from

Colonel L. When he retired, he disappeared from the radar, and I was never able to contact him again. Today, with the electronic searches available on Google and Facebook, I could probably locate him, but they weren't available in the 1970's.

Richard Nixon won the presidential election in November 1972, and under the Paris Peace Accords between the North Vietnamese Foreign Minister, Le Duc Tho, and the U.S. Secretary of State, Henry Kissinger, American forces continued to withdraw from South Vietnam and prisoners were exchanged.

Kissinger's statement that "Peace is at hand" proved to be premature by several years. As U.S bombings of North Vietnam were suspended, the ARVN and Viet Cong forces accelerated their forays into the south. They looked eagerly at the prospect of invading Saigon and destroying the South Vietnamese forces being abandoned by the Americans and their allied forces.

Chapter 9
Tobacco Road

When I returned from Vietnam in late 1972, I was assigned to Seymour Johnson AFB in Goldsboro, North Carolina. A Strategic Air Command (SAC) base, which normally supported the 68th Bombardment Wing B-52 bombers, it was a caretaker base when I arrived.

All the B-52 Strategic Bombers and their KC-135 tanker support aircraft were deployed to Utapao Air Base, Thailand to support the continuing war in Vietnam that Secretary of State Kissinger had proclaimed would be over imminently. Tactical Air Command (TAC) also had a unit assigned to the base. The 4th Tactical Fighter Squadron, had rotated their F-4 Phantom II's to Ubon Air Base in Thailand for fighter operations starting a few months before I arrived.

Goldsboro was in the Piedmont area of North Carolina in the middle of the tobacco growing region. Over a hundred miles from the scenic mountains of the Blue Ridge Parkway to the west and nearly as far from the Outer Banks of the Atlantic Ocean to the east, it rested on a plain that boasted broad open fields that stretched as far as the eye could see in any direction.

As I drove through the country on my way to my new assignment, I thought about Erskine Caldwell's novel, *Tobacco Road*. The phrase actually originated from the title of his novel, which was set in Georgia, but it naturally migrated to North Carolina because of the state's primary role in tobacco production.

In 1972 a new car cost just over $2,000, a gallon of gas was 50 cents, a new home about $30,000, and a ladies stylish over the knee boot was around $20. It was a dark time in the history of the International Olympic Games when Arab gunmen killed 11 Israeli athletes in Munich, Germany. The Watergate Scandal began with the burglarizing and wiretapping of the Democratic National Committee's headquarters. In Iceland, where I had been stationed, American Bobby Fischer beat Russian Boris Spassky to become the World Chess Champion. In Washington D.C. the Equal Rights Amendment to provide sexual equality was passed by the Senate.

The first *Godfather* movie played at theaters and *Hawaii Five-O* was popular on television. At the same time, HBO launched as the first subscription cable service. The Eagles, along with Michael Jackson, Elton John, and Simon and Garfunkel, were getting major play of their music.

The wing commander, who welcomed me to Seymour Johnson, told me he had reviewed my records and wanted me to take over as the commander of the Airborne Missile Maintenance Squadron (AMMS). He told me I would be the only captain in SAC holding the title of squadron commander.

I wasn't sure if I should be thrilled by the new assignment when I walked into the AMMS orderly room. Although it wasn't as bad as the squalid Aircraft Maintenance Squadron at Tan Son Nhut, it wasn't a sharp military unit. Responsible for the maintenance and installment of the non-nuclear missiles AGM-69 Short Range Aerial Missile (SRAM) and the ADM-20 Chaff Dispenser, the large open hangar bay was nearly deserted. Only a few of the weapons were left at the base after the Southeast Asia aircraft deployment. We had no idea when the airplanes would return to the base, so our mission was to maintain the AMMS facility to receive them when they arrived.

The first thing I did as commander was to organize the unit into three groups: Red, Blue, and White. I challenged them to compete with each other for the AMMS Squadron Cup. The competition included work performance, proficiency testing, and sports competition. The winner of each three-month period would receive a large presentation cup I had designed and built by a local business and several cases of cold beer.

The men accepted the challenge and their spirits went up as we got into the competitions. Some of the volleyball and softball games were pretty rough as the Reds prevailed for the first quarter.

Just as we were going into our next phase of competition, the wing commander showed up un-announced for an inspection. After he and his inspectors finished their white glove assessment, he called me aside. "I don't know what the hell you've been doing out here, Captain," he said. "I've never seen a better unit than this. We could eat off the hangar floor, I can see my reflection."

As the next months passed, being a caretaker squadron commander weighed me. During the summer, I was able to spend some time with my sons, Alan and Mike, before they returned to Florida to be with their mother.

Then, as the fall turned the tobacco of the Piedmont into brown and the deciduous leaves of the trees on the North Carolina Skyline Drive into various shades of russet, umber, and red, the demands of being a commander of a stateside caretaker squadron hearing reports of the continuing war efforts half way around the world in the tiny country of Vietnam began to bother me.

The war was the central issue of the 1972 presidential election. Richard Nixon's opponent, George McGovern, campaigned on a platform of total withdrawal from Vietnam. About that time, Henry Kissinger, in secret talks with North Vietnam's Le Duc Tho reached an agreement to a peace accord. However, South Vietnam president Thieu demanded changes to the accord and the war dragged on.

To placate Thieu and force the North back to the negotiating table, Nixon ordered Operation Linebacker II, a massive bombing of Hanoi and Haiphong. The offensive destroyed much of the North's economic and industrial capability and was instrumental in bringing about the Paris Peace Accord early in 1973, which started a 60-day withdrawal of U.S. forces and the release of American prisoners, some of whom had spent over eight years in prisons.

One evening at the officer's club I met a retired U.S. Air Force colonel, who was an F-105 pilot during the Vietnam Conflict. He was shot down by a ground missile and spent over seven years in various North Vietnamese Prisoner of War (POW) sites including Hanoi Hilton, the infamous prison near Hanoi that included many American officers including John McClain who later became the senator from Arizona.

Over the next few weeks and more than a few drinks with the colonel he related to me the horrible travails of the loss of his aircraft and the subsequent imprisonment and torture by the North Vietnamese. Through it all, he said, "I never gave up hope I would survive and get back to my family again."

After several years of being rushed about many jungle stockades, suffering from injuries, dysentery, and brutal beatings from the guards, he said when he finally arrived at the Hanoi Hilton, he thought the worst was over for him. He said he quickly found out that was not true. The Vietnamese interrogators there, trained by the Chinese, probed deeper into his physical and mental capacities than he ever thought it was possible to go.

"They isolated me from other prisoners in a cell with no windows, bars on the door, and two buckets, one for water such as it was and the other one for a toilet. I was told by my interrogator I was to be totally silent, and any noise would result in another beating. One night I screamed out in my sleep and was whipped with a hose. I don't know how long I was in the cell. I tried to mark a calendar on the wall, but many days I didn't update it."

The colonel took a hefty swig of his Scotch before going on, "Then I decided they were not going to break me. Each day I paced my cell and built an imaginary home I would build for my family when I returned to America. It took me many months to finish it in my mind. When I was repatriated, I built that house near here. Just like I imagined it, down to the color of the paint on the walls, the design of the cabinets, and the work benches in the garage."

I picked up the phone one day and called the officer's assignment office at Randolph Air Force Base in San Antonio. A friend of mine, who I had gone to Squadron Officers School with, was now in charge of the office.

By the time I hung up, I received an assignment to report as the assistant avionics officer at the F-111 unit in Takhli, Thailand. They were providing continuing bombing support for the ARVN against the advancing NVN and Viet Cong forces closing in on the Saigon area of South Vietnam.

The memories of my tour at Tan Son Nhut were never far from my mind. I couldn't forget the anguished look on Anh Thu's face when she told me her sister Linh had been killed by ARVIN forces while she was going to the market to buy food for her daughter. The face of the young waif, Phu, also haunted me. I wondered what had happened to her as the world of war closed down on her without her mother to support her.

I couldn't get back to Vietnam, but I could get close. Maybe there was something I could do to help during the withdrawal of our forces in the face of the advancing North Vietnamese army.

Chapter 10
Kraits and King Cobras

When I reported to the Air Force unit at Takhli, Thailand, the commander of the 347th Tactical Fighter Wing welcomed me and others with a lecture in an open hangar next to the flight line. It was hot and humid in the huge building even though the doors were rolled open. A gecko lizard, high in the metal rafters, kept chirping during the colonel's speech.

It was difficult for us in the audience to keep from laughing because it sounded like the creature was using the four letter "F" word and spewing "F*** You, F*** You."

The commander cautioned us to be aware of deadly local serpents, which included Kraits and King Cobras. "The Kraits," he said, "are nicknamed 'Step and a Half' because if one bites you on exposed skin, you will be dead in a step and a half. Their venom contains powerful neurotoxins, which cause muscle paralysis. So keep your fatigues buttoned up, don't wear shorts, and stay out of the wooded areas where they live."

The colonel stared up at the pesky gecko before going on, "Now the Cobra, who roams all around, will stand up in front of you, stare you in the eyes, spread his hood, and then strike from several feet away. If you meet one, don't look in his eyes and don't move; eye contact and movement pisses him off."

I was later to have up close and personal meetings with both of those venomous serpents. And in both instances, I didn't heed the wing commander's warnings.

Takhli was a Royal Thai Air Force Base in central Thailand, about 150 miles northwest of Bangkok. Under Thailand's "gentleman's agreement" with the United States, they let us use the facility but maintained command authority. The official reason for the agreement was for the U.S. to aid Thailand in resisting the spreading communist aggression and subversion threatening all of Southeast Asia.

Our aircraft were under the regional control of the Pacific Air Forces (PACAF) 13th Air Force headquartered at Clark Air Base in the Philippines. Starting in the early 1960's, we flew covert air missions into Laos and, after the 1964 *Gulf of Tonkin Resolution* effectively started the Vietnam Conflict, overt missions into Cambodia, and South and North Vietnam.

When I arrived in 1973, we were flying General Dynamics F-111 aircraft assigned out of Mountain Home, Idaho. Until August 15, the 347th flew combat missions into Cambodia. After the Vietnam cease fire on that date, the wing maintained combat ready status for possible peace fire violations.

I was assigned as the deputy commander of the Avionics Squadron reporting to Major C. who had been on the base for six months. He was a bright, self-assured officer with a fastidious nature. Even during the oppressively hot and humid days, he wore neatly pressed fatigues and didn't appear to perspire. The men in the squadron respected him, although they remained aloof from him.

He had a strange habit of driving his truck out to the revetments when the F-111 aircraft taxied out for take-off. He would get out of the vehicle, stand at attention, and salute the pilots as they passed him.

Unfortunately, I was only able to work with him for several weeks. We were standing outside the Avionics building one morning discussing the daily maintenance meeting coming up. About 10 steps away from us a thin, spindly papasan (Thai man hired by the USAF) was operating a power mower; or the mower was operating him because he was so light.

Suddenly, in the middle of a sentence, something struck Major C.'s head, and he dropped to the ground. As I knelt over him, I looked around, suspecting that someone had shot him. But I didn't recognize a threat, and I hadn't heard the report of a gun, just a sharp whack when the major was hit.

He was lying on his back and holding his hand over his eye with blood streaming from between his fingers. Then I saw a small, bloody rock on the ground next to him. Looking back at the papasan, who was staring at us in surprise, I realized what happened. The mower had picked up a rock and flung it through the air striking Major C. in the eye.

The base ambulance came within a few minutes and two corpsmen covered the major's wound with a bandage and loaded him inside. The doctors at the local hospital couldn't manage the injury, so they air evacuated him to the regional hospital in the Philippines. Later, the wing commander told us he might lose sight in the eye; the ophthalmologist surgeon may even have to remove it.

That was my welcome to Takhli. It felt like Icelandic déjà vu; once again I was put in charge of a squadron because of the commander's ill fortune.

The poor papasan who ran the mower was very distraught. He came into my office and, sitting in a chair, started crying. He blamed himself for the accident. I couldn't console him since I couldn't speak his language, and his knowledge of English was very limited.

The Thai Air Force had an avionics building next to ours, and I had met one of the lieutenants who spoke English, so I called him to come over. After a long conversation in the sing-song rhythmic Thai language, the lieutenant assured the papasan the accident was not his fault, and he shouldn't blame himself.

The Thai language was a pleasant change from the chaotic, guttural murmuring of Vietnamese. For example, "hello pretty woman" in Vietnamese was a sharp "*Chao co dep lam*" with the harsh emphasis of rising and falling inflections. In Thai it was a musical "*Sway mock poo ying,*" that came easily to the tongue and ear.

A few days later, the papasan came in the open area outside my office. I had just come out when he walked up to the First Sergeant's desk rubbing his stomach. "Ooh," he moaned, "Number ten."

The sergeant looked over at the chief clerk sitting across from him. "Hey, Stan," he said. "Give the papasan an Alka-Seltzer."

Stan took one out of his desk, removed it from its wrapping and handed it to the papasan. Before anyone could react, the papasan popped the tablet in his mouth. Almost immediately, foam began to pour out of his mouth, his eyed widened in anguish, and he turned and ran out the door.

"My God!" the first sergeant shouted. "You could have at least put it in a cup of water."

I don't know what the papasan thought of the American medicine Stan gave him that day. We never saw him again. When he didn't show up for work for several days, we had to hire a replacement for him.

When the swing-wing F-111 fighter-bomber aircraft, called the Aardvark, was first assigned to Thailand in 1968 it was one of the most controversial planes ever built in the United States. Harshly criticized by the press for its excessive cost over-runs and poor performance, the first three F-111's launched out of Takhli never returned from their missions. Investigation revealed that none of them were downed by enemy fire. A malfunction in the flight control systems caused the deadly sorties.

By the time I arrived in Thailand in 1973, the manufacturer had solved the flight system failures and, except for one unexplained crash, the aircraft had been performing well, especially in adverse weather conditions that would have grounded most other airplanes.

Our avionics squadron had several General Dynamics technical representatives assigned to support their company's product. One of them, Dale Brawner, was to become a life-long friend and the reason I was later to become a General Dynamics employee after my retirement from the Air Force. Dale was the most knowledgeable fire control systems engineer I ever met. I think he played a major role in the success of the F-111's in Southeast Asia.

Later, Dale was to become the acknowledged world-wide F-16 Fighting Falcon fire control systems expert. When he retired, Lockheed (who purchased the General Dynamics Aircraft Company) elected him to their Hall of Fame.

Dale and several other civilian employees lived in the town of Takhli at a place called Winnie's Bungalows. Winnie was a middle-aged Thai woman who owned a restaurant next to a number of rental units.

It was at Winnie's where I learned to love the complexity of Thai cuisine. Their food, normally served with rice, emphasizes dishes with strong aromatic components carrying a spicy edge. The interplay of three or four tastes in each dish incorporated sour, sweet, salty, bitter, and spicy flavors. Many Americans, not used to the jumble of tastes in their food, didn't cater to it, but I really enjoyed it.

I had an interesting experience with the locals one Saturday afternoon at Winnie's. I had a lunch at the restaurant of pork fried rice with vegetables topped with a fried egg. Then I walked outside to a small lake on the property where I had seen Thais fishing from the shore.

I carried with me a Pocket Fisherman I had owned for several years. It was only about 16 inches long with a short flexible tip and a wide grip that housed the spool of line. I could cast it long distances and had caught a lot of fish with it in Florida, Vietnam, and North Carolina.

On that day, when I walked out on the short pier extending into the lake, there was no one else around. After several casts, using a bobber and a piece of pork I salvaged from lunch, I had a strike and pulled in a colorful, fat sunfish type of fish I was not familiar with. I took it off the hook and released it back into the water.

As I stood up to cast again, I heard a murmur of voices behind me. Turning, I saw a gathering on the shore of ten or twelve young men and one older gentleman wearing a wide-brimmed straw hat. They stared at my Pocket Fisherman as I cast out into the water. I couldn't understand what they were saying, but I could see they were excited.

When I pulled in another fish, they crowded out onto the pier with me. I started to toss the fish back when the old man waved his hand and reached out for it. I gave it to him and he put in the pocket of his bloused shirt. Then he put his hand out and gestured at my Pocket Fisherman.

When I just looked at him, he reached into his pants pocket and removed some Thai currency. Holding it out to me, he flashed me a broken tooth smile.

I shook my head at his offer, and he turned to the crowd around him and said something sharply in Thai. I couldn't believe the response he got. All the others dipped into their pockets and came up with coins and bills and handed them to him.

I was at a loss on what to do. I didn't want to give up my Pocket Fisherman, but when I saw the determined look of the old man and his companions, I decided that discretion was the better part of valor. I handed him the pole and waved at the money like I didn't want it. But as I tried to push my way off the pier, the old man grabbed my arm and thrust the money in my hands.

When I got back to my hooch on base later, I took all the money the group at Winnie's had given me and tossed it on my bed. After counting it and computing what the exchange rate was, I realized I had sold a $20 Pocket Fisherman for over one hundred dollars.

One afternoon I decided to return to my room at lunch time to change into clean fatigues since I had spent most of the morning on the sweltering flight line under a bright sun helping maintenance technicians trouble shoot a wiring problem on one of the F-111's. It was difficult to find the malfunction and we were all soaked with sweat by the time we finished.

As I walked out of the sunshine into the shade of my hooch, my eyes adjusted to the change in light, and I found myself staring into the eyes of a massive King Cobra, his hood raised in anger and his forked tongue flicking toward me with a hissing sound. The snake was so big his face was almost at eye level with me even though over half his body was still coiled on the ground. I recalled the warning the wing commander had given during his welcome speech: don't look a King Cobra in the eye and don't move.

Well, I had already looked the monster in the eye. So I turned and ran. If someone had seen me, I think they would have noticed that my feet didn't even touch the ground while I was running. My older brother, Charlie once told me he was so fast he could turn out the bedroom light at the wall switch and be in bed before the room was dark. I think I was faster than Charlie that day as I left the menacing snake behind in the shade.

There was a Royal Thai Air Force security post near our hooch building. I made a beeline for it and, after finding one of them who spoke English, told him about the snake. They called their command post and within minutes the area was flooded with security personnel. They cornered the Cobra under the steps leading up to my hooch and killed it with a hail of bullets.

The Thais who killed the Cobra held it up for photographs after measuring it. The snake was over eight feet long. They had it skinned and mounted it above the entrance to their security headquarters.

About a week later, I met the second venomous serpent the commander had warned us about, the even deadlier Krait.

We were playing a softball game between our squadron and some of the pilots, and because of the heat, all the players, including me, were wearing shorts and t-shirts. The outfield bordered the exterior fence of the base with an entry gate just off the first base foul line. The Thai guards were watching the game with interest, cheering good and bad plays.

I was playing right field when a big left handed batter on the pilot's team came to the plate. He had already hit a home run and a double. With a powerful swat of his bat he hammered a ball high in the air down the first base foul line toward the entry gate. I knew as soon as I heard the crack of the impact that it was going over my head, but I turned and ran back hoping to shag it down.

The ball soared just beyond me and headed toward the entry gate, which was now open. Just beyond the gate several youngsters were gathered watching the ball game from outside the fence. As I ran back, I stumbled as the ball bounced near the gate and then skidded across the perimeter road and into thick foliage beyond.

I started to cross the road to get the lost ball when I remembered the wing commander's warning about staying out of trees and underbrush and stopped. I didn't think the ball was worth facing a deadly Krait.

One of the boys, who was about ten years old, watching the game decided otherwise. He was bare chested and bare legged, wearing only a pair of shorts. Without hesitation, he ran into the dense foliage in pursuit of the ball. A few moments later he emerged with the ball and a wide grin on his face, chattering in Thai.

I looked down and saw something black with thin white stripes slivering in the grass behind him. I shouted at him, but it was too late, a Krait about three feet long bit the boy on his heel and then slunk off into the underbrush.

I picked up the youngster and ran to the Thai entry gate. "Krait...Krait," I yelled. The guards stared at me when I put the boy down in front of them and hollered again, "Krait!"

By the time the Thais were able to transport the boy to their hospital, he had progressed from abdominal cramps into total paralysis. They didn't have any anti-venom, and he died a horrible and debilitating death during the night while I waited outside the hospital room with his mother and father.

I have never been able to shake the feeling that if we hadn't played that softball game, or if I hadn't stumbled and was able to stop the hit down the foul line, that young Thai boy would have lived. His family moved away from Takhli after his death, and I was never able to contact them. To this day, I don't know what I would have said to them. I didn't even know the boy's name.

Not long after that terrible event we were notified the wing, with all personnel and aircraft, was being transferred from Takhli to Korat Royal Thai Air Force Base. When we left in July of 1974, Takhli was turned back over to the Thais and all the remaining U.S. personnel left soon after.

Gerald Ford took over as U.S. president in August after Nixon resigned due to the Watergate scandal. Democrats in congress immediately voted on restrictions on funding and military action in Vietnam. The North Vietnamese forces took advantage of the withdrawal of American support and accelerated their drive south toward Saigon and the puppet government trying to stem the tide of communism.

The epigraph in my novel, *Evening of Pale Sunshine*, is taken from Ernest Hemingway's *In Another Country*, "In the fall, the war was always there, but we did not go to it anymore."

And that is the legacy of the United States in the Southeast Asia conflict; the way history will record our participation. We never admitted defeat nor victory, the war was still there, but we just didn't go to it anymore.

I wasn't at Korat very long when I received a call from the officer's assignments unit at Randolph Air Force Base in Texas. Normally, one of the staff officers would contact me when I was due for re-assignment. But this time, the colonel in charge of the unit phoned me.

"Captain Miller," the colonel said, his voice echoing from the many exchanges the call had to go through to get from Texas to Thailand in the middle of the night. "We want you to report to Hickam Air Force Base in Hawaii right away. General W. in charge of the logistics division has asked for you by name. He needs you to head up his maintenance department for the draw down after the withdrawal from Vietnam."

So I left Thailand several months early of my normal 12-month assignment. I had no idea who General W. was or why he wanted me on his staff. As I packed up for departure, my thoughts turned back to Vietnam. I wondered what had happened to those I met during my tour there: Colonel Than, Phu, and Anh Thu. I knew Anh's sister, Linh, was dead; killed by her own security force. I hoped Anh was able to join her American soldier fiancé in the United States.

By the end of 1974, the provincial capital of Phuoc Long was captured by the North and the fall of Saigon was assured when the Americans abandoned their longtime allies in the south. As the ARVN tried to disengage from the superior attacking NVA forces, refugees mixed in with the line of retreat. Panic set in as the soldiers and civilians were shelled incessantly. By the 30th of March of 1975, over 100,000 leaderless ARVN troops surrendered in the face of the Northern forces.

Chaos and panic broke out as South Vietnamese officials and civilians scrambled to leave Saigon. American helicopters began evacuating South Vietnamese, U.S., and foreign nationals from the American embassy compound. In the early morning of April 29, 1975, the last U.S. Marines left the embassy as civilians swamped the perimeter and poured into the grounds hoping to be rescued by the Americans. Many of them had been employed by the Americans and were left to an uncertain fate.

I met one of the last Americans to evacuate from Saigon years later when I went to work at General Dynamics. John Gilbert, who became a good friend of mine, was a retired Marine and a civilian employee of the Americans when he had to scramble to the top of the embassy to catch one of the last helicopters flying to aircraft carriers in the ocean off the coast.

Thanks to John's remembrances of that time and his friendship with a young Vietnamese boy who later migrated to the U.S. after the conflict, I wrote my second novel, *Weep Without Tears*. It was about *Operation Baby Lift*, the story of children of American servicemen who were left in South Vietnam after the war.

They were ostracized as outcasts. Called *bui doi*, dust of life, by their country because of their mixed heritage, they were persecuted by children and adults who would not accept them into the new society ruled by the communists from Hanoi far to the north.

John told me that the scene around him when he boarded the helicopter was the most chaotic he had ever seen. Vietnamese men, women, and children poured through the embassy gates and climbed over the walls in a frantic effort to get on the aircraft. He said when they lifted off, one woman grabbed the landing skid and was lifted high in the air before she lost her grip and plummeted to her death in the riotous streets below.

On April 30, NVA troops entered Saigon and captured the city. The South Vietnamese president surrendered, and the flag of a united Vietnam was raised over the city for the first time in over half a century.

Did the North Vietnamese extend their military supremacy past the borders of their united country, even as far as Australia and other Southeast Asia countries as the "Domino Theory" espoused by U.S. leaders going back to President John Kennedy said they would? No, they did not. That was never their intention. Our foreign intelligence community, as before and often since, was wrong; very wrong.

Over 55,000 Americans and their allies, and over 3 million Vietnamese, Cambodians, and Laotians died because of their failure to recognize the North Vietnamese leaders wanted only one thing since the early 20th century occupation by the haughty, formally dressed French and the later imposition by the pale skinned and cruel Americans; they wanted the united country their ancient forefathers had envisioned when they emigrated south from China centuries before. They wanted one Vietnam.

Were the North Vietnamese kind and benevolent conquerors of the South? Not really. Following the communist takeover, several million South Vietnamese were sent to re-education camps to rid their minds of the poisonous thoughts given them by the Americans and the puppet government in Saigon. It would take a long time, several generations in fact, before the memory of the many deaths and injuries caused by the exploding bombs, napalm, and other horrendous weapons delivered by U.S. aircraft and ground forces became gentle on their minds.

Over a hundred thousand South Vietnamese were executed or died from hard labor in the camps. Thousands of others died at sea as "boat people" when they fled the retribution of the North.

I was never able to find out any information about Linh's sister, Anh Thu, or Colonel Tan. Many South Vietnamese were able to make it out of the country in the years after the fall of Saigon, and they established communities in countries throughout the world. I wasn't successful in locating any of my friends. I thought one of them might read my books about Vietnam and contact me, but it has not yet happened.

Today, after many years, the U.S. and Vietnam have established official communication, and the country is open to mutual trade and tourism.

Chapter 11
Aloha Hawaii

"Captain Miller," General W. addressed me in his office on the third floor of Pacific Air Forces Headquarters on Hickam Air Force Base, Hawaii the afternoon I arrived on station. "Welcome to paradise. Although you will be so busy, you won't think of it as that."

I smiled as I recalled the many long days and nights I worked in Vietnam and Thailand. I certainly didn't expect a Hawaiian assignment to be any harder. I was soon to be proven wrong.

"I hope you haven't unpacked your suitcase," the general continued. "You have a 0500 C-130 flight to Clark Air Base."

Glancing up at the clock on the wall, he smiled thinly and added, "That gives you about 13 hours to check in at the BOQ and rest up before reporting to base ops."

General W. was a thin, fit looking man with sandy brown hair cut just longer than a crew cut. He had a habit of narrowing his eyelids over his piercing gray eyes when he wanted to emphasize a point.

"We have a hell of a mess in the Far East with the draw down from Vietnam and Thailand. There's aircraft and personnel all over the damn place; from Japan to Korea to the Philippines. I want you to report to the 13th Air Force Logistics Commander and get a list of type and number of aircraft and logistics personnel and where they're located. Our supply chain is backed up here at Hickam and in the states. We don't know what to send where. Also make sure my office is copied on all supply requisitions from the units. By the time they go through Clark they're as screwed up as Hogan's goat."

I was exhausted from the overnight flight from Thailand, but I had enough energy to nod and say, "Yes Sir."

Then I added, "Why did you pick me for this job, Sir?"

General W. smiled again, "You worked for a Chief of Maintenance at Tan Son Nhut who is a close friend of mine. He's now retired, but I called and asked him who he thought could get the job done. He said you could."

So Colonel L. recommended me, I thought. I had never worked for an officer I respected any more than him.

"By the way, Captain," the general said. "You are representing me and PACAF Headquarters. Don't take any shit from 13th Air Force or any of the bases out there."

"I'm only a captain, Sir," I said.

"You are also the logistics representative from PACAF, young man," General W. said through his narrowed eyes.

"By the way," he added. "You aren't eligible for promotion to major for over two more years. But I am going to do something about that. I am on the advisory board for below the zone promotions. I intend to see you're on the next list. Now get out of my office and go to work."

That was my Aloha to the Hawaiian Islands. Before I could take a deep breath of the warm tropical air or put a lei around my neck, I was on my way back across the Pacific in a roaring, pitching C-130 turbo-prop aircraft bound by waist and shoulder harnesses to the cabin wall next to large, rolling and snapping belted pallets of supplies bound for the Philippines.

Clark Air Base is located on Luzon Island near Angeles City and about 40 miles from the capitol city of Manila. The base was a stronghold of the combined Filipino and American forces during World War II and a backbone of logistics support during the Vietnam War. Now filled with American aircraft and servicemen filtering back from bases supporting the war, it was the host of 13th Air Force Headquarters.

Angeles City bars and brothels were legendary throughout the military. As a result, Clark had numerous servicemen's clubs and theaters open 24 hours a day to try to keep the restless men from venturing into the city's dens of iniquities.

After several days at Clark Air Base and many meetings with logistics personnel, where the General W. and PACAF Headquarters names opened doors, I got the information the general wanted on our far-flung aircraft fleet. I faxed pages of data to him and prepared to return to Hickam hoping to unpack and settle down and get some rest.

I should have known better. A return fax from the general gave me new directions in terse language, "Problem at Yakota. Relieved COM. No knowledge of fleet status. Go there ASAP."

So, instead of returning to Hawaii, I was manifested on the next military aircraft going to Japan to see why the Chief of Maintenance had been removed and report on the fleet status. Fortunately, I had blanket orders signed by General W. that authorized me priority travel on any military aircraft, billeting in BOQs, emergency cash funding, and civilian travel if I needed it.

Just outside my VOQ (Visiting Officer's Quarters) room at Clark was a tennis complex with a number of courts. I had played a little tennis before, but I was still a novice. One morning, when I had a few spare hours, I took lessons from one of the tennis professionals, a slender young Filipino with good command of English. After my lesson, I bought a new racquet at the pro shop.

As I boarded a Lockheed C-141 Starlifter aircraft assigned to the Military Airlift Command (MAC) headed for Yakota, Japan, I was carrying a military B-4 folding suitcase, a briefcase, and my new tennis racquet. The C-141, with a wing span of over 150 feet and a cruising speed of 500 miles per hours, was powered by four jet engines. It was a pleasant upgrade over the old prop churning C-130's I was used to riding on. It had somewhat comfortable front facing and cushioned seats.

Apparently, someone had notified Yakota Air Base the C-141 I was on was carrying someone from PACAF Headquarters. I don't know if it was the flight crew or someone at Clark Air Base, but I was about to receive a very strange welcome to the Japanese unit.

After we landed and taxied up to our parking spot next to one of the hangars, the aircrew opened the main door as the landing crew rolled up a set of stairs. The aircraft commander, a major, stuck his head out the door and then quickly stepped back.

"Captain Miller," he said. "I think you better go out first."

I couldn't imagine why he would say that. During the flight from Hawaii I had dozed off and on. When I stepped to the door carrying my B-4 bag, briefcase, and my tennis racquet the bright sunlight outside caused me to squint my eyes as I looked out. At the bottom of the stairs stood several Air Force colonels at attention flanked by other officers and sergeants lined up on either side as if they were expecting a general officer to disembark.

As I walked down the steps, the colonels smartly saluted me. Then they looked up to see who was accompanying me. When they didn't see anyone else, one of them, who was the wing commander, snarled, "What the hell is going on, Captain? We were expecting a formal inspection."

I shifted my tennis racquet to my left hand and returned the colonel's salute. "You're welcoming a representative of PACAF, Sir," I said crisply.

I can't imagine what the top ranking officers on Yakota thought when they stormed out to our landing aircraft and lined up in formal order expecting an inspection team from PACAF Headquarters, which should have included at least a general officer, when I, a lone captain, walked down the landing stairs with a tennis racquet in my hand.

When we got inside the logistics facility, Chief Master Sergeant S. met me. "What can we do for you, Captain?" he said in a haughty manner.

"You can give me a yellow pad and a couple of pencils, Chief," I said. "I'm here to inspect your unit."

The sergeant quickly responded to my request. As we walked around the maintenance and supply buildings, I scribbled down comments as if I was really there on an inspection. I did notice things that were amiss: dirty work stations, out of uniform technicians, racks of aircraft systems over-due repair, electronic and other test equipment that needed certification, and a general laisse faire attitude by all the personnel up to and including the officers. I could see why General W. had relieved the Chief of Maintenance.

As I was about to walk out the door to get a base taxi to take me to the VOQ, I saw a Staff Sergeant who looked familiar to me.

"Captain Miller, how are you?" the young man said as I walked by.

"Sergeant T.," I responded. I recognized him from my tour at Takhli Air Base in Thailand.

He seemed hesitant to talk to me in front of the Chief so I took him aside so we could speak privately.

"Captain," T. said. "I don't know why you're here, but we've got real problems."

"What do you mean?" I asked.

"Well, Sir," Sergeant T. said quietly, not meeting my eyes. "We have a lot of aircraft here that came from Thailand and other bases after Vietnam crumbled. We don't have an enemy any longer. The communists aren't coming after us so our officers and senior sergeants don't even bother to show up for work. The problem is no one cares if they fly or not. I thought I wanted to make the Air Force a career, now I just want to get out of this uniform and go home."

Suddenly, I realized the dilemma General W. faced. It wasn't the war in Vietnam, which had demanded the full attention of our armed forces, our national press, and our president and congress; it was the aftermath, the withdrawal from the front lines and the vacuum the violence created that no one wanted to confront.

How did we accept military forces who fought a war in a country half-way around the world that was not approved by the majority of Americans back into our society? How would we embrace the returning warriors from a conflict that we lost to an enemy of inferior firepower who carried in their backpacks decades of hatred for foreign intruders invading their country with no intention of returning that homeland to them? Could we Americans forgive a gentle Asian nation who worshipped their forefathers and only wanted a united Vietnam free from outside aggression?

After I finished my trip report, including my analysis of the post-Vietnam war problems, to General W. with the late morning sun brightening his office windows at Hickam Air Force Base in Hawaii two days later, he looked at me for several moments with his eyes narrowed in retrospect.

Finally, he said, "Okay, Captain. I appreciate what you're saying. I have had the same thoughts. What do you think we should do? We have a lot of units in the same shape as Yakota."

"Bring them home, Sir," I said after some hesitation.

I was tired from all the travel and the transition through the time zones from Japan, but I had to speak my mind. "The communist threat no longer exists in the Far East. I know we are still in a Cold War with Russia, but our units in Asia are too far away to combat that. Their morale is so low discipline is a real problem. If we don't get them out of that environment, you are going to have to remove more senior officers."

"What do we do with them after we bring them back?" General W. asked quietly.

"I don't know, Sir," I answered as I took a deep breath. "That's above my pay grade. I think SAC, MAC, and TAC should consolidate their units in stateside bases while we re-evaluate the global threat to the U.S. I really don't know what that is now."

"Hmm," General W. said after looking out of his window at the Hawaiian landscape stretching downward toward the Naval Station at Pearl Harbor. "I don't know what that is yet, either, Captain Miller. It's a bit over my pay grade also. I report to the PACAF Commander who reports to the Chief of Staff of the Air Force who reports to the Chairman of the Chiefs of Staff who reports to the Secretary of the Air Force who reports to the Secretary of Defense who, finally, reports to the President of the United State."

General W. narrowed his eyes as he continued, "Harry Truman's statement that the buck stops there is not entirely correct. The president is held responsible to the people of the United States through the Senate and House of Representatives and the national voters. It's quite a chain of command, Captain. Withdrawing military systems and forces from overseas, and downsizing personnel will be a long and complex procedure."

General W. paused and took a deep breath, before he continued, "I know you're tired. Get some rest, and then check into your office. You've done a fine job. We need on the ground information like you put in your report. I agree with your premise, and I intend to pass it up the line."

Until then, I didn't even know I had an office, but I was to find I did. I even had a secretary and a staff of five senior enlisted personnel on the third floor down the hall from General W.'s office.

The office was authorized one additional sergeant and one of my first official requests was to transfer in Staff Sergeant T. from Yakota.

As the aftermath of the Vietnam withdrawal continued, travel requirements for me and my staff increased. It was a rare day to find more than two or three of us in the Hickam office at the same time. Our travel wasn't limited to Far East locations as we had to visit stateside air bases, headquarters, and depot facilities.

One of my staff, Senior Master Sergeant Frank G., and I traveled together quite often. Frank was a special person; intelligent, motivated, friendly, and extremely small. I was really surprised when I first met him. I thought the Air Force had a minimum height standard but, if they did, Frank must have been right on the lower edge. Even wearing custom made shoes with elevator heels, he only came up to my shoulder and I'm just five foot ten inches.

One day Frank and I were in the Honolulu Airport waiting for a flight to San Francisco. Both of us were wearing Class A uniforms, which included long, dark blue blouses with our medals and rank on them. The stripes on Frank covered his entire upper arms from his shoulder to his elbow. From a distance, he looked like a little boy dressed up like an airman.

Just then, Wilt Chamberlain, the Hall of Fame retired basketball player, walked toward us. I had read in the newspaper he was playing in a professional volley ball tournament in Hawaii. Wilt towered several inches over seven feet tall.

When he saw Frank, he stopped and bent over to him, laughed, and said, "Hi sonny. Does your mommy know you're dressed up like a soldier?"

Then Wilt reached out with his huge hands, grabbed Frank by his shoulders, and lifted him up to his eye level in one swift motion.

I could see the anger well up in Frank as he dangled in the air. He was very sensitive about his height.

Cocking his head back, he said through his clenched teeth, "I'll have you know I'm a Senior Master Sergeant in the United States Air Force. Now put me down."

Wilt started to laugh, then, seeing how serious Frank was, carefully placed him on the floor. "I'm very sorry, Sir," Wilt said contritely. "I didn't mean to insult you. I'm proud of you servicemen. I tried to join, but they wouldn't take me. I'm too tall."

Elvis Presley owned a home on the north shore of Oahu and he came to visit several times while I was there. One day I was at the airport when his black jet aircraft arrived. As he entered the arrival area, a number of reporters swarmed around him and his Memphis Mafia entourage. One of them held a microphone up in front of Elvis and asked him why his aircraft vertical tail had the letters "TCB" printed on it.

Elvis smiled and answered, "That means I'm taking care of business."

Several months after arriving at Hickam, I was able to get a two-bedroom duplex from base housing. It was very close to my office building. My wife, Carolyn, moved from Mississippi to join me. When I was able to schedule time off from my demanding job, we were able to get to know and love the islands of Hawaii.

The year of 1974 was a momentous one worldwide. Most of the countries on the globe, including the United States, were mired in a recession and inflation soared into double digits. Richard Nixon became the first U.S. president to resign his office as a result of the Watergate Scandal.

The average cost of a new car was just under $4,000 and a gallon of gas was 55 cents. Muhammad Ali regained his heavy weight boxing championship when he knocked out George Foreman in the "Rumble in the Jungle" in Zaire. The Sears Tower in Chicago became the tallest building in the world. Popular musicians included ABBA, Beach Boys, Carpenters, Alice Cooper, Dolly Parton, and Eric Clapton who sang "*I Shot The Sheriff.*"

In September of that year, the Kootenai Indian tribe near my hometown of Bonners Ferry, Idaho declared war on the United States to gain attention to the tribe's land lost to the federal government. The U.S. deeded the tribe an additional 12.5 acres of land for their reservation to end the war.

Oahu, the volcanic island where Hickam was located was not very large, only 44 miles long and 30 miles wide. One Saturday morning Caroline and I drove southeast past the Ala Moana Shopping Center and the Aloha Tower through Honolulu. We went by Waikiki Beach where the tourists crowded into hotels and onto the blue ocean beach, which stretched for miles. Past that we skirted Diamond Head, a symbol of the island where Punchbowl Cemetery was located, the resting place of thousands of Americans who died during the Second World War.

Then, as we turned west, we drove by Hanauma Bay, the site of the famous Blow Hole, which periodically shoots ocean spray into the air through a narrow opening, and Kaneohe Bay, the home of Sea World and its exciting porpoise and Orca shows.

Finally, going north, we passed Kailua Bay on the windward side of the island before stopping at the Polynesian Cultural Center, a theme park that preserves the history and culture of the Polynesian forefathers of Hawaiians. With native Hawaiian hula dancers and sumptuous luaus, the attraction draws many thousands of visitors every year.

After leaving the cultural center, we turned toward the North Shore, best known for its massive waves—most notably in the Bonsai Pipeline—which attracts surfers from around the world. Swinging south from there, we passed through pineapple and sugar cane farms. We stopped at one of the pineapple plantations where they had a welcome kiosk with cold, sliced pineapple. We ate so much of it, both of us developed blisters on our lips from the acetic acid.

Past the plantations, we drove by the U.S. Army facility at Schofield Barracks on the way back to Hickam. That was where my father was billeted during the early morning of December 7, 1941 when the Japanese attacked Hawaii.

The Red Hill Project Dad was working on back then as a civilian was still highly classified when I was there, and I couldn't get in with my Air Force clearance. The massive underground tanks, as large as tall office buildings, are still in use today as the primary fuel storage area for the Pacific Naval Fleet and Air Force.

To get through the stressful days at the office and the wearisome travel requirements I had started jogging several miles each day. Early one morning, I was surprised to see General W. pass by me at a quick pace. When I asked him about it later, he told me, "I don't have time to jog, Captain. I get my three miles in and then come to work."

And come to work he did. He was in his office every morning except Sunday by six. On Sundays, he attended church with his wife and teenage son, and after lunch at the officer's club reported for duty by 1 pm. It seemed he never went home at night.

Several times, after going to a movie on a Saturday evening, as I drove by the general's office around 11 pm his light was still on, and I could see his shadow on the window.

One day I was shopping at the Base Exchange (BX) and met General W.'s wife. She was buying a suitcase. I had met her on several occasions at official functions. When I asked her why she was buying the travel bag, she responded, "We're leaving in the morning for a vacation to Napa Valley where my parents live."

"That's interesting," I said. "General W. has called for a meeting tomorrow afternoon. I didn't know he wouldn't be here."

"Oh," she said. "He'll be there. My son and I are going alone. My husband never takes leave."

I couldn't believe what she said. The Air Force gives us 30 days of vacation leave every year. "Never?" I asked.

"No," she said sadly. "In the twenty-two years we've been married, he has never taken a day of leave. I have to go without him."

A few days later, I was jogging—not running like the general—along the street beside my house when I stepped off the curb and severely sprained my ankle.

After several months of rehabilitation at the base hospital, I was still limping badly and favoring the ankle. One of the sergeants in my office was married to a woman of Polish descent who was a nurse at a children's clinic in Honolulu. When she heard about my ankle problem, she had her husband bring me to their house one afternoon.

After stripping off my shoe and sock, she said, "Tsk...Tsk...Tsk."

"What does that mean?" I asked her.

"You have poor circulation in your ankle," she said. "That's why it's not healing. But don't worry, I'm going to fix that."

"You are, how?" I asked.

She didn't answer as she went into the kitchen, and I could hear the clanking of pots and pans. About twenty minutes later she came into the living room carrying a large pot full of water with ice floating in it. Going back to the kitchen she brought out another pot with steaming hot water.

She set both pots in front of me and grabbed my sore ankle and thrust it down in the freezing water. She held it down in the pot even though I tried to pull it out.

After several minutes, while my foot and ankle lost all sensation, she pulled it out and thrust it in the hot water. Wow! Beads of sweat popped out of my forehead as she held my foot in the torrid water. After a few minutes, she repeated the process; first emersion in the cold water and then in the hot. This went on for about fifteen minutes, and then she let me have my foot back.

The next morning, I got out of bed and went into the bathroom to brush my teeth and shave. I was looking at my image in the mirror when I realized I had walked without a limp or pain in my ankle. I don't know if any medical study has ever evaluated the Polish cure for a sprain, but it sure worked for me.

My secretary, Mary Kaolin, was Hawaiian. She told me she could trace her ancestors through stories and songs back to the original settlers of the islands who had traveled thousands of miles across the South Pacific Ocean many generations before.

She explained that the hula, the traditional dance of the islands, was based on ancient lore. When the dancers moved in sensuous rhythm they were miming stories handed down from thousands of years before. The flutter of their fingers told of the fall of rain from the sky and the motion of the waves in their ancestral homes far to the east. The languid movement of their hips and the sliding steps of their dance spoke of the canoes—large enough for many families with their livestock, bread fruit, fresh water, and other plants—that carried them to their new land where the volcanoes beckoned: the wonderful islands of Hawaii.

A few months after I arrived at Hickam, Mary gave me a wonderful pencil drawing of a Hawaiian beach with palm trees framing a setting sun for my birthday. It was a work of art by a true professional.

When I asked about the artist, Mary hesitated for a moment, and then said he was her uncle.

When I told her I would like to buy some of his art, she wouldn't look at me as she answered, "I'm sorry. That is not possible. He is in the leper colony, Kalaupapa, on Molokai."

Molokai, known as the "Friendly Island," is very small, only 38 by 10 miles in size. About 25 miles east of Oahu where Hickam is located, the lights of Honolulu reflecting against the clouds are visible across the waters from its western shore. Formed by two extinct volcanoes, the island is split into two areas; the western half is dry and sparsely covered in vegetation. The eastern portion is a high plateau rising up to nearly 5,000 feet in altitude. It is covered with lush forests that get over 300 inches of rain each year.

Kalaupapa, located on an isolated peninsula on the north side of Molokai, was the site of a leper settlement starting in 1866. Thousands of men, women, and children from throughout the Hawaiian Islands diagnosed with Leprosy (also known as Hansen's Disease) were forcibly exiled to the colony by the government and legally declared dead. They were not allowed to leave the settlement and were forced to live out their days in the isolated settlement.

When I arrived in Hawaii in the mid 1970's, there were no longer any active cases of leprosy because of the development of specific medications, but there were some patients who chose to continue to live in the Kalaupapa settlement because of the social stigma their disfigurement would bring to their families. Mary's uncle was one of those who, after over twenty years there, wanted to stay.

"Does your family visit your uncle?" I asked Mary.

"Yes," she answered. "He will have his 60th birthday next month. That is a time of special ceremony for our people."

"I would like to go with you," I said. "I want to meet the artist who drew this picture. I think he is a kindred spirit."

Mary looked at me strangely, "I will ask my family," she said. "No one has ever wanted to go to the leper colony with us."

The charter boat from Honolulu docked at the west coast of Molokai because the crew, still haunted by the ghosts of generations of lepers living on the north coast, refused to put in at the beach fronting Kalaupapa. To get to the colony we had to mount sure footed donkeys that carried us up from the coast and along a high ridge on a narrow trail overlooking the vast ocean surrounding the tiny island.

As I rode along the path, I felt like I was being transported back over a hundred years into the past when the leprosy colony was first established. On the cliffs above us wild white goats cavorted on the steep hillside.

Mary, her father, mother, and her aunt, rode ahead of me on the trail of memories. Her family had welcomed me with open arms and the wide smiles prevalent among Hawaiians at the dock in Honolulu.

As we descended from the high plateau down a winding road, I could see that the north coast, where the Kalaupapa settlement nestled on a verdant peninsula against the rocky cliffs, was isolated from the rest of the island where most of the residents lived. For over a hundred years, thousands of men, women, and children lived and died in the leper colony.

The small church built by the Roman Catholic Father Damien a hundred years before in 1874 still stood among the small dwellings, mostly abandoned. The Father, venerated as Saint Damien of Molokai, volunteered to live and preach among the diseased outcasts. After 16 years of caring for the physical, spiritual, and emotional needs of those in the leper colony, he contracted and died of the disease.

Mary's uncle lived in a tiny thatch roofed shack close to the beach and the roar of the surf pounding the shore. As we climbed down from our donkeys, I saw a pair of eyes staring out a window at us.

Mary's father went into the hut alone and talked with his brother for a long time. Finally, he came out and said his brother, Kekoa, was embarrassed because I was with the family, and he didn't want me to see his disfigurements.

"Please tell him I have a beautiful drawing he made of a Hawaiian beach," I said. "Mary gave it to me. I came to see him because I know he has the soul of an artist. What he looks like is of no concern to me."

Mary's father started to go back into the shack when a stooped man with scraggly gray hair wearing a long sleeved blue shirt, a pair of worn Levis, and leather slippers shuffled out into the sunlight. Scars of long ago pestilence wracked his face and narrowed his nose to tiny slits. He was missing several fingers on his right hand and his left thumb. But, very noticeable was the intelligent gleam in his dark eyes.

"Thank you for coming to see an old man," he said to me, his voice raspy and weak as if he had suffered from a long bout with a cold. "My Mary works for you."

Then he added with a tinge of humor, "My family likes you or you would not be here."

Mary's mother spread a blanket on the ground near the beach and set out the birthday meal she had prepared. It included Kalua pork with cabbage wrapped in ti leaves, poi, sweet bread, ahi tuna limu, lomi salmon, and kava liquid.

As we sat on the sand with the meal before us, Kekoa told me he had made the drawing Mary had given me many years before when he still had all his fingers. Pointing toward a large rock by the beach, he said that was where he had sat while drawing the scene.

After the delicious meal, we all gave Kekoa a birthday gift, called "makana" in Hawaiian. Following Mary's suggestion, I gave him a box of chocolates.

When we prepared to leave, so we could traverse the treacherous cliff path back to our boat before dark, Kekoa, touched each of his family on their shoulders with his right hand.

As he turned to me, I suddenly thought about a scene from the movie, *Papillon*, which had been released a year before. It was based on a true story about a man sentenced to life imprisonment in the notorious French penal colony on Devil's Island off the coast of French Guiana. As he was escaping, the man, played by Steve McQueen, met a group of lepers deep in the jungle.

The leader of the outcasts took a cigar out of his mouth and handed it to McQueen, expecting him to reject it. But McQueen took the cigar and puffed on it before returning it. Later he said he did it because he knew leprosy was not contagious. I think I was comforted by that movie gesture.

I reached out and touched Kekoa on his right shoulder. He looked into my eyes and returned the gesture with a smile.

When I returned from Molokai, I took art classes in the evenings at the base servicemen's club. After years of observing drawings and paintings, I thought I would try to be an artist. I had a pretty good understanding of linear perspective from my engineering training, but lacked an appreciation for color application.

I remember the art teacher telling us, "A color is the color it is because of the color it is next to." Under her tutelage I began to paint landscapes and seascapes in oil and water color. After many, mostly failed, experiments, I decided I was a good technician but lacked the artistic ability to produce real works of art.

While assigned to Hawaii, several family members came to visit, including my brothers Jerry, Charlie, and Joe.

Joe met his former high school mate Alice Douglas there. He had just finished working on the Alaska Pipeline as a welder. Alice was employed then as a teacher in Australia. Joe later joined her and they became Australian citizens and had two children, Joel and Kaylin. They still live there near Perth in Western Australia.

One of the favorite Hawaiian tourist attractions was the Arizona Memorial in Pearl Harbor. Straddling the sunken hull of the battleship, the memorial marks the final resting place of 1,102 sailors who were killed on the USS Arizona during the Japanese surprise attack on December 7, 1941.

The memorial, built in 1962, was only accessible by a U.S. Navy shuttle boat. Small replicas of the Arizona were for sale to tourists. Quite ironically, they were made in Japan. There was quite a heated discussion at that time in the state legislature about the source of the mementos. It was later changed to an American manufacturer.

In March of 1975 my third son Brian was born at Tripler Medical Center. Known as the "Pink Elephant," the massive hospital overlooked Pearl Harbor directly in front; the downtown Honolulu area, Waikiki Beach, and Diamond Head to the left; Pearl City to the right; and, beyond, stretching to the horizon, the massive sweep of the Pacific Ocean. Behind the main structure and its smaller outlying buildings loomed the Koolau Mountains.

When it was constructed in 1948, the huge sprawling coral pink hospital had been the tallest skyscraper west of San Francisco. During the Vietnam Conflict and for several years afterward it was the largest military medical facility in the Pacific area, with the responsibility of servicing over 50 percent of the earth's surface. Its staff of over 2,000 cared for U.S. military members and dependents in Hawaii and far to the west, which included Brian as he was issued into the world.

Eighteen years later Brian would graduate from high school in Taiwan, Republic of China, as my travels as a sojourner continued to take me around the world for many years to come.

Later in that year of 1975, I saw the "Thrilla from Manila," in the Philippine Islands when Mohammad Ali fought Joe Frazier. I was on temporary duty at Clark Air Base and was given a free ticket and a bus ride to the fight. I called my father later and told him about the match, which Ali won after a brutal battle in a steaming arena.

During my tour in Hawaii, I visited most of the major islands. Maui, the second largest island, became my favorite. My brother, Charlie, and his wife, Lilly, visited it with me. We rode bikes down from the summit of the dormant volcano Haleakala, which rises over 10,000 feet high.

I used Maui as a setting for one of the scenes in my novel, *Weep Without Tears*.

A large hydroplane hovercraft boat built by Boeing Company ran out of Honolulu to the other islands. With my military discount, I could visit Kauai, the Garden Island, and the large island of Hawaii for ten dollars for a round trip.

Another advantage of being in the military then was free tickets to Don Ho's show. Ho was a traditional Hawaiian singer, musician, and entertainer. Best known for the songs *Tiny Bubbles* and *Pearly Shells*, he was a U.S. Air Force veteran who had served at Keesler Air Force Base in Mississippi. He said he would have made the military a career, but he returned home to Honolulu to care for his ill mother.

At his show, very popular with tourists, his children often worked with him. Every night he would acknowledge the veterans in the audience, many times calling some of them up on the stage to be with him as he performed.

I shot my all-time lowest golf score at the Navy Marine golf club on Oahu in 1976. I had a three under par 69 on the Par 72 course using a set of Wilson Sam Snead metal shafted irons and an original laminated McGregor Jack Nicklaus Crown persimmon wood driver.

During my business travels while at PACAF Headquarters, I enjoyed playing at courses in the Philippines, Japan, South Korea, Okinawa, Thailand, and several places in California and other states.

One afternoon, while I was having lunch at the Officer's Club, I received a message to report to General W. in my office. I thought that was strange. Why wouldn't he order me to report to him in his office?

When I walked into my office all my staff was there with General W. I was trying to think of what I had done to warrant such a welcome.

"Thank you for reporting promptly," General W. said through his narrowed eyes. "I can see I need to make more visits to my staff offices. You people think you can get away with anything as long as I'm in my office, including being out of uniform."

I could not imagine who the general was referring to. One of the things I was very strict about was everyone reporting for duty in the proper uniform.

The general turned to me and said, "You're the one I'm talking about. You've been wandering around with the insignia of a captain on your lapels." Reaching into his pocket, he withdrew the gold oak leafs of a major.

I stood at attention as General W. stepped up to me, took off my silver captain's bars and pinned on the major's leafs. Then he stepped back, saluted me, and said, "Congratulations Major Miller."

While he shook my hand, the staff applauded. Then Mary uncovered a large cake on her desk. She smiled as she showed it to me. It was white and embossed with a gold leaf and the words, "Aloha Kakou, Major Ken Miller."

While on one of my business trips to the CONUS, as we called the Continental United States, I visited my brother, John, who lived in Fort Worth, Texas. John was the co-owner of a food delivery business. He had moved there after serving in the U.S. Army. During my visit with him, I was also to spend some time with my older sister, Lavina, who worked for John.

Lavina was born in the small town of Hoehne, Colorado during my father's sojourning days of the Great Depression. She was one of those very special people I have had the pleasure of knowing. She had a zest for life, a free spirit, and a yearning for adventure. She was a beautiful woman with dark hair, penetrating eyes, and an enigmatic smile that reminded me of my mother's.

I recall her driving up to our house on Camp Nine Road in Idaho one time in her Model A and giving several of us kids a ride. I never forgot that special moment as we stormed down a country road with Lavina driving and my brother, Bob, sitting in the right front seat. I was in the rear with my sisters, Kate and Carole.

Suddenly, Lavina turned to Bob and asked him if he wanted to drive. When Bob grinned in reply, Lavina slackened speed a bit, opened her door, and jumped out. Bob did the same on his side of the car. They ran around to the rear of the Model A and reversed positions, running forward to catch up. Unfortunately, the road pitched downward and the car picked up speed leaving them behind.

Ahead was a steep drop off to the Kootenai Valley far below. As the Model A hurtled toward it, my sisters began shrieking in fear. At the last moment before we plunged over the edge of the abyss, Bob was able to put on a burst of speed, jump into the driver's seat, and bring the Model A to a screeching halt.

Unfortunately, a few months after my visit with John and Lavina in Texas, I received a phone call from John that Lavina, learning she had incurable breast cancer, decided to end her life on her own terms instead of trusting it to the doctors who had given her no chance to survive. Her death in Fort Worth was to become the first of many coincidences that would become a part of my life for many years to come in that city.

I attended Lavina's funeral at the windswept Grand View Cemetery overlooking the winding Kootenai River near Bonners Ferry, Idaho. She was the third of my siblings to be buried there. The only one not resting beside her, Clifford, and Paul was my brother Leonard Keith, who was born in 1935 in the same small Colorado town, Hoehne, Lavina was born in. Leonard died as an infant, and he was buried near Hoehne.

As the reduction of military forces in the Pacific continued after the Vietnam Conflict we began to feel it at PACAF Headquarters. General W. was transferred to Warner Robins Air Force Base in Georgia, and I lost several manpower authorizations.

One of the sergeants who worked for me had often complained he didn't like Oahu because it was too small. He said he liked to get in his car and drive longer distances. I was in the office the day he received transfer orders to Minot, North Dakota. I think, to this day, he blames me for an assignment from a warm tropical climate to one of the coldest bases in the continental U.S., although I told him I had nothing to do with it.

Randolph AFB Officer's Assignments called me one afternoon and asked me if I would be interested in being an Intercontinental Ballistic Missile (ICBM) Minuteman Launch Control Officer at Maelstrom AFB in Montana.

We were still immersed in the Cold War with Russia and our nuclear forces, which included a number of ground based missiles and many armed B-52 and B-58 aircraft, hopefully served as a deterrent against the soviet threat to annihilate our nation.

It didn't take me long to respond negatively to the assignments officer. I had a lot of respect for the men and women who supported the Minuteman Program, but the thought of spending long hours in a missile silo deep under the frozen ground of Montana did not appeal to me.

So my next—and final—assignment as an Air Force officer was to the Armament Development and Test Center (ADTC) at Eglin AFB, Florida. I was about to say Aloha to Hawaii and hello to my second tour in the sunshine state of Florida.

Chapter 12
Oysters and Hushpuppies

Eglin AFB was located in the northwest panhandle of Florida. Like many Air Force bases, it was named after a deceased pilot, Frederick Eglin, who died during a crash in 1937. The base was the home of the USAF Tactical Air Warfare Center, which was responsible for the development, acquisition, testing, and deployment for all Air Force non-nuclear armaments.

When I reported, I was put in charge of a group of military and civilian technicians and engineers evaluating aircraft armament and security systems.

A number of auxiliary fields had been developed on the massive Eglin military facility for testing and certification of airborne weapon systems. While I was there I saw many different types of ordnances fired on targets: incendiary and napalm free drop bombs, laser guided bombs and missiles, and Gatlin and machine gun bullets.

Unfortunately, I also witnessed several airplane accidents caused by weapons malfunctions, airframe and engine problems, and pilot errors; some of them resulting in the injury and death of aircrews.

One of the tests assigned to my office was to evaluate the usage of laser systems to protect B-52's armed with nuclear weapons. The lead engineer I put on the project was known by the name of Tiny. Tiny was a legend at Eglin AFB and in the Florida panhandle. Standing six and a half feet tall and weighing nearly 500 pounds, Tiny was the largest person I ever met. At one time, about ten years before, he had topped the scales at 920 pounds and was known as one of the heaviest men in the United States.

I saw a photo from a newspaper when Tiny was on a local high school football team about 20 years before. The shot was taken behind the opposing quarterback looking toward Tiny lined up in a one-hand stance. It had to be intimidating for that youngster to see a monster over 400 pounds who was so broad he took the place of two normal size teenaged players.

After Tiny maxed his weight out, he went on a diet under a doctor's care and over the past ten years had lost half his weight.

Tiny had several impressive attributes. Even as large as he was, he was very nimble on his feet. I once saw him climb over a high chain link fence fleeing from a savage dog nipping at his heels. And Tiny was incredibly intelligent. He had a photographic memory and was an excellent test engineer whose reports were the best I had ever read.

One summer evening our office had a party on the bright white sand at Fort Walton Beach near the base. In addition to fried fish, hush puppies, and tubs of cold beer a fisherman friend of Tiny's brought several barrels of shelled oysters.

"Watch this," one of my staff told me. "You are about to see an amazing feat."

I couldn't believe what I was seeing as Tiny began snatching oysters out of the barrel, cracking them open with a knife, and sucking the raw oysters off the half shell through the air from his meaty raised hand. Everyone stopped what they were doing to stare in fascination as Tiny ate over half of a 55-gallon drum of oysters while inhaling nearly a case of beer, throwing the shells and cans on the ground to create a massive pyramid. When he finally finished, he received a round of applause as he belched like a bull elephant and bowed.

The hush puppies we had at the beach party were a traditional southern dish of fried or baked cornbread batter, usually served at seafood restaurants. Their history goes back centuries to the Native American Indians who grew and milled the first corn (maize) available in the world. They were also known as "hoe cakes" or "fritters" or "Johnny cakes." In the movie that won John Wayne his only Academy Award as Best Actor, *True Grit*, he kept a saddle bag full and called them "corn dodgers."

Most of the systems we used and evaluated at Eglin were of U.S. manufacture. But many companies had international partners who contributed to their products. Some of our test equipment was built by a British company.

One day an English representative of the company came to visit us. Since it was the first time he had ever been to America, I took him to lunch at a seafood restaurant overlooking the bay leading to the ocean. I wanted him to taste the local food.

After we were seated, the Englishman looked at the menu and asked me to order for him.

I ordered fried shrimp, cold slaw, and hush puppies with iced tea. He looked at me strangely when I said, "iced tea."

"Unlike you Yanks," he said with a superior air. "We drink our tea warm with cream and sugar as it is meant to be."

I laughed and told him he should try it, but he declined, sipping a glass of water.

After the waitress delivered our order, I took several hush puppies off the serving plate and ate one of them.

"What is that?" he asked.

"Hush puppies," I answered.

"I'm sorry," he said with a disdainful look. "We don't eat dogs in England."

A few years later when I left the Air Force and went to work for General Dynamics in Fort Worth, Texas, I met a man from North Carolina who said he had met the woman who was responsible for the name "hush puppies."

He told me that back in the depression days of the 1930's a woman who was a friend of his mother in the small town they lived in lost her husband in an accident. She had a number of children and to make ends meet opened the kitchen in her house to the public as a restaurant.

Not wishing to waste any food, the woman was frying some left over corn bread when neighborhood dogs, foraging for food, began baying at the back porch. The woman went to the door, hollered at the dogs, and tossed them some of the fried remnants. She shouted at them, "Hush puppies."

A newspaper reporter from the state capital of Raleigh happened to stop in for lunch one day and was enjoying some of the cooked corn bread. He noted what the woman said when she fed the dogs. Later he reported in his column he had a delicious meal at the restaurant, especially the "hush puppies," which was fried corn batter.

While I was at Eglin, my sojourner father and Mom moved from Idaho to a farm near Natural Dam, Arkansas. My brother, John, who had a business in Fort Worth, Texas bought the property and asked them to come live there. I know Mom didn't look on it favorably, because it would take her out of the cool dry mountain air and away from her children and grandchildren. But she showed her love and support for Dad and moved with him to the hot, humid farm.

When they had their 50th wedding anniversary, most of our family joined them for a celebration in Arkansas. We roasted a pig over a fire pit and told stories late into the night. As we were all leaving, I noticed Mom seemed tired and withdrawn.

I called her later from Florida, and she told me they weren't happy living there. She was frightened of the many poisonous snakes that seemed to like to use the porch for siestas. She said Dad, who loved to work in the garden, would come in after a few hours streaming with sweat from the high humidity. She cried and said she missed her family in Idaho.

A few months after that, I got a phone call from Dad. He said when he came in from working outside Mom was gone. She left a note saying she was ill, and she wanted to die in Idaho. She had packed a few clothes and other things and had left in her car. Dad was very upset. He asked me if I could come and help him move back to Idaho.

I, and my son Mike who was staying with me during his high school vacation, caught the next airplane to Little Rock, Arkansas. I rented a car and when we pulled up at the farm Dad was packing up a U-Haul truck. After we filled the truck there was still more furniture and other items to move, so we went to the nearest town where we left my rental car and picked up another U-Haul truck.

When we headed north from the farm, Dad drove in the lead with me and Mike trailing him. This was in the days before mobile phones and internet connections, so Dad had no idea where Mom was. He worried she might have had an accident or passed out somewhere on the highway. He said when she became ill her skin had turned yellow, but she didn't want to go to a doctor.

We drove late every day and started early the next morning. Each time we stopped for the night or to eat and re-fuel, Dad would call my sisters, Eileen and Penny, in Idaho for word about Mom. But after two days, no one had heard from her.

The third morning on the road, we had breakfast at a gas station in north Wyoming. Dad picked at his food, saying he wasn't hungry, and I could see how worried he was.

I noticed a poster on the wall advertising the Little Bighorn Battlefield National Monument just across the Montana state border on the highway we were traveling. I had visited it several times, but I knew Mike hadn't been there. I asked Dad if we could stop and make a quick drive through the memorial site. He told me we couldn't take the time. We had to get on to Idaho.

A few miles from the turn off to the National Monument Dad pulled over on a turnoff and stopped. I drove in behind him. When I got out of the truck, Dad was looking at one of the rear tires on his truck.

"I have a problem with one of these tires," he said not looking at me. "While I fix it, why don't you take your truck and drive Mike through the Custer Battlefield."

I knew there was nothing wrong with Dad's tire, but I pulled out around him and Mike and I drove through the National Monument. We circled around the hillside graves of the buried soldiers still interred at the battlefield and made a quick stop at the visitor's center.

When we exited back onto the highway, Dad was waiting for us and we fell in behind him as he turned north and headed for the panhandle of Idaho.

We arrived at Penny's house near Naples, Idaho to find Mom ill in a bed there. She had arrived the day before, and Penny had taken her to a doctor, who gave her medicine for jaundice. When Mom had arrived in Idaho, she couldn't even get out of her car without help because she was so sick and stiff from her long, arduous drive.

Somehow, Mom had driven over two thousand miles by herself while she was so ill she was sure she was dying. But she had the strength to finish the trip she thought would be her last. She wanted to die in Idaho near her family.

Strangely, I didn't remember Mom ever being sick when I was a kid. All of us children were, most of the time. We had every illness known to man, and some that weren't: chicken pox, measles, mumps, colds, scarlet fever, and others. I guess the only one we didn't catch and pass on to others was mad cow disease, although we had a lot of mad cows. As a matter of fact, I don't know that we ever had a happy one.

But Mom always seemed to be healthy. Her day started early before the rest of us crawled out of our sleep cocoons and staggered rubbing our eyes to the kitchen for breakfast and her warm from the oven rolls.

Mom recovered from her Arkansas illness and she and Dad moved into a temporary house until they could buy back the Camp Nine farm north of Bonners Ferry, Idaho. Dad's days as a sojourner was over (except for several driving trips they made to the west coast and down to Texas to visit their far flung family), and they stayed there until both passed away; Mom in 1989 and Dad in 1992.

During the summer of 1978, I gave some thought to leaving the Air Force. I could retire at the age of 39 with another career to look forward to. My wife, Carolyn, and I separated and she moved back to Biloxi, Mississippi with my son, Brian. The work at the development center, while interesting, had ceased to be a challenge to me.

The Cold War was still of concern to our country, but I couldn't see a real threat on the horizon from the Soviet Union. At that time, working for a civilian contractor appeared to be very lucrative. With my engineering degree and experience in aircraft operations, testing, and development, I could look forward to promising offers from many companies.

When I told my supervisor at ADTC I was considering retirement, he tried to talk me out of it. After reviewing my record and calling Air Force Headquarters, he told me I was under review for a below the zone promotion to Lieutenant Colonel. He also told me if I stayed in the military promotion to Colonel and possibly General was in my future.

But, in the meantime, I had called Dale Brawner, the General Dynamics F-111 field engineer I met in Thailand. Dale told me they wanted to offer me a position in the Logistics Department as a Product Support Engineer.

"This is an exciting time for us," he told me. "We are developing the new generation high performance air superiority aircraft for the Air Force, and it's going to be the front line fighter for countries around the world for years to come. Come join us and be a part of the F-16 program."

I left the northwest corner of Florida, took off my uniform after 20 years plus three days, and moved to Fort Worth, Texas.

Chapter 13
Cowboy Boots and Camels

The General Dynamics (GD) manufacturing plant, located in the southwest part of Fort Worth was across the active runways from Carswell Air Force Base, a Strategic Air Command (SAC) base with nuclear armed B-52 bombers and KC-135 airborne tanker aircraft. The huge facility was originally built in 1940 by Consolidated Aircraft to support the expansion of the Army Air Corps. In the ensuing years, it transitioned into building aircraft to support the Second World War, the Cold War, and the international conflicts afterward.

I was assigned to the Logistics Department when I was hired by GD and helped develop aircraft support proposals for the new F-16 aircraft program. My first day, I sat across the desk from K. who was the manager. The first thing he said to me was, "Ken, I hope you don't mind traveling. We'll have to do a lot of it with a small staff. Our prime customer is the U.S. Air Force, but we hope to sell the F-16 to countries around the world."

K. would prove to be an accurate seer of the future. The F-16 would sell like hotcakes globally, and I would have to swap my military B-4 bag for a large suitcase. In the next few years I would travel many times to the main F-16 depot in Ogden, Utah; the avionics depot at Warner Robins, Georgia; the Pentagon in Washington D.C.; and to numerous countries around the world where we marketed the best lightweight jet fighter aircraft in history.

In 1978 the average cost of a new home had gone up to over $50,000, a Dodge Charger went for $5,000, a gallon of gas was 63 cents, and the price of gold reached an all-time high of $200 an ounce. The Internet was still far in the future, and one of the first home computers—the Radio Shack Tandy TRS80—was retailing for about $400 using floppy discs for memory storage. The Bell Company introduced the first ever cellular mobile phone system, an expensive and bulky instrument. *Grease* and *Close Encounters of the Third Kind* were showing in theaters. The Bee Gees, Rolling Stones, and Commodores were high on the music charts. *Happy Days, Little House on the Prairie, Wheel of Fortune*, and *Charlie's Angels* were playing on television.

When I told my brother, John, who lived there at the time, I was coming to Fort Worth to work for General Dynamics, he wrote me a letter telling me I had to do several things when I arrived in Texas: I had to buy a pick-um-up truck with a gun rack in the back window for a shotgun and a deer rifle, a ten gallon wide-brimmed hat, cowboy boots, and a pair of blue jeans with a stretched back pocket so I could put a bottle of long neck beer in it while I was dancing the two step with a West Texas cowgirl.

I didn't buy a truck, a shotgun, or a deer rifle. I did buy jeans, cowboy boots, and a hat, which I never wore and gave to my Idaho brother-in-law Dean Burley. I never danced with a West Texas cowgirl, probably because I couldn't do the *Cotton Eye Joe* without tripping over my own feet. The blue jeans are still hanging in my closet, and the gray ostrich quill boots are on the floor beneath the jeans.

But travel I did. Lots of travel. In the next few years, I flew so many miles that, early in the frequent flyer days, I had so many free trips I couldn't even give them away to family and friends.

Today, U.S passports are issued for a ten-year period. Back then, they were only good for five years. I filled up so many passports with country visas I had to carry several with me every time I flew internationally. When I went to Egypt I had to use a different passport than the one I traveled to Israel with to avoid customs harassment for visiting both Muslim and Jewish countries.

One of the things I had to get used to in transitioning from a military career to one with a defense contractor was the change in clothing. For the past twenty years in the Air Force I wore the uniform of the day: fatigues, short sleeved shirts with blue slacks, or, on rare occasions a Class A uniform with a jacket, tie, and a brimmed hat.

General Dynamics required its salaried employees (as opposed to union represented people) to wear a suit or sport coat with a tie. I started off by buying three suits, two sport coats, and a number of slacks, white shirts, and ties. I was soon to realize that was not enough.

The Marlboro Man was still advertising cigarettes on television and our company, like most of them in the United States during the 1970's and 1980's, did not have a non-smoking policy. Almost every male (I was a rare exception) and many of the females smoked. And they lit up everywhere: desks, conference rooms, restrooms, cafeterias, outside areas (except for the flight lines and hangars where aircraft operated or were parked), and on all commercial airplane flights.

I still have a copy of a Life magazine with ads from the 1970's that states, "7 out of 10 doctors recommend Camels," and "Come to where the flavor is. Come to Marlboro Country."

At the end of a day at GD, I would go home with my clothes reeking of cigarette smoke. I would have to take a shower and shampoo my hair to get rid of the stench. The next morning, when I opened my closet, I could smell the lingering odor, and I had to put on a fresh suit. I segregated my smoky clothes in the closet and found myself driving by a dry cleaner every few days to drop off those I had only worn one time.

One of the men I worked with daily didn't smoke, but he chewed Day's Work, a strong tobacco leaf. He carried a cup around with him to spit into but, over time, much of the spittle dropped down onto his wide ties. One day, several of us were discussing the distasteful habit of our tobacco chewing friend. I just happened to be reading a Fort Worth Star Telegram article nationally syndicated as "Dear Abby." It was an advice column where readers submitted concerns for Abby to address.

On the spur of the moment, I decided to ask Abby for advice on how to control our tobacco chewing comrade. I was truly amazed when several weeks later the newspaper published my request and Abby's response.

Dear Abby,
My co-worker has a nasty habit of chewing tobacco and dribbling it down on his tie. By the end of the day, it is a horrible mess. What can we do for him? A concerned co-worker.

Dear Concerned,
Tell your uncouth friend to buy a tobacco colored tie,
Abby

The day after Abby's response was in the newspaper, our sloppy co-worker found several tobacco colored ties on his desk when he came to work, including one from me.

The F-16 aircraft depot facility for world-wide support was established at Hill Air Force Base in Ogden, Utah. I had to make a number of visits to the depot in support of our government proposals. During one of those trips, I accompanied one of our vice presidents and his staff to Ogden. We arrived in the evening and decided to stop at a restaurant on the way to our motel.

As we were driving to the restaurant, one of the staff members, B, a retired Air Force Chief Master Sergeant who had a wry sense of humor, told our driver to pull over to a pharmacy on the way. We thought he might need aspirin or something for a headache. But he didn't say anything when he got back into the car.

When we got to the restaurant, B ordered soup with his entrée. When the waiter brought the soup, B reached into his pocket and extracted the purchase from the pharmacy and dropped it in his bowl. It was a cloth zipper like you would sew into a pair of pants you were making.

We all stared at B as he hollered, "Waiter, come here. I've got a fly in my soup."

B was an amazing person. He could carry on a conversation while drinking beer and tossing peanuts up into the air and catching them in his mouth while he continuing to talk.

After B retired from General Dynamics, I walked into the men's restroom at the company Squaw Creek Golf Course in a beautiful valley west of Fort Worth. B was standing in front of one of the urinals.

"Hello," I said. "Does it get longer after you retire?"

"No," B replied without looking back to see who was talking to him. "But you have more time to play with it."

Several years later, when B was dying from cancer, he wrote his own obituary. It was published in the Fort Worth Telegram after his death.

In it B said he was sorry he had to leave his family and friends before them. "But," he wrote, "I'm already in Heaven with an early morning tee time. Wish you could be here with me. I'm hitting it longer than ever. If you come, better bring some money."

I wasn't in the Logistics Department very long when our marketing department sold some of the F-16 aircraft to Venezuela. When new country contracts were signed, the Program Office established program managers to support the individual buyers. A friend of mine from Engineering, Bob Drewry, was assigned to Venezuela. I had worked with Bob on several aircraft support proposals in the past.

Bob was one of those true southern gentlemen I had the fortune of knowing. Tall, handsome, with silver hair neatly combed, he was raised in Alabama and graduated from Auburn University with a degree in engineering. Soft spoken and always gracious, when Bob asked me to become his deputy for the Venezuela Program, I accepted readily.

But before I could move to the Program Office, another tragedy struck my family; the horrible mutilation and death of one of my brothers.

Chapter 14
Johnny's Salt

I like to cook and one of the pleasures of that pastime is selecting various herbs and spices to give food a special flavor and taste. In my kitchen cabinet are several containers of a seasoning called "Johnny's Salt." Its ingredients include sea salt, pepper, paprika, garlic, and various spices. Manufactured in Tacoma, Washington it is not available from stores in Texas where I live.

Several years ago, during a visit with my older brother, Charlie, in Otis Orchards, Washington we had a breakfast that included scrambled eggs. Charlie sprinkled something on his food and handed it to me. "You can't eat eggs without Johnny's Salt," he said.

As I was using it, Charlie added quietly, almost reverently, "Every time I use it I think of Johnny."

When I left Charlie's he gave me a large container of Johnny's Salt. Over the next few years, I used it up because I couldn't think of eating eggs without it. My sister, Carole, during one of her visits to Fort Worth replenished my supply. I found I shared Charlie's sentiment: I couldn't use it without thinking of Johnny.

John E. Miller was the 12th of 17 children of my parents, Charles and Ruth Miller. Johnny, as we all called him, was born on July 5, 1943 in Bonners Ferry, Idaho. He was the only one of us who didn't have a middle name; only the initial "E." The family lore is that when Johnny was born, Mom looked at him and shrieked, "Eee," because he was so small. We were told he was so tiny he slept in a shoe box in a dresser drawer.

Johnny grew into a normal sized boy and man with a charming personality, clear blue eyes, and curly blonde hair, which later turned to light brown. He had the enigmatic smile with one side of his mouth that Mom had, and I think he inherited her sense of humor and her giving nature.

I was four years older than Johnny and one day, when he was about six years old, he told me he didn't like his curls; all the kids at school made fun of him. I took him out to Dad's work shed and cut all his curls off with a pair of scissors. I have to admit, I made a horrible mess of it. He looked like a sheep that had been sheared by a drunken shepherd.

When Mom saw Johnny, she didn't wait for Dad to come home

before administering ADD (Adult Daily Discipline). I thought Dad whacked us hard with his belt, but Mom went him one better as she beat me and Johnny that day.

As Mark Twain so aptly put it, "My mother had a great deal of trouble with me, but I think she enjoyed it."

After high school, Johnny joined the Army and was sent to Addis Abba, Ethiopia where he served with the U.S Embassy staff. I got a letter from him with a photograph of him riding an ostrich. His enclosed letter said everyone in Africa was so black he bought dark sunglasses so everyone would look the same.

After leaving the Army, Johnny met a man from Texas, Ross Bruner, in New York City. Together, they went to Fort Worth and began a business named "International Pizza and Deli Supply." The company became very successful. Their customers included the theme park "Six Flags Over Texas," and many local restaurants.

One of Johnny's early customers was "Margie's Italian Gardens," a long established Fort Worth restaurant.

I want to take a moment to note one of the many unique coincidences that have occurred over the years between my Miller family and Fort Worth, Texas.

Margie and her husband immigrated to the United States from Italy during the latter years of the Second World War. She was a most unusual woman with a friendly, outgoing personality. When anyone visited her restaurant, she would greet them at the door and ask their names. Repeat visitors, even after years of absence, would be greeted by her cheerfully welcoming them by name.

After I moved to Fort Worth to work for General Dynamics, Johnny took me to Margie's for dinner. She welcomed us with open arms and a special dinner of Italian cuisine. Her son, Doyle, who was the head chef, joined us that night and told a most unusual story.

Several years before, he related, he had a run in with his parents and left Fort Worth to drop out of the mainstream of society. He wanted to be a street person, he said, a vagabond who just traveled around as his whims led him. He admitted he sampled various drugs and alcohol on his sojourns.

After about six months, Doyle told us, he woke up one morning somewhere in Florida and wanted to come home. He called his parents and asked them for money to return. But when he got the funds, he said, he got high and hit the road again. A while later, he found himself in New York City with no idea how he had got there. Again, he asked his parents for money to return to Texas. They sent it to him, and he disappeared into the vagabond society again.

I looked at Johnny and he just smiled and shook his head at me. Later he told me he had never heard Doyle talk about his life.

"Then one day," Doyle said. "The bus I was on stopped at a small town in the Northwest. My ticket had run out and the driver told me to get out. I found myself in this small town with mountains all around. I had no money and no food. Then this stranger, dressed like a cowboy with the boots and wide hat and all, came up to me and said he wanted to take me to lunch. 'You look a little peaked,' he said."

"Well, where were you?" Johnny asked.

"Oh, some little place, you wouldn't know about," Doyle answered. "After the cowboy bought me lunch he took me home and I stayed with him and his wife. Then he put me to work with him for a couple of weeks, and he and his wife talked me into coming back to my family here in Fort Worth. You know, he logged timber with Shetland Ponies. Can you believe that?"

Johnny and I looked at each other in surprise.

"Oh my God," Johnny exclaimed. "What were their names?"

"Oh, Dean and Eileen Burley," Doyle answered off handedly.

"My God," Johnny said. "Doyle, you met my sister Eileen and her husband Dean Burley in Bonners Ferry, Idaho."

My brother-in-law Dean Burley was quite famous for logging with Shetland Ponies. He was allergic to gasoline so he used horses to skid logs through the forest. Why he used ponies instead of mules or large horses no one ever understood, but it was unusual. Several times, he was written up in local and Spokane newspapers for his strange choice.

In addition to the coincidence of Doyle meeting my sister in Idaho, my older sister, Lavina, died in Fort Worth. John and I came here for business reasons, my elder sister, Louise, moved here in the late 1980's from the West Coast to be near her daughter, Robyn, who married an ex-marine from the area. Then in the 1990's, my sister, Carole, transferred from Washington D.C. here as a result of de-centralizing in the Department of Agriculture.

But the most unusual coincidence would happen later when I moved to Taiwan, Republic of China and met a Chinese-German whose mother lived on the north side of the Kootenai River in Bonners Ferry. As my brother Charlie would say, "Truth is stranger than fiction."

I was amused and concerned when Johnny called me one day and said he was definitely going to quit smoking. He had told me several times he was giving up the habit, but was never able to kick it. He tried nicotine gum, staples in his ears, shots in his sinuses, and high filter cigarettes without success.

This time, he said he found a hypnotist who assured him he could help him. I told him to call me each day and let me know how he was doing. He called me on the first, second, and third day telling me he had not smoked. But he didn't call on the fourth day. I waited several more days before I phoned him.

"I couldn't do it any longer, Ken," he said. "I had a stressful situation at work and went outside and had a cigarette. I'm back to smoking."

I sympathize with Johnny. I know it is hard to quit highly addictive cigarettes. As Mark Twain said, "To cease smoking is the easiest thing I ever did. I ought to know because I've done it a thousand times."

Johnny was adored by his employees and their families. Each Christmas, he would have an office party and dress up as Santa Claus and give out gifts to everyone. He told me one time that since he grew up in such a large family he could relate to all of his Texas workers because they made him feel wanted.

Then, during the night of November 30, 1982 I received "the call." The call is the one you dread and try not to think about. The call is one of deep tragedy, one you cannot anticipate nor ignore.

It came to me from Johnny's partner, Ross Bruner. "Johnny is dead," he said in a halting voice. "Someone murdered him in his house."

Tom Anderson, a Fort Worth Star Telegram, writer wrote an article about him:

The 38-year old owner of a Fort Worth pizza supply business was found fatally stabbed in the dining room of his Meadowbrook area home early today.

Police identified the victim as John E. Miller of 5604 Shadow Ridge Court, whose body was found by his business partner, Ross Bruner, shortly before 1 a.m. today.

Fort Worth homicide detective Joe Tiroff said there were no suspects this morning.

Tiroff said Bruner told him he had gone to the Greyhound bus station downtown about 11:15 to ship several packages to Oklahoma City. When Bruner returned shortly before 1 a.m. to the house that he and Miller shared, Tiroff said, Bruner found Miller's body in the dining room.

A bloodstained pair of blue jeans found hidden behind a box in the garage were submitted to the police crime lab for analysis, Officer T.J. Brown said.

Brown said Miller's body bore numerous stab wounds to one arm and the back and that a wooden-handled steak knife was protruding from the victim's right arm.

Miller was owner of International Pizza and Deli Supply at 5901 Tension Drive. The company provides ingredients for pizza restaurants in Fort Worth and North Texas.

Tiroff said that other than blood on the floor near the victim's body, there were "very minimal signs of a struggle." Miller's body was found kneeling face down against a dining room wall, Brown said.

Tiroff said robbery did not appear to be a motive.

Brown said a chair in the kitchen was overturned and several items had been taken out of the kitchen cabinets. A 16-gauge shotgun was found on the floor.

Bruner said that when he opened the unlocked front door a small piece of paper that apparently had been jammed between the door and the facing fell out.

That night was the start of many nights, many days, many months, and many years of anguish for me and my family over Johnny's murder. I have never met a kinder or gentler person than Johnny and his loss grieved me deeply. In the ensuing years, I spoke to the detectives investigating his murder many times. But when it went from an active to a cold case I, like many in my family, gave up hope that it would ever be solved.

I escorted Johnny's body to Bonners Ferry, Idaho where we buried him in the Grand View Cemetery near his brothers Clifford and Paul and his sister Lavina.

My father could not understand how someone could be killed without swift justice. In Boundary County, Idaho where he lived, there had not been anyone murdered in many years. It was hard for him to relate to violence in a city like Fort Worth. Dad was a man of action, and it wasn't long before I received a call from the head of the Fort Worth police department.

When I walked into the Police Chief's office, the investigating detective, Joe Tiroff was with him.

"Please sit down," the chief said as he waved to a chair across from him. Looking down at his desk, he started speaking, "Uh, the governor has called me about your brother's murder case. It seems he got a letter from your father asking him to look into it."

I just looked at him. Dad had written a letter to John Connelly, the governor of Texas about Johnny. Maybe, I thought, now we can make some progress. I had never been impressed with Tiroff's interest in the case. In fact, two days after Johnny's murder, Tiroff had taken a three-day vacation. After two months, there were still no suspects. Johnny's partner, Ross, had been considered for a while and then discarded as not having any part in the killing.

"Uh," the chief said, finally looking up at me. "Please tell your father we are doing everything we can to find the culprit. Isn't that right, Sergeant Tiroff?"

Tiroff was a small man with a narrow face. If I was to liken him to an animal, it would be a weasel. I had met with him a number of times after Johnny's murder, usually at my insistence. Whenever he spoke to me it was in an aloof, offhand manner as if he had better things to do with his time.

"The chief's right," Tiroff said while staring out the window. "We've run the fingerprints—got some good ones because of all the blood—but haven't turned up anything. We checked with the bus and train station to see if anyone suspicious left that night, but came up with nothing. We are thinking it was a random act. Someone just wandered in off the street and attacked your brother when he came home and then disappeared into the night."

"I understand that," I said trying to get Tiroff to look me in the eyes. "I've talked to all Johnny's employees and most of them said you didn't even talk to them. Instead of blaming it on a random act of violence, have you tried to see if anyone here in Fort Worth had an issue with him? I think it's called establishing a motive. Several of them told me he and his partner were having some problems working together."

The police chief stared at Tiroff as he waited for him to respond.

"Well," Tiroff said, still not looking at me. "His partner had an airtight alibi. He was with a friend that night who took him to the bus station at the time of the murder."

I left the police office frustrated and angry at the perceived disinterest and shoddy investigation by the detective and the lack of support from the chief. Even though my brother Jerry later proved through handwriting analysis that John's partner had his will changed and his signature falsified so he would inherit Johnny's estate nothing came of it.

I talked to Dad many times, but the months and years went by with no resolution and no closure on Johnny's murder. Dad died in 1992 never knowing who took the life of his son.

Then on the 13th of April, 2010, 27 years 4 months and 14 days after Johnny died, I received a phone call from Detective O'Brien of the Fort Worth Police Department Cold Case Unit. He said he was reviewing John's case file and it aroused his interest. He found a cigarette butt in the evidence file from the murder scene.

They didn't have DNA analysis back in 1982 so he sent it to the state and national DNA laboratories for testing. It came back with a signature that did not match Johnny. They did come up with a match to a man named Russell Morris. Morris, who had a long list of felonies on his record, was in the Texas prison at the time for sexual assault, but he was close to being released on parole. O'Brien said he interviewed Morris in prison and he confessed to Johnny's murder.

I couldn't believe what I was hearing, and it took me a long time to compose myself and respond to O'Brien. After we finished our conversation, I called and e-mailed all my family and told them that at last we had some closure. The man who killed Johnny had finally been identified.

The Fort Worth Police issued an arrest warrant for Morris and he was transferred from prison to the Fort Worth jail. Two years later, after a plea bargain with the District Attorney for an additional 12 years of incarceration, Morris was scheduled for sentencing at the court house. I was there when the judge convened the session, and I read the following letter from the family into the court record.

August 9, 2012
From: John Miller Family
To: Whom It May Concern
Subject: Family Statement (Case Number 1201361)

John Miller was killed in his home on November 30, 1982. As the years passed, we had given up hope that his murderer would be found and we would receive closure on his passing.

We want to express our heartfelt appreciation to the Fort Worth Police Department Cold Case Unit Detectives O'Brien and Reyes for re-opening John's case and pursuing it until a suspect was indicted. We also thank the District Attorney Office and Arthur Clayton for prosecuting this case in an expeditious and professional manner. The personal attention given to our family by Laura Flores of the Victim Assistance Unit was a special help during this difficult time.

John Miller was born in Bonners Ferry, Idaho on July 5, 1943, the 12th of 17 children of Charles and Ruth Miller. After graduating from high school, he joined the US Army, serving at the embassy in Ethiopia. After his discharge, he went to Fort Worth, Texas and established a successful food distribution company. His co-workers, employees, and customers praised John as hard-working, honest, and very caring. One employee said that he felt like he was a member of a large, extended family, not a business organization. Christmas was a special time for John because he got to play Santa Clause and pass out bonuses and presents to his employees and their families.

John's father and mother were alive when he was brutally murdered at the age of 39. Since then, they have passed on, carrying the open wounds of losing their son and not seeing justice done. Eight of John's siblings are still alive. We all remember him fondly after nearly 30 years. His older sister, Louise, said that when she thinks of him, she remembers his wonderful smile. His brother, Ken, who identified John's body the night of his death, is still haunted by the memory. His sister Carole said that she would keep her kitchen light on until his murderer was convicted. Now she can turn out the light.

As a family, we hope that Mr. Morris is never free again, not only as punishment for killing John, but to ensure that he never commits another crime like this.

To you, Mr. Morris, we can never forgive you for taking John from us. We can only pray that God will have mercy on your soul.

The John Miller Family

While I read the letter, I looked at Morris, who was wearing a jail jumpsuit and handcuffs, but he stared down at the table beside his attorney and never acknowledged me. The last view I had of him was when he was escorted out the rear of the court room by several deputies.

Less than two years later, on July 29, 2014, I received a letter from the Texas Department of Criminal Justice stating that Morris had died while in their custody. They did not list the cause of death.

Morris never implicated anyone else in the murder. Johnny's partner, Ross, who many suspected of being involved, couldn't run their business by himself and it soon went into bankruptcy. He moved to Central America and later went into a nursing home in New Jersey where he died.

Carole has turned off her kitchen light at night, and I use Johnny's Salt whenever I cook, not just for eggs. I use it very sparingly, but when I run out, I'll get some more.

Chapter 15
Angel Falls

Bob Drewry and I were responsible for coordinating every facet of engineering, development, manufacturing, delivery, supply, and field support for the Venezuela Air Force as they became the first Latin American country to take ownership of the F-16 aircraft.

Talk about travel; it was about to increase. Travel to the depot support facility at Ogden, Utah, to the Air Force Headquarters at the Pentagon, to meetings in Panama, and, long trips to Caracas and the operational unit at El Libertador Airbase in Maracay, Venezuela.

After I moved to the Program Office in 1983, I bought a new Cadillac, the first unused car I ever purchased. That year the cost of a stamp was still 20 cents, gas had increased to $1.25 per gallon, a new house in the Fort Worth area was approaching $90,000, and a new car sold for about $6,000.

That was about what I paid for my new Cadillac. It was a beautiful automobile with all the bells and whistles available back then. When I sold it four years later, it was under strange and humorous conditions.

I put an ad in the local newspaper and received a number of responses. One of them was from a black woman who said her husband was a pastor at a Baptist Church south of Fort Worth. She said they were looking for a white Cadillac to enhance his image.

They came to look at the Cadillac one morning and bought it on sight at the price I wanted. When we went to the Credit Union to transfer the title and deposit the sales money, the pastor's wife brought a large paper bag inside with her. When the teller asked her if she had a check for the transaction, she said no and put the bag on the counter in front of her. As I watched with my eyes wide open, the teller impatiently counted out $3,000 in cash, the largest being $20 bills. I suddenly realized the car was being bought with the pastor's church congregation donations.

During one program review trip to Panama City for the Venezuela Program, I had a free afternoon and visited the Panama Canal. An open-air train ran along the canal and I went from the Atlantic Ocean side nearly 50 miles to Balboa on the Pacific Ocean. Watching the locks fill with water as the huge ships traversed the canal, which opened in 1914 after over 20 years of construction at a worker death toll in excess of 22,000, was fascinating. Prior to the canal, which has been named one of the seven wonders of the modern world, seagoing vessels had to sail or steam around the southern tip of South America through the hazardous Cape Horn route.

It was in Panama City that my usually unerring direction ability failed me. One afternoon, I was driving a rental car, with Bob Drewry as a passenger, going from our review meeting place to our hotel near the beach several miles away. The traffic, as in most Latin American cities, was horrendous: bumper to bumper, horns blaring, signal lights in-operational or ignored, and thousands of flitting motor scooters and cycles weaving in and out of traffic like water bugs.

I was headed in the right direction when an accident, one of many I would witness during my travels to South America and Asia, caused me to turn off the main thoroughfare to a side street. Unfortunately, it was a one-way road going the wrong direction. After several more turns, I was lost. I knew the general direction to the beach because of the location of the sun, but I couldn't go that way because of traffic.

Then I saw a taxi parked on the street curb and pulled up beside it. I got out and gave the driver, who spoke no English, a business card from our hotel and a hand full of money. Pointing at the card, I signaled that I wanted to follow him to the hotel. The driver stared at me perplexed for several seconds. Then he smiled and nodded. I was able to trail the taxi through the convoluted and congested streets and get back to the hotel.

Bob and I took a company sponsored Spanish class several hours a week when we were in Fort Worth. Our instructor told us we only needed to learn one sentence to get along in any Spanish speaking country, "*Una mas Cerveza por favor*," which means "one more beer please."

I learned to read somewhat but never became proficient in the language. Bob, on the other hand had many problems with Spanish. Soft spoken with a distinct southern United States accent, he just couldn't speak the language.

One lunch time, Bob and I stopped at a McDonald fast food restaurant in Venezuela and Bob said he wanted to order for us. "*Dos hambergesa e papa's fritas*," he said in his Alabama drawl. He was trying to say "two hamburgers and French fries."

The girl behind the counter stared at Bob for a moment, then she turned and motioned at several other workers to come to her. When they gathered around, she smiled at Bob and said, "*Senor, de nuevo por favor*," which meant "Sir, again please."

When Bob repeated his order, all the servers burst into laughter. Bob's face turned red and he said to me, "I'll never speak this language again."

And he didn't. During the next few years while I worked with Bob on the Venezuela Program, he never again tried to speak Spanish. But he really didn't have to. Most of the civilian and military people we communicated with spoke English, many of them trained or educated in the United States. For those who didn't, we always had a proficient translator.

When I wasn't out on a business trip, I had to prepare a weekly briefing on our program status and present it to the vice president of country programs Dr. M. and his staff.

It was like attending Alice in Wonderland's "mad tea party" along with the Mad Hatter (Dr. M.), the March Hare (Dr. M.'s loud and obnoxious assistant), and a very tired Dormouse (the technical publications director) who falls asleep frequently, only to be violently woken up by the Mad Hatter.

As I sat through the tedious and uninteresting briefings (which were a trademark of most defense contractors), I kept waiting for the staff of male White Anglo Protestants (Wasps) to give me a riddle like the famous "Why is a raven like a writing desk?" the Mad Hatter gave to Alice. But that never happened, the meetings just droned on and on with a noticeable lack of humor or levity.

Dr. M. (the Mad Hatter) was a round faced man with a mouth that turned perpetually down in a frown. Sparing gray hair over dark plastic framed glasses made him look like everyone's idea of an accountant working for the Internal Revenue Service. He could walk into an empty room and blend right in.

His secretary, who had worked for him for over 30 years, once told me the last time she heard him laugh was when he watched the Chairman of the Soviet Union Nikita Khrushchev pound his shoe on the table during a General Assembly meeting at the United Nations in 1960. She said she lived in dread for the day when Dr. M. would strip off his shoe and pound the desk at one of his weekly briefings.

I never saw Dr. M. pound for attention with his shoe, but I did see him take his ball point pen out of his suit jacket pocket and tap it on the table in impatience when some of the briefings went on too long even for him.

When the Supply Director droned on ad nauseam over the backlog (orders to suppliers) for left-handed electronic veeble fetchers and other assorted miscellaneous items, the Technical Publications Director enumerated the number of misprints reported in the overhaul manual for the F-16 right manifold pressure thing-a-ma-gig, or the Indonesian Program Director hesitantly reported the IAF sortie rates had fallen below 50 percent on time because the witch doctor the technicians depended on to exorcize the demons out of their test equipment had died and they couldn't find a replacement, out would come Dr. M.'s pen and the tap-tap-tap would begin.

When the Mad Hatter reveals they have tea all day because time has punished him by eternally standing still at 6 pm (tea time), Alice becomes insulted and tired and leaves, claiming it was the stupidest tea party she had ever been to. Unfortunately, I couldn't get up and leave even though I thought they were the stupidest and most time wasteful meetings I had ever been to.

Then one day I chanced upon a strange photograph in a magazine. It was a comic sketch of a hammer unlike any I had ever seen. It had two heads, one facing 90 degrees from the other one on a single u-shaped handle. As I looked at it, a bemused thought came to me, and I smiled the secret smile my mother would use when she wanted to inject humor into times of stress.

I took the photo to a friend who worked in the graphics department and explained what I wanted. He looked at it for a moment, then he laughed and said, "Can do. Wish I could be there when you show it."

At my next briefing, updating the status of our Venezuelan Program, I asked my friend Bill Littell to flip my overhead charts. He had tried to talk me out of showing the strange hammer picture, but I insisted on using it.

Near the end of my briefing, which I had deliberately delivered in a monotone voice (immediately putting the Supply Director to sleep) Bill put up the hammer chart. The graphics arts technician had interposed it on a Support Equipment form with the heading in large red letters, *Aggie Hammer, PN10012AH*.

In an upbeat voice, I said, "We have added a newly developed piece of support equipment to assist the aircraft technicians beat out dents in the wing skins of the F-16. The official name is the Aggie Hammer."

Gasps spread throughout the room just before it went totally silent and everyone at the table and on chairs against the walls looked open-mouthed at Dr. M. for his reaction.

For a moment, a very brief moment, I thought I saw a flicker of emotion in Dr. M.'s eyes behind the coke bottle lens of his glasses. But then it was gone, his hand poised above the table as it was ready to tap the table.

He didn't tap his pen. In an impassive voice, he simply said, "Who is the next briefer."

I no sooner returned to my office when Bob Drewry, who had not attended the meeting, called me.

"What did you do during the briefing?" he asked in his quiet and respectful manner.

I showed Bob the Aggie Hammer chart. He had a chuckle over it before telling me one of the meeting attendees, an Engineering Director who was an Aggie, was very upset, and he wanted me to personally apologize to him.

I made the apology straight away.

Texas A&M (Agriculture and Mining) was established in 1876 as the state's first public institution of higher learning. Up until 1965 the Corp of Cadets (a pseudo military organization) referred to as the "Guardians of Tradition" was mandatory for all students and female undergraduates (who were few and far between). The Aggies, as they became known, historically outnumbered commissioned officers from any other university in the nation other than the military academies.

General Dynamics in Fort Worth was a bastion of Aggies; let me qualify that as male Aggies since there were few female Aggies in the company and none in management positions then. The president, many of his vice presidents, directors, and managers were graduates from the hallowed halls of learning in College Station, Texas. As a result, Aggie stories and jokes proliferated throughout GD.

One of my first experiences with Aggies occurred at a Texas A&M versus Texas Christian University (TCU) football game in Fort Worth. I bought a ticket not looking at the seating chart, and I found myself right next to the Corp of Cadets.

They did not sit down the entire game. They stood up and bent over with their hands on their knees blocking my view of the entire left side of the field from the 50-yard line. They also chanted incessantly like a large group of Buddhist Monks begging for alms, which drowned out the game announcer's commentary on the progress of the game. As a result, I only got to see half the game, that half played to my right side.

I'm not sure if it arose from that football game experience, but I became the unofficial keeper of Aggie stories for GD, maintaining a running log of Aggie jokes. It wasn't long before I was being contacted by many others in the company who wanted me to share my research with them. I received calls from all over the world asking for jokes.

One of our engineering field representatives in Egypt called me and said he was expecting some company visitors; two of them being Aggies. He wanted some new jokes to use during their visit. After running down my list, I was able to pass on several he could use.

One of the Aggie football stories I passed on came to me as I reflected on the game where I sat next to the Corp of Cadets. Late in the 4th quarter of a game between the Aggies and TCU in Fort Worth the score was tied. TCU had to punt with less than a minute left. Just as an Aggie caught the ball and was tackled, a whistle sounded from a nearby train. The TCU players thought the game was over and they left the field. It then took the Aggies four plays to score.

I think the touchdown occurred on the left side of the field where I couldn't have seen it.

I was elected the president of the National Society of Logistics Engineers (SOLE), an organization that included several hundred aircraft manufacturers and suppliers. At the dinner where I was inducted in Washington D.C. I arose to give the keynote speech.

When I stepped up to the microphone, I appeared nervous and knocked over a glass of water. "Good evening," I said hesitantly. "I almost didn't make it here tonight. I was attacked in the parking lot by a man with a razor."

When the oohs and aahs and what happened comments finished, I added, "Yes. I was attacked in the parking lot by an Aggie with a razor. Fortunately, the cord was too short and he couldn't reach me."

After my speech, a GD vice president who I had worked for many years came up to me. Z was an Aggie.

"Ken," he said with a frown and pursed lips. "We are going to make you an honorary Aggie." Then he added ominously, "Posthumously."

During one of our visits to El Libertador Airbase to meet the pilots and support personnel who would receive the F-16, Bob Drewry and I were taken to lunch at the Officers Club. The food was served cafeteria style with the food warmed by overhead lights. Normally, the club would be the cleanest place to eat on the base, but after our visit there I'm not so sure.

As Bob and I got in line, we noticed there were no eating utensils next to the plates. One of the Venezuelan officers with us shouted at a heavy-set cook standing behind the food line wearing a dirty white apron and smoking a cigarette.

The cook, who appeared to be upset because the officer was yelling at him, reached into a bucket where previous diners had deposited their used utensils, pulled some out, and wiped them on his filthy apron before slamming them down in front of us.

Bob and I looked at each other and took a deep breath before we picked up the recycled utensils and went down the food line because we didn't want to insult our guests, all young officers who were trying to impress us.

The food, which was piled in metal serving trays, looked very unappetizing. The lights shining on it had dried the meats out and the vegetables looked wilted. There was a pot of beef broth soup still steaming so I opted for a bowl of that.

After we sat down at one of the tables, I stirred my soup and, as I pulled my spoon up, a dead roach floated to the top. Neither Bob nor I ate any lunch that day, and we avoided the Officers Club after that.

Although the food on El Libertador was unpalatable, many of the restaurants in Venezuela were very good. One near the hotel where we stayed in Maracay served great paella, a saffron flavored dish with rice, meat, seafood, and vegetables with a bubbling sauce. And on most street corners in Maracay and Caracas, push cart vendors hawked hot and tasteful quesadillas, enchiladas, tamales, and tacos de carne.

Maracay, established in 1701 by the Spanish Bishop Diego de Banos, was named after a local chief whose name meant tiger. One of the most important cities in Venezuela, it was an industrial and commercial center. Sugarcane, tobacco, coffee, and cocoa were its main products. Heavily influenced by the military base at El Libertador, Maracay was the cradle of Venezuelan aviation.

After we established the F-16 fighter aircraft there, changes in their national political arena caused separation between them and the United States. Today, although they still have the F-16, we no longer support it and as the years have gone by, the aircraft is nearly grounded by lack of support and supplies.

About 25 miles from Maracay was one of the strangest towns I have ever visited anywhere during my days as a sojourner: Colonia Tovar. It was founded by a group of Baden, Germany immigrants seeking religious freedom in 1843. Several years later when I went to Germany, I realized the village was an exact duplicate of those in the mountains of the home country.

Through all the years, they maintained their original culture, religion, and architecture. Like a Shangri La amidst the native population and Spanish settlers, Tovar was known as "the Germany of the Caribbean." Maintaining their pure German bloodline meant they had to import new young men and women of child bearing age over the years.

But as I walked around the village of over 3,000 people during my visit there about 140 years after it was established, there was evidence of family inbreeding: children and adults with blonde hair, blue eyes, and vacant stares.

A Venezuelan Air Force Colonel had driven me and Bob Drewry to Tovar for our visit. To get there, we exited the main highway connecting Maracay and Caracas onto a narrow paved road that switch-backed up a steep mountain slope in the foothills of the Andes Mountains that stretched for several thousand miles down the continent. The road was narrow, single lane at times, and the drop off below precipitous. We could see crosses and flowers by the side of the way where travelers from years past had lost their lives in accidents on the hazardous mountain side.

When we topped the crest of a high ridge, Colonia Tovar appeared below perched on the down slope like an alpine medieval European township above the Rhine River. Far off in the distance we could see the glimmer of the Atlantic Ocean.

We arrived near mid-day, and the colonel escorting us drove directly to a restaurant where the sound of a German oompa band poured out into the street.

The lunch was superb with German wurst (sausage), sauerbraten (sour roast), and a local Tovar beer. The wait staff and the musicians were gracious; while remaining aloof as if they resented us coming to their closed community.

After we finished eating, we walked around the center of the quaint village. Passing the Tovar Brewery, dating back to mid-1800, we strolled by the Church of St. Martins of Tours, the Casa Codazzi, and many cafes and craft shops.

We were about to return to our auto when we heard the excited sound of voices on the street below us. Looking that way, we could see a plume of dark gray smoke billow up overhead.

Joining the locals crowding to a balustrade at the lower perimeter of the town, we could see far below us, on the steep slope from the valley, the bright red glow of a brush fire leaping upward toward Tovar. It was fueled by the dry brush and trees suffering from a long drought caused by a high pressure area that had settled into the coastal area.

As we watched, the conflagration expanded rapidly until it filled the gulch leading up to us. I took several photos with a small camera I carried. Later, when I had the film developed—this was in the days before digital cameras—I could see startled looks on the faces of the Tovar residents as they stared down at the threatening fire rapidly hurtling toward them.

Our Venezuelan escort shouted at us as he ran back up the street toward our car. Bob and I followed him as quickly as we could. When we left Tovar, speeding over the crest of the mountain and down the narrow road beyond, we could see smoke billowing up over the village behind us.

Later we heard that, thanks to the supreme efforts of Tovar's fire department and volunteers, the village was spared from the ravenous fire with only the loss of a few outlying buildings.

During one of my trips to Venezuela, I had the opportunity to visit the highest uninterrupted waterfall in the world, Angel Falls, in the southern part of the country. The torrent of water drops nearly 3,000 feet over the edge of a high mountain escarpment. It was born many thousands of years ago when a massive earthquake lifted a portion of the land containing a river upward in a cataclysmic moment of time creating the monumental cascade.

According to historical accounts, the first European to observe the falls was Fernando de Berrio, a Spanish explorer in the 17th century. It was not known to the outside world until American aviator Jimmie Angel flew over it in November of 1933 while searching for a valuable ore bed.

Angel returned four years later with several companions including his wife Maria. He tried to land his airplane near the top of the falls, but the plane was damaged when the wheels sank into the marshy ground. Forced to descend around the falls by foot, it took 11 days for Angel and his party to make it back to civilization. News of their adventure spread world-wide and the waterfall was named Angel Falls in his honor.

Angel's airplane remained on top of the falls for 33 years before being lifted out by helicopter. Restored, it now sits outside the commercial airport at Maracay. The cremated ashes of Jimmie Angel, who died in 1956, were cast into the river at the top of the falls in 1960 by his wife, his two sons, and several of his friends.

Getting to see the falls was a complicated trip that took me two days because it is located in an isolated jungle. I had to fly a small charter airplane to reach Canaima Camp, the starting place for the river trip to the base of the falls in wooden curiaras (canoes) oared by the Pemon guides.

One of our guides, who spoke English, told us not to put our hands in the water because it was full of piranha, a flesh eating fish. He said if we fell overboard to remain still because motion would draw the blood thirsty creatures. I could just see myself falling in the river surrounded by piranhas and not moving. I would be flailing my way back to the boat like a swimming extra in the movie *Jaws*.

We paddled up the dark, roiling river bounded by overhanging trees and vines. The flora of Venezuela consists of a huge variety of unique plants; over a third of the estimated 21,000 species of plants found in the country are endemic to Venezuela. Native orchids peeking through the rain forest gave it a vibrant and colorful life.

Suddenly a horrible shriek tore through the jungle frightening everyone but the guides who laughed at our consternation. It was a Howler Monkey one of them told us.

On a later trip to Costa Rica with my son Mike and his family, I was to run across that strange creature again. They had one of the loudest cries of any animal on earth and could be heard from miles away. Their sound is formed when the monkey forces air through its large, hollow hyoid bone, which is between its lower jaw and larynx. The deep, resonating howl vibrates through the jungle with immense intensity and echoes all around until it seems to come from every direction and it's impossible to locate the source.

I have visited waterfalls all over the world during my travels: Niagara Falls in New York, Gullfoss in Iceland, Yosemite Falls in California, Wailua Falls in Hawaii, Rhine Falls in Switzerland, Kbal Chhay Waterfall in Cambodia, Hannoki Falls in Japan, Camaya Falls in the Philippines, Jurong Falls in Singapore (which is actually an artificial waterfall), Shifen Waterfall in Taiwan, Phu Fa Waterfall in Thailand, Dam Ri Waterfall in Vietnam, Falling Foss in England, Bow Glacier Falls in Canada, Glassimine Falls in North Carolina, Kootenai River Falls in Montana, and many others. They have all been very impressive in their majestic power and beauty.

But none of them inspired the feeling of overpowering awe I felt when I visited Angel Falls. The downpour was from so high up its origin was obscured by mist. As I stood looking up in wonder, I thought it must start up in the heavens above where the river gods are pouring their waters down on the pool far below.

We had just delivered the first group of F-16 aircraft to Venezuela when I received a call from the manager of the Logistics Training Center, Gordon Brownlee. I had worked with Gordon on several training issues and had a lot of respect for him. A retired Air Force colonel, he had a quiet strength about him I respected.

The center was located off the manufacturing facility grounds in a two story office building in Southwest Fort Worth. Gordon said he was thinking about retirement and he was looking for someone to replace him as the training manager. He wanted to know if I was interested in the job.

After talking the opportunity over with Bob Drewry and finding someone to replace me in the Venezuela program, I accepted Gordon's offer and moved on to one of the most interesting and challenging assignments I would ever have in my military or civilian career. I never realized just how much was involved in training the many pilots and support personnel it takes to design, manufacture, test, maintain and operate an advanced high performance jet aircraft like the F-16 Fighting Falcon.

Chapter 16
Goats in the Bathtub

The Logistics Training Center was established in 1979 to provide customer classroom, laboratory, and on-site training in General Dynamics products that included the F-111 and F-16 aircraft and other aircraft related systems and subsystems. In addition to training at the center with its classrooms, simulators, and laboratories, the instructors took the students to the main plant's flight line where they received hands on work on aircraft flying checkout sorties before delivery to USAF and foreign air forces around the globe.

I had visited several of the classes for the students of my Venezuelan Program, and I was very impressed with the quality of the facility, instructors, and management. They had the latest state-of-the-art computers, simulators, training materials, scheduling displays, and multi-media. By the middle of the 1980's they had provided training to over 5,000 U.S. and worldwide servicemen and civilians with a staff of 110 management, administrative, and teaching personnel.

When I sat down across the desk from Gordon Brownlee, I thought about what an important function the training department had. I knew it would take me some time to get familiar with all the personnel and the vast scope of the responsibilities they had. But Gordon immediately dispelled any hope I would have time to gradually fit into the organization. I should have had a clue when I saw a suitcase next to the window behind his desk.

"Welcome aboard, Ken," Gordon said in a deep, modulated voice. He still wore a military style crew cut, which was graying over his tanned face.

"I would take you around and introduce you to the staff, but I have to leave," he went on. "Most of them know you anyway. And by the way, we have some Turkish officers coming in the morning."

Gordon picked up a stack of overhead transparencies from his desk and handed them to me. I looked questioningly at him.

"You'll have to give them the briefing on our department and the training their students will get when they arrive next month," Gordon said with a smile. "I'm on my way to the Pentagon to talk to the F-16 Air Force Program Office, and I have to pick up my wife and take her to lunch before I leave."

With that, Gordon stood up, grabbed his suitcase and patted my shoulder as he walked by me and out of his office. I sat at the desk and stared at the stack of briefing transparencies. Welcome to the Training Center, I thought.

Somehow, by studying the briefing charts late into the night, and by calling on other staff members when I was unsure of factual information, I made it through the session with the Turkish Officers. I not only had to hit the ground running but, it seemed at times, swim upstream against the current. My baptism under fire impressed the training staff, and I quickly fit into the unit.

A few weeks later, I received a visit from two of our students from Egypt. We had rented apartments for them near the training center. They had only been in them a few days when they came in to complain they were so close to the interstate highway they couldn't sleep because of the noise.

I called the apartment manager and he told me he could relocate the students further down into the complex where it was quieter and closer to other Egyptians. Then I located a moving company who would move the students that afternoon. As they left my office, I thought the problem was solved.

However, that was not the case. Later in the day, the apartment manager called me. He sounded very upset as he told me when the moving van arrived at the student's apartment they told him they wanted to stay where they were.

When I arrived at the Egyptian's apartment they met me at the door. I could hear a television blaring in the background. We had included cable TV in their rental agreement. I asked them why they didn't want to move. They wouldn't look me in the eye as they blocked my view of the TV and just said they wanted to stay where they were.

The next day one of the instructors came in my office laughing so hard he couldn't catch his breath, "Do you know why those two Egyptian students didn't want to move?"

"No," I responded. "Why?"

"The previous tenant had cable TV with the Playboy Channel. Apparently it never got turned off when our guys moved in. You know they never see anything like that in Egypt. The only naked women they've ever seen was probably in their dreams."

At the request of the supervisor of the Egyptian students we cleaned out one of our classrooms that faced toward Mecca, the birthplace in 570 AD of Muhammad the founder of the Muslim religion, so the students could perform their daily *salat* (prayer) which is compulsory in Islam. The *salat* is usually performed five times each day starting at dawn and consists of bowing on small prayer rugs accompanied by appropriate chants from the *Quran*, the religious text of Islam.

Since the students training day started at 7 am each weekday, we worked out a schedule so they would perform their *salat* mid-morning and early afternoon at the training center.

I discussed the Playboy Channel two of the students had with their supervisor. At his insistence, we had it removed from their cable input. Strangely, they never asked to move away from the freeway traffic noise afterward. I think they stayed where they were hoping the channel would mysteriously appear again.

As I settled into the Training Center routine, the many responsibilities we had never ceased to amaze me. Students (officers, enlisted personnel, and civilians) poured in from all over the world as the F-16 Program grew in leaps and bounds.

The General Dynamics manufacturing plant had to operate three shifts to keep up with the demands of customers from all over Europe, Asia, the Middle East, South America, and the United States wanting the lightweight fighter aircraft.

And as the customers queued up, I found myself traveling to destinations I had never imagined I would go to. I flew to Indonesia, Turkey, Singapore, Egypt, Israel, Germany, Spain, Portugal, France, Italy, England, Belgium, and all over the United States to discuss training requirements with the many users, co-producers, and support organizations.

Then one morning there was a note from Gordon Brownlee to come to his office. When I walked in, he was filling boxes with items from his desk and photos off the walls.

Gordon looked at me and said, "This is it, Ken. I'm out of here. It's time for you to take over. I talked to the vice president. He's not going to interview anyone else. The training center is yours. I leave it in good hands."

Gordon looked tired and his eyes were teary as he continued, "I'm going to take my family to Phoenix. Time for a change of scenery."

I didn't know what to say. Gordon had been under a doctor's care for heart problems for several years. The increasing demands of travel and student requirements on our department had worn him down.

I helped Gordon finish his packing and shook his hand as he left the office that suddenly had become mine. I went behind the desk and sat in the chair with a view of two windows overlooking an apartment complex on one side and a busy highway arterial on the other. I knew I would need help to be a successful manager of the training center.

Fortunately, that assistance was readily available to me in the fine staff, from my new secretary, the experienced planning unit, the excellent instructors, and the student support personnel.

Among those who I leaned heavily on were Ted Byers who was the Chief of Student Training with an engineering degree and over 20 years of General Dynamics experience, and Al Hatsell, a retired USAF Chief Master Sergeant, who was in charge of support functions.

Al's mother lived in a small North Carolina town not too far from Atlantic Beach where my son, Alan, served as a police officer. During one of my visits to see him and his family, I visited Al's mother.

Her house, an old wood framed single story building sat back from the narrow highway behind a well tended garden of flowers, vegetables, and herbs. I walked up several creaking wooden steps to the porch. It was late spring and the door was open behind a screen door.

I knocked on the door frame and announced myself so I wouldn't startle her, "Hello Mrs. Hatsell. I am Ken Miller from Fort Worth, Texas. I work with your son, Al."

A thin, frail gray haired woman stepped up to the screen door and peered out at me. "Who did you say you were?" she demanded in a loud, raspy voice as if she suspected I was a door-to-door salesman.

"Ken Miller from Texas," I responded.

"No you're not," the woman said sharply. "You're not Ken Miller."

"Well I'm pretty sure I am," I responded.

"No you ain't," Mrs. Hatsell barked. "My son told me I would have to widen my door to let you in because you are so big."

I was finally able to convince her I was indeed who I said I was, and we spent several hours talking over tea and cookies before I left.

When I got back to the training center in Texas I collared Al and asked him why his mother thought I was so big.

He laughed and said he told his mother another member of the training center with a different name might stop by to see her. And that person was very large with a wide body. She must have been confused.

I thought the problems with the Egyptian students were solved until I received a call late one afternoon from their apartment manager who was extremely agitated.

"You better get over here now!" he shouted. "The police and a SWAT team has broken down the door of one of the apartments. A neighbor called 911 and reported someone was being murdered in there."

It took a while to sort out what happened after I arrived at the Egyptian apartment. The police had cordoned off the area and wouldn't let me in until I persuaded them I was in charge of the students. The scene in their apartment was still chaotic. The SWAT team had left but about a dozen police officers milled in and around the apartment.

Four of the Egyptian students were huddled on a sofa wide eyed in terror while being harangued by one of the policemen. As I entered from the hallway I could smell a horrible stench I couldn't recognize.

After I stopped the police officer, who was so mad his face was flushed, from berating the students, he took me to the bathroom and told me what happened.

Hanging upside down from the shower head over the bathtub by a rope was a large black goat. Its throat had been sliced open and the blood was running down into the tub.

"When they killed it," the policeman said, finally calming down. "The poor creature cried out. Someone in the next apartment heard it and thought someone was being murdered in here. They called 911. What in the hell were those idiots thinking?"

"They are Muslims from Egypt," I said. "They are supposed to only eat *halal* which means lawful meat in Arabic. They don't eat pork, but goat is okay. The goat has to be killed with a sharpened blade and hung upside down until the blood runs out."

"My God," the policeman shouted. "Don't you guys at General Dynamics feed them so they won't have to do this?"

After the police left, the goat removed by the city animal control services, and the apartment scrubbed by a cleaning service, I sat down with the students and their supervisor. They assured me they would never again try to cook a goat in their apartments. When I asked them where they got the goat, one of them said his instructor, who lived in the country west of Fort Worth, sold it to them.

After I had an all-hands meeting of training center personnel and told them what happened, I was assured that no more goats were available on the open market.

Most of the foreign students who attended our training courses had some knowledge of English from their home schooling. When they were selected to come to the United States, they were sent to English Language Training for almost a year at the USAF Randolph AFB in San Antonio, Texas.

By the time we received them, the students had some proficiency in English since that was the language we taught in, the operations and maintenance manuals were printed in, and the aircraft systems displayed in. In fact, since the end of the Second World War, the international language of aerospace has become English. Nearly all air traffic controllers, pilots, and support personnel have some proficiency in the language.

But it wasn't until we had some difficulty communicating with our students from Indonesia I realized how difficult our training syllabus with computer interfaces could be for technicians who were only one generation removed from village life without television or even electricity.

One day an instructor came to me and said he couldn't complete the block of training that called for computer interaction from his Indonesian students.

"They refuse to interact with the computer," he said. "They think there is an evil spirit inside the box."

After consultation with the student's supervisor, we came up with a solution to the problem. The instructor would take the place of the computer and the students would respond to his questions and answers. I approved the work around and handed out graduation certificates to the students at the end of their training, even though I had reservations about their ability to support the F-16 systems when they were delivered to their country.

I made it a point to travel to Indonesia several months after the students graduated. When I landed in Jakarta I was met at the airport by the Indonesian Air Force (IAF) colonel in charge of F-16 support. He took me to dinner that evening to one of the most expensive (and in retrospect, one of the most disgusting) restaurants in the bustling city. The local cuisine was influenced by Chinese, Sudanese, Javanese, Indian, Arabic, and European culinary tastes, and usually very good.

Jakarta is the most populated metropolitan area in all of Asia and the second largest city in the world. Nicknamed the *Big Durian*, after the thorny strong smelling fruit native to the area, it is the center of the Hindu religion outside of India.

The colonel and I joined six other diners, one of them a silver haired friend of his who owned an export business. We sat at a large round table with a Lazy Susan rotating platform in the middle where the waiters placed large platters of steaming rice, vegetables, fish, shrimp, chicken and lamb. It was a very good meal and I thought I would recommend it to other General Dynamics travelers. However, I was about to change my mind.

When I entered the restaurant I hadn't noticed a small round table with a hole in the center sitting in one corner. Now I did as two waiters carried in a squealing monkey from the kitchen area, which drew everyone's attention.

For the first time, I realized there was not a single woman there; only men. The waiters strapped the noisy monkey in a harness under the small table with the top of his head showing above the hole.

The colonel turned to me and said, "This is a very special and very expensive event."

Nodding toward his businessman friend, he whispered, "He has purchased it in your honor."

As the colonel and his friend rose from our table to go to the monkey table, I said quietly, "Tell him I appreciate it, but I cannot participate."

One of the waiters removed a long knife with a serrated edge from his sash and cut the hair off the crown of the monkey's head and then sawed around his skull with a flourish. After he removed the bony cover, the colonel and his friend scooped out portions of the poor animal's brain with long handled spoons and ate it while the monkey shrieked in pain and anguish.

I knew I was causing the colonel to lose face with his friend who had paid for the expensive evening, but I couldn't stand it any longer. I left the restaurant and made it back to my hotel room before I threw up.

I had seen a lot of disgusting things in my life, but eating the brains of a live monkey topped them all. I knew many societies ate live creatures from oysters, to fish, to animals, and even to other humans, but I couldn't accept that educated people would participate in horrific ancient rites going back thousands of years.

The next morning when I met the colonel outside my hotel for the ride to the Indonesian Air Base where the F-16 aircraft were based, he was very quiet and respectful. As we sped through the bustling city and the verdant countryside, we said very little. I didn't speak of the past evening and he also avoided mention of it.

During the ride, I thought about the Indonesian student's fear of interacting with computers because they thought they housed evil demons. I wasn't sure what to expect when they had a modern high performance aircraft to support.

After I returned to Fort Worth from Indonesia, I recommended to my supervisor, the Director of Product Support, the addition of an on-site technical representative qualified in the F-16's fire control system. From my observations of the technicians at the IAF base, I doubted they could maintain the system without assistance. My boss agreed and an additional field engineer was added to the Indonesian Program.

The supervisor of the Israeli students at the training center was an interesting man with an open and friendly demeanor, Colonel Katz. A branch of his family owns the famous Katz's Delicatessen on the Lower East Side in Manhattan, New York City. The deli was founded in 1888 and is widely known as one of the best kosher style restaurants in America.

During World War II, Katz's encouraged parents to "Send a salami to your boy in the army," which became one of the deli's noted catch phrases. Katz was the site of Meg Ryan's famous fake orgasm scene in the movie *When Harry Met Sally* followed by Estelle Reiner's iconic line, "I'll have what she's having."

I planned to visit Colonel Katz at his family deli in New York City during one of my business trips to the Northeast, and get an introduction to his family. But he couldn't make the connection, so I went by myself. I had one of the most delicious and humongous corned beef sandwiches I ever had anywhere.

Colonel Katz didn't stay in Fort Worth during the entire Israeli training program but he did make several visits over the course of instruction. During one of his visits, he told me the students wanted to go to Dallas and see where President John Kennedy was assassinated.

I accompanied Katz and the Israeli students on their bus trip to Dallas. I am continually amazed at the fascination so many in the world have about Kennedy's murder. I think it speaks highly of the esteem most people in the world had for our charismatic former president, and the horror they felt at his violent early demise.

We visited the Kennedy Museum just above the street where Kennedy was supposedly shot by the lone gunman Lee Harvey Oswald from the third floor of the Dallas Book Depository on November 22, 1963. They showed the film of the fatal shot to the president's head from the home movie Abraham Zapruder took as the motorcade passed through Dealey Plaza. The Israeli students were fascinated by the film and asked to see it several times.

After we left the scene of Kennedy's murder, I asked the bus driver to take us on a tour of Dallas. One of the stops we made was at the oldest building in the city, the Sharrock Cabin built in 1846. It was a rickety assemblage of logs with a small sign proclaiming its prominence.

When we got back on the bus one of the students, who was not impressed by the old cabin, said, "That is less than 150 years old. In Israel when we turn over a rock we see thousands of years of history."

At the graduation ceremony for the students, Colonel Katz invited me to visit him in Israel. I told him I would certainly do that. In addition to seeing how the students were applying the training from us, I wanted to experience the thousands of years of history the student was talking about.

In April of 1987 I flew to Tel Aviv, Israel and, after spending the night in an airport hotel, took a taxi to Haifa in the northern part of the country near the air base where the Israelis were operating the F-16 aircraft they had purchased from General Dynamics.

Israel is a small country on the southeastern shore of the Mediterranean Sea. It shares land borders with Lebanon to the north, Syria in the northeast, Jordan on the east, and the Palestinian territories to the south.

Declared a Jewish state in May of 1948, the new country, with a population now about the same as New York City in an area approximating the state of Rhode Island, has been at war with its neighboring Arab countries ever since with intermittent and short lasting periods of cease fire, peace talks (which should be called war talks because there will never be peace between the Jews and the Arabs), and mutually suspicious détentes.

An interesting fact about the country that seems to be contradictive: Israel has one of the highest life expectancies in the world. I guess if they can make it alive through the years they would normally serve in the military (which is mandatory for males and females) they live to an old age.

Haifa is a beautiful city perched high above Mediterranean Sea sand beaches, which offer the best surfing in Israel. Known for its exquisitely landscaped Bahia Gardens, established by the Islamic sect Bahia, sitting above the picturesque German Colony, which was founded in the nineteenth century by German Templars who came to establish a Christian community in the Holy Land, the city personifies the diverse nature of Israel.

The country is home to settlers over the centuries from many nationalities throughout the world. As I was to find out later during a tour of Jerusalem, without outside agitation the many cultures and religions in Israel have learned to live, work, and worship together in a cautious spirit of harmony.

I met Colonel Katz and the former students from my training center at a building outside the Israeli air base. I was not allowed to go onto the military site, which was screened from view by high fences covered by camouflaged canvas.

The Golan Heights, not too far to the east, was only a short ground-to-ground rocket shot away from Arab armies that occupied the mountainous area. The enemy air forces were only several hundred miles away, but the Israeli Air Forces ruled the skies above the country, launching armed F-16 patrol sorties throughout the day and night.

I could hear the scream of the aircraft engines as they took off and landed throughout my meeting with the Israelis. Their students had been the best we ever trained in Fort Worth. I had gotten to know most of them well. Their command of English was excellent of course, but their technical knowledge and ability to understand the operation and support of the new F-16 systems was heightened by the daily threat of the Arab forces surrounding their country: forces committed by their religious leaders to annihilate them and their faith.

After our business review was over we went to a local restaurant where they hosted me for dinner. After the meal we went into a back room reserved for us with a local band.

As the evening progressed, and the ingestion of beer and spirits increased, I found myself dancing the strenuous traditional Israeli Hora. Starting the dance, we formed a circle, holding hands, and stepped forward toward the right with the left foot, then followed with the right foot. The left foot was then brought back, followed by the right foot. This was done while holding hands and circling together in a fast and cheerful motion to the right. I tried to keep up to the accompaniment of the cheers of Colonel Katz and the former students who accompanied me on the dance.

When Katz picked me up in his car at my Haifa hotel early the next morning, I was still feeling the effects of the late and boisterous evening before. It wasn't long however until I sat up straight and looked carefully at the sights on our drive south to Jerusalem. I didn't realize that we were driving to the east until I saw a highway sign that proclaimed: "Bethlehem of Galilee, Birthplace of Jesus Christ."

On the outskirts of the small town was a large and colorful billboard with an automobile advertisement: "Israeli Volkswagen."

I glanced over at Katz but he seemed oblivious to the strange dichotomy of a German auto dealer in the land where the Nazi government during the Second World War had been determined to eradicate the Jewish population wherever they existed.

When we drove through the village, Katz pointed out a building fronted by street vendors with kiosks peddling carpets, vases, crude paintings, and other memorabilia commemorating the birth of the Christ child.

"That is the Church of the Nativity," he said with a flat tone and a shake of his head. "It was built over the manger where Jesus of Nazareth was born, according to legend,"

He was wearing a kippah, or yarmulke, a small cloth cap worn by Jews to fulfill the customary requirement of orthodox authorities that the head be covered at all times. It was the first time I had seen Katz wearing the distinctive hat. During his visits to my training center in the United States, he didn't wear it.

I was overcome with emotion as I thought about the Christmas day a few thousand years before when Mary brought the baby Jesus into the world. This dusty town, baking in the late morning sun was the birthplace of the founder of Christianity, one of the world's largest religions. Although it was only a few miles from Jerusalem, it took Jesus over 30 years to reach there as he fulfilled his biblical destiny and founded his religion before facing his tragic death on a cross on a hill above the tumultuous city, which was of historical importance throughout mankind's recorded history.

While I traveled around the United States and the world, I studied many of the faiths, large and small, that have shaped the destiny of the human race from the days many hundreds of thousands of years before when modern man migrated from the heartland of Africa: Hindu, Islamic, Shinto, Christian, Catholic, Mormon, Animism, Judaism, Buddhism, Taoism, Korean Shamanism, Vietnamese Caodaism, Indian Sikhism, Baha'i Faith, and many indigenous sects developed on every continent including Africa, Australia, Asia, Europe, and the Americas as the population of the human race exploded to the billions that populate it today.

Daniel Defoe, the prolific 18th century author of over 500 books, pamphlets, and journals, including the classic *Robinson Crusoe*, wrote, "Religion is properly the worship given to God, but 'tis also applied to the worship of idols and false deities."

When I studied the world's religions during my travels as a sojourner, I kept in mind Defoe's admonishment to differentiate the worship given to God versus the worship of idols and false deities.

Since reading the Old Testament tales of Moses' expatriating Israelites worshipping the golden calves in the Sinai wilderness to the modern day suicide followers of James Jones in Guyana, the drinkers of poison of the Halley Bop sect, the radical Muslim fanatics like Al Qaida and the Islamic State of Iraq (ISIS or ISIL as it is known widely), and the believers in otherworldly religious applications like

Scientology, I realized for many there is a fine line between the worship given to God and that applied to idols and false deities.

Marcus Aurelius the Roman Emperor, philosopher, and writer of the 2nd century, wrote in *Meditations*, "Live a good life. If there are gods and they are just, then they will not care how devout you have been, but will welcome you based on the virtues you have lived by. If there are gods, but unjust, then you should not want to worship them. If there are no gods, then you will be gone, but will have lived a noble life that will live on in the memories of your loved ones."

But, before we get too serious about religion, remember what Mark Twain said about it, "Heaven goes by favor; if it went by merit, you would stay out and your dog would go in."

As we approached Jerusalem, we were stopped at a barricaded gate in a fence topped with concertina wire. When the Israeli guard, armed with an Uzi submachine gun glanced at Katz's identification, he stepped back and with a smart salute opened the gate to let us pass.

We parked outside one of the main Jerusalem gates. Divided into four quadrants, the ancient city was surrounded by a high wall built many centuries ago to protect the inhabitants from marauding bands of foreign armies bent on rape, looting, and destruction of the inhabitants of the central city in the "Promised Land," the land promised by God to Abraham according to the Hebrew Bible and *Genesis* in the Old Testament.

The "Promised Land" concept, the main tenet of Zionism, was the driving force behind descendants of Abraham when they established the modern Jewish state of Israel in 1948 surrounded by Arab states fiercely vowing its destruction.

During its long history, Jerusalem has been destroyed several times, besieged over 50 times, and captured and recaptured over 40 times. In the 16th century the walls were built that define the Old City, which is divided into four quarters: Armenian, Christian, Jewish, and Muslim.

Colonel Katz, who had lived for several years in the city as a teenager and knew it intimately, gave me an interesting tour. We walked to the Temple Mount, the holiest Jewish site; the al-Aqsa Mosque, where Muslims believe the founder of their religion Muhammad ascended to heaven; The Church of the Holy Sepulchre (also venerated as Calvary of Golgotha), where Christians believe Jesus was crucified, buried, and resurrected; and the Western Wall, a remnant of the wall surrounding the Jewish Second Temple.

Although a mutual peace prevailed in Jerusalem while I was there, the hustle and bustle of the diverse people held an undercurrent of tension and distrust of each other.

Katz took me through the ancient city, chattering endlessly about his boyhood experiences and the many friends he had made with boys and girls of other than the Jewish faith, and the many religious shrines and their historical importance. He was at ease in his old home and downplayed any fears he had, even though he was a Jewish military officer, of armed conflict between the inhabitants.

My impression of the holy city: there was too much to comprehend in such a short time, about an hour in each of the four quarters. I do know I could spend many days there, hopefully with Katz as my guide. But that was to be my last visit to Jerusalem as my life as a sojourner would take me to many other countries and cities in the coming years, but never back to Israel or Jerusalem.

Later I learned Katz retired from the IAF and was able to fulfill his lifelong dream: he became a history teacher at a small university in the northern part of the country. I am sure he mesmerized his students as he did me during my tour of Jerusalem that day.

Chapter 17
The Tree of Life

The Director of the Product Support Department, who was my boss, received a special assignment away from Fort Worth and I was selected to replace him. Leaving the training center as its manager was difficult, but I was just moving up one echelon since they would still report to me. In addition, I supervised the in-house field engineering department and the field service engineers who supported our world-wide customers.

From being the manager of just over one hundred personnel at the Fort Worth Training Center, I now had the responsibility of over 250 men and women assigned around the globe with an annual multi-million dollar General Dynamics budget.

One of my first trips as the director was to Turkey where I visited Istanbul, Ankara, and Incirlik. During my introduction to this memoir, I mentioned an engraved display dish presented to me by the Turkish officers at my training center. When they were to receive the first shipment of their F-16 Fighter Aircraft, they extended me an invitation to be at the presentation ceremony at Incirlik Air Base.

My first day in country, I toured Istanbul, the largest city in Turkey. Considered a transcontinental city in Eurasia, it straddles the Bosporus Strait near the Black Sea. Founded in the 7th century BCE (Before Common Era) as Byzantium, it developed into one of the most significant cities in the history of mankind. It served as an imperial capital for the Roman, Byzantine, and the Ottoman empires, and was instrumental in the advancement of Christianity before it was transformed into an Islamic stronghold.

What struck me the most in my tour was the amazing condition of administrative and religious architecture after thousands of years of existence. The Hagia Sophia built in the 6th century AD for example, which was originally a church and then a mosque, looked so clean and fresh it was hard to believe it had not just been recently constructed.

The next day I traveled to Ankara, the capital of Turkey, to visit General Dynamics' co-production facility. One of the interesting aspects of the world-wide F-16 sales programs was the introduction of the buyer's co-production contracts. Although many of the major and minor construction and support components of the aircraft were manufactured at Fort Worth, most of them were produced at companies around the United States and in the foreign countries where the aircraft were delivered. Not only did that reduce the program cost to the customers, but it provided companies overseas and in the United States with lucrative contracts.

I'm sure in the process that many millions of dollars from the contracts lined the pockets of politicians, custom agents, company directors, military leaders, and sundry other grubby individuals. Contract kickbacks are an overt business process in most countries in the world. In the U.S., it happens frequently but more under the table than elsewhere.

The General Dynamics advisor supervisor at the Ankara manufacturing plant was Van Gilley. Van was a most unusual man, tall and thin, he possessed the largest hands I've ever seen except for Wilt Chamberlain's. When Van briefed me on his facility, he waved his long fingers in the air in front of him as if he was conducting a symphony orchestra. It was difficult to listen to him without following his rhythmic gestures.

Van had an interesting family history. One of his cousins was Mickey Gilley, the country singer and the one-time owner of "Gilley's" in Pasadena, Texas, the largest honky-tonk saloon and performance venue in the United States until "Billy Bobs" in Fort Worth took over that honor. Van was also related to the singer Jerry Lee Lewis and the Louisiana televangelist Jimmy Swaggart, who made his infamous "I have sinned" confession to the world after investigation revealed he had solicited prostitutes.

Van also had a son named Rod, who I was to work with in Taiwan several years later. Rod would become a close friend and one of the most personable people I have ever met.

I stayed in a hotel in Ankara for several days. The morning I was to leave for Incirlik Air Base I looked out my room window, which overlooked one of the main city streets. Although I was only on the third floor, I couldn't see the street below because of the oppressive pollution. Overhead, the sun in a cloudless sky, looked like a dim flashlight with a weak battery as it tried futilely to penetrate the heavy mists of polluted air.

It was winter then and Ankara like many Eurasian cities and towns, used bituminous (soft) coal for heating and electricity generation. The residue from the generators, stoves, and furnaces poured unfiltered into the air where it was caught in a temperature inversion above the metropolis and sent back downward to mix with the oil and diesel pollutants ejected from the many vehicles crowding its streets to pollute the air and blacken buildings, vehicles, animals, and people's eyes and lungs.

I thought I would never again see such heavy pollution, but I would. When my sojourns took me to Taiwan, I would see up close and personal an island nation that was poisoning its air and water in a horrendous scale to feed the voracious business appetites of its political and business leaders.

Incirlik Air Base is located about 35 miles from the Mediterranean Sea. Although the Turkish Air Force owns and manages the base, the U.S. Air Force has maintained a large force of men and aircraft there for many years. Francis Gary Powers launched his U-2 Spy Plane from Incirlik in 1960 before it was shot down by Soviet surface-to-air missiles.

When I arrived there, the base was in a festive mood as they awaited the first delivery of General Dynamics F-16 Aircraft to the Turkish Air Force.

Unfortunately, it was to turn out to be an inauspicious occasion that caused the Turkish officer, who was the wing commander and who had presented me with an engraved display plate while I was at the training center, to resign in disgrace.

While the initial fleet of twelve F-16's was in route from the United States, the wing commander, hoping to impress the visiting military and political VIP's had the main runway covered with a new surface that caused it to shine and gleam under the afternoon sunlight. Unfortunately, the surface treatment was also slippery. When the first two aircraft swooped down for a landing accompanied by the flourishing sound of a military band and the cheers of thousands of on-lookers, they hit the slick surface side-by-side and slid off the runway and into rope barriers on the over-run.

The sound of the music and the raucous roars of the crowd quickly faded out. Fortunately, an alert air traffic controller saw what was happening and warned the trailing aircraft. Their pilots, at the last moment, made a touch and go and soared back into the sky to avoid sliding into the first aircraft ensnarled in the barriers. After several minutes of confusion, they were able to descend again and land on an alternate runway far from the suddenly stunned visitors and the irate General of the Turkish Air Force.

Along with thousands of others, I was ordered to immediately evacuate the area and leave the air base. I heard later the wing commander, who ordered the new runway surface installed, was stripped of his rank and forced to leave the military. I don't know what happened to him, but his loss of face was monumental in Turkey. In years past, he would have been put to death, but I was assured by my on-site field engineers that didn't happen to him.

Enroute back from Turkey, I stopped over in England for a few days. Our U.S. Air Force had a squadron of General Dynamics F-111's at Upper Heyford and Lakenheath Air Bases. Since I had supported those ugly Aardvarks, that looked like a South American Condor with its ominous drooped nose and swooping wings, while I was in the USAF and stationed in Thailand, I felt like I was going home for a visit.

I spent the first day in London, one of the world's most interesting cities. The weather was as I recalled from my other visits to the North Sea Island city: cold, rainy, and windy. I don't think I would have felt comfortable with mild sunny weather because it wouldn't suit the ambiance of the historic metropolis. Fortunately, I had a long waterproof overcoat well named for the occasion: London Fog.

On the River Thames, London has been a major settlement for over two thousand years, its history going back to its founding by the Romans. A major world cultural and financial capital, London is the most visited location measured by international arrivals. A diverse city with a wide range of people and religions, more than 200 languages are spoken in the metropolitan area.

Although London has one of the largest areas of any city in the world, it is amazingly easy to navigate. All you have to do is pop down a staircase below the raucous, thrashing wet street traffic to the Underground, a subway system unparalleled anywhere.

Using the wonderful London Underground Map on the walls that presents stations in logical sequence with their interchanges colorfully laid out, I was able to travel to the Tower of London, the Palace of Westminster, Westminster Abby, and the National Gallery of Art all in one afternoon and return to my hotel in time for dinner.

Although Lakenheath was a Royal Air Force (RAF) base, it hosted USAF's 48th Fighter Wing. The F-111 unit was assigned to the United States Air Forces in Europe and Africa.

Just before I arrived, the Fighter Wing had participated in Operation El Diablo Canyon, the bombing of Libya's forces under the despot Muammar Kaddafi. During the strike one of the F-111's was shot down by Libyan ground fire and the two crew members were killed.

The Libyan government eventually returned one of the pilot's bodies, however there is still controversy over the remains of the other missing pilot. The bombing of Libya prompted the mock acronym. Lakenheath Is Bombing Your Ass (Libya).

After spending several days at Lakenheath visiting with the field service engineers who worked for me and their USAF counterparts, I was able to play golf at one of the local courses. Although rain had subsided for the afternoon, the cold wind still howled over the flat, open course pushing balls willy nilly through the air like ping pong balls caught in a thunderstorm.

After the exhausting round of non-productive golf, I went into the clubhouse bar to warm up and have a drink. I thought of Mark Twain's statement about the tiring experience I had that afternoon, "Golf is a good walk spoiled."

Behind the bar was an interesting looking fellow with thinning gray hair, a florid complexion, and a wart on his nose exuding a long black hair, quite darker than that framing his protruding ears. He spoke with a raspy voice as if his vocal cords were wrapped in a whisky drenched cloth. I had no idea what he was saying. Although I was sure he spoke in English, it was totally unintelligible.

As I looked at him, I thought he might be a character from one of Charles Dicken's novels of Victorian England. Uriah Heathcliff, would be his Dicken's name. And his profession? Why a seaside pub tender of course. He would be serving beer in dirty glasses to scruffy, cantankerous sailors just off whaling ships after a yearlong hunt in the southern oceans.

I finally was able to get through to the bartender that I wanted to order Scotch. He mumbled something back to me. The only thing I could make out was the single word, "American," spoken in a decidedly negative way.

When my drink was pushed back across the bar to me it was in a small glass that had been washed so many times it looked like it had been dragged behind a New York City garbage truck the length of Manhattan. It held a few ounces of amber liquid that stared back at me.

I pushed the glass back across the bar and said, "Ice. I want some ice."

The bartender looked at me like I was crazy. After repeatedly asking for ice, he finally reached behind the bar and picked up a tiny piece of ice in his grubby hand and plopped it in my glass while muttering again. I'm sure I heard the word "American," spat out again.

As I looked down into my glass, the ice so reluctantly thrust into the Scotch had already melted. I took a tiny sip but couldn't stand the heavy taste of the liquid. I waited until the bartender was distracted by another golfer who had sought the sanctuary of the bar, plopped down a few English pounds, and slunk out into the blowing wind.

I added the experience to my growing store of knowledge: you don't spit on Superman's cape, you don't cut your spaghetti with a knife in Italy, you don't point your chopsticks at other diners in Asia, and you don't order Scotch with ice in England.

When I arrived back in Fort Worth I received another one those calls everyone dreads, my mother had been diagnosed with cancer and wasn't expected to survive. I immediately flew to Coeur d' Alene, Idaho to join my family where she was hospitalized. The prognosis was not good for Mom. Apparently the cancer, which had started in her lungs although she had never smoked cigarettes, spread into her lymph nodes and other bodily organs.

After 82 years of life, which included giving birth to 17 children, and raising to adulthood all but one of them, Mom's body failed her.

She was transferred to a hospice unit at the hospital in Bonners Ferry and we prepared for the worst. The doctors sedated her with morphine as the ravages of the cancer surged through her body. Near the end, just when we thought she would succumb to the terrible disease, she rallied and reached out to us with tears in her eyes.

Suffering horribly, she held on until my brother Joe finally arrived from Australia. Then, in one quiet moment, she left us. Her pain and anguish finally conquered through the release of her death, and Grand View Cemetery took another member of my family into its windswept bosom.

There are times in our life when we contemplate our mortality. Sometimes it is because of our own illness, injury, or bodily threat but usually it comes at the loss of our parents: our father who sired us and gave us guidance and love, and our mother who birthed us and gave us life that would reach down through the ages that would follow long after our own demise.

I didn't have long to grieve my mother's death before I had to travel to Bahrain. The first Gulf War was on the horizon and the American military might and the resolve of the first Bush administration was about to be tested in the Middle East cauldron of Muslim extremists. Sadam Hussain was rattling his Sunni power sword and threatening to invade Kuwait to expand his influence.

Operation Desert Shield, the code name for the buildup of the coalition forces from 34 nations led by the United States presaged Desert Storm, the attack against the Iraqi military invasion of Kuwait.

Our company's F-16's were at the forefront of the attack against Hussain's army, many of them based out of the island country of Bahrain near the Persian Gulf. I flew there to visit the air forces flying our aircraft to ensure they had adequate product support from Fort Worth.

A small country, Bahrain is only 34 miles long and 11 miles wide.

Saudi Arabia lies across a causeway to the west and Iran is just over a hundred miles to the north across the water. Everywhere the ground wasn't watered artificially it was just sand: miles and miles of sand, blowing and sifting in the gulf breezes. It was strange not to see tropical foliage on the island but it never seemed to rain there.

Fortunately, oil reserves provided the Kingdom an immense amount of wealth. Lawns, gardens, and parks proliferated in the capital city of Manama where a vast amount of the oil income was spent on spectacular high rise buildings surrounded by well-watered grounds, ponds, small lakes, and waterfalls creating shiny rainbows in the clear sunny air.

During my taxi ride from the hotel to the air base at the other end of the island, we entered a flat world of sand that stretched on either side of the single road bisecting the island all the way to the gulf water on both sides.

Then, strangely, I noticed the flag sticks of a golf course near the road. But I couldn't see any grass fairways or greens. I asked the driver, who spoke fluent English about it. He told me it was a sand golf course. The caddy carried a piece of indoor/outdoor carpet for you to put on the ground and hit your ball from. The greens were rolled and lightly oiled. When you putted you could see the trace your ball made. After putting out, the caddies would use a roller to smooth the surface for the golfers behind.

I laughed as we sped by the golf course. I was spoiled from playing spectacular, lush venues around the world, and there was no way I would step on that goat pasture.

Actually I did play there before I left Bahrain. It was quite an interesting experience. It took me several holes to get used to hitting off the carpet and putting on the oiled greens, but it was enjoyable. I don't remember my score; I think it is called selective memory loss. I do recall on one par four where I took six strokes, but when I looked at the scorecard, the caddy had jotted down a four. He smiled at me in anticipation of a larger tip.

A few miles past the course I saw a strange sight off in the distance. There was a lone tree out in the middle of the sandy landscape. The driver turned to me and said, "That is the Tree of Life."

"Tree of Life!" I said incredulously. "What is that?"

"Why it is a tree from the Garden of Eden," the driver said seriously.

I knew he was a Muslim and it surprised me he would make reference to the Christian *Old Testament*. "I want to see it," I said.

The spreading tree, a prosopis cineraria about 30 feet tall, stood on top of a high sandy tell that had formed around an ancient fortress, which had disintegrated through the ravages of thousands of years of wind and occasional rain storms leaving no trace. The site is a local tourist attraction since it is the only tree growing in the area as far as one can see, and there is no visible source of water.

The tree is visited by over 50,000 tourists every year. It is believed to be the site for cults practicing ancient rites. Recently archaeologists have unearthed pottery and other artifacts in the vicinity of the tree dating to the Dilmun civilization, which goes back to over 2,600 B.C.E., one of the oldest civilizations in the Middle East. The Sumerians described Dilmun as a paradise garden in the *Epic of Gilgamesh*. Some biblical scholars think the location may have been an inspiration for the *Garden of Eden* story in the *Old Testament*.

The Bahrain air base was a maelstrom of activity. There were so many aircraft of different types from so many nations it appeared the island would sink into the gulf water from the excessive weight. After spending several hours with our F-16 units, the constant whine of aircraft engines deadened my hearing senses. I couldn't image the Iraqi ground and air forces standing up to the ferocious military might that was about to be unleashed on them.

And the truth is, they couldn't. The allied forces pushed Hussain's army and small air force back into Iraq in a blitzkrieg maneuver. Then, just as they had the dictator withdrawing with his tail between his legs into Baghdad, President Bush called off the hounds and ended the campaign.

Bush received a lot of criticism, in the U.S. and abroad, for not capturing or killing Hussain. His son, George Bush, after attaining his presidency, used false intelligence about weapons of mass destruction, and finished the coup de gras during the Second Gulf War. Our forces captured Hussain, which led to his death after a military trial by his countrymen.

Several years later I read an intelligence report outlining the reasons the senior Bush terminated the First Gulf War early. He and his allies certainly had the military advantage to go into Baghdad and capture Hussain. But his foreign advisors told him if they did a civil war might erupt in Iraq between the Sunnis (Hussain's minority party), the majority group the Shiites, the Kurds in the northern part of the country, and the Turks to the north who were poised to protect their borders from the Muslim factions to the south.

Today, after all the events that have unfolded in the Middle East over the past decades, the turmoil from the Gulf Wars still haunt us. The major Muslim religions, the Sunnis and the Shiites, splintered by the radical Al Qaeda and ISIS sects hold the area and the world in their spotlight. Human rights violations, women oppression, and refugees flooding out of the powder keg of the Middle East headline world news nearly every night.

A Muslim follows an Abrahamic religion based on the Quran. They consider the Quran to be the verbatim word of God as revealed to the prophet Muhammad. "Muslim" is an Arabic word meaning "one who submits to God." Most Muslims will accept anyone who has publicly pronounced the declaration of faith as a Muslim.

Their *Shahadah* states: "There is no god but God and Muhammad is the messenger of God." Islamic beliefs held by Muslims include: God is eternal, transcendent, and absolute; God is incomparable, self-sustaining and neither begets nor was begotten.

Islam is the complete and universal version of a primordial faith that has been revealed before through many prophets including Abraham, Moses, Ismael, and Jesus. The religious practices of Muslims are enumerated in the *Five Pillars of Islam*, which, in addition to *Shahadah*, consist of daily prayers, fasting during the Islamic month of Ramadan, alms giving, and a pilgrimage to Mecca (hajj) at least once in a lifetime.

After Muhammad died in 632 AD in Medina, Arabia his religion was split between conflicting groups of his family and evolved as the Sunni and Shiite factions. Over the ensuing centuries, they were not compatible and actually became sworn enemies.

When Sadam Hussain took over Iraq, his Sunni followers were among the minority. To consolidate his power and maintain control over his ancient kingdom, he became a despot, oppressing and slaying his opposition and gathering the wealth of his kingdom into his Bagdad palace. After his downfall during the Second Gulf War, Iraq became a festering whirlpool of intrigue and instability as the diverse groups of Sunnis, Shiites, Kurds, Christians, and other factions rattled their swords in ancient animosity.

That instability has given rise to the anti-western factions of Al Qaeda and ISIS of today. The maelstrom whirling around them threatens the stability of the entire Middle East, Israel, Europe, and the United States. Where that will lead, no one can predict.

I do think if Jesus and Muhammad had lived at the same time they would have walked hand-in-hand together preaching against wars (including the *jihad* holy wars of radical Muslims) and inhumanity. They would gather the lame, the weak, and the oppressed to their bosoms.

After visiting the Desert Storm units, I flew on to see our European regional manager at Ramstein Air Base in south-western Germany. Ramstein serves as headquarters for the United States Air Force in Europe and Africa. Its main hospital treated the injured evacuated from the Desert Storm battlefields, and the base provided most of the logistics support for that war.

While I was there visiting the base, aircraft traffic nearly rivaled the frenetic activity I had observed at Tan Son Nhut Air Base in Saigon during the mid-1970 Southeast Asia conflict. Takeoffs and landings at short intervals took place around the clock every day of the week.

After several days of meetings and discussions with the Air Force personnel supporting the American and foreign F-16 units, the regional manager took me to dinner at an ancient castle overlooking the Rhine River and the Black Forest beyond.

Surrounded by vineyards, the views from the castle tower was spectacular. A former master of the castle, the Count of Drachenfels, had a large winged, fire-spitting dragon constructed from stone to commemorate where Siegfried is reputed to have slain a dragon.

At dinner, which included a sumptuous feast of breads, vegetables, and fish and venison from the local area, the waiter offered us a wine menu. At our request he brought us a bottle from the local area. It was an excellent light red wine. When I asked the waiter where it was from, since the label was printed in German and I couldn't read it, he smiled and pointed out the window at the vineyard tumbling down the steep hill toward the river.

I had no idea, sitting there above the Rhine River that night I was only a few miles from Sulzbach, Bavaria, Germany where my 11th Great Grandfather Adam Mueller was born in 1530 and died 60 years later. At that time, I did not know my father, who was still alive then, had a long line of ancestors stretching back to Germany and beyond to Switzerland. It would be another ten years before I would discover the truth about my heritage.

The next few years were filled with more business trips for me around the United States and to European and Asian countries as the world-wide fleets of F-16 aircraft continued to expand to 25 customers. Over 4,500 Fighting Falcons were built at the Fort Worth plant and supported by co-production facilities around the world. Scheduled to remain in service with the U.S. Air Force until 2025 as it is gradually replaced by the F-35 as a multi-role aircraft, the F-16 has been the most successful and largest income producing airplane ever manufactured.

Now my career was about to change drastically. The previous Product Support Director returned from his special assignment, and I and my son Brian were to move to Taichung, Taiwan.

I was given the opportunity for a long term assignment as the Logistics Advisor to a Chinese colonel and his staff in support of the development of a fighter aircraft manufactured by the Aerospace Industry Development Corporation (AIDC), a company under the auspices of the Republic of China Air Force (RCAF).

My life as a sojourner was to take me back to the Far East to one of the most challenging and interesting assignments of my military and industrial careers.

Chapter 18
No Feng Shui

Brian was living with me in Fort Worth and attending a local high school when I received the offer to go to Taiwan. My concern over his education was alleviated when we learned there was an English speaking school in Taichung: Morrison Academy.

Established in 1952, it offered a college preparatory and American based Christian affiliated education to expatriate children living in Taiwan. Although it was set up to serve the families of missionaries assigned around the world in countries where English schools were not available, it supported businesses like General Dynamics and others operating in Taiwan and other countries.

Formerly known as Formosa, Taiwan, which is east of China, west of Japan and north of the Philippines is officially the Republic of China (ROC). One of the most densely populated countries in the world, slightly larger than Switzerland, it was originally inhabited by aborigines until the Dutch and the Spanish discovered it in the 7th century. Following the Chinese civil war after the 2nd World War, the Chinese nationalists, led by Chiang Kai-shek, evacuated the mainland and took control of the island.

The rapid industrialization of Taiwan since the 1950's has made it one of the "Four Asian Tigers" alongside Hong Kong, South Korea, and Singapore. The cultures of Taiwan are a hybrid blend of traditional Chinese, Japanese, Confucianism, and Western values. Even today the issue that Taiwan, a democratic republic, is not a part of China is officially ignored.

AIDC was established to develop Indigenous Defense Fighter (IDF) aircraft to support their armed forces in case of attack by foreign aggressors, primarily the growling tiger across the Straits of Formosa, China, whose communist leaders were devoted to bringing the breakaway republic back under its dictatorial control. Working together with the American developer of the F-16 aircraft General Dynamics, AIDC was developing the Ching-kuo (named after the son of Chiang Kai-shek) fighter aircraft.

As we will see later, even the name of the project would elicit negative comments when translated into English.

The first weekend after we arrived at the American compound in Taichung, Brian and I were invited to a dinner hosted by the general in charge of AIDC. Unfortunately, our household goods shipment from Fort Worth did not arrive intact. We were expected to dress for the dinner in business suits. We had no problem with the suits, but only one of Brian's black shoes made it. He couldn't wear my shoes, so we made a grand entrance in front of the Chinese general and his staff with Brian in a suit and tie wearing a pair of scuffed tennis shoes.

Later on the track coach at Morrison Academy asked Brian to join his team as a discus thrower and shot putter. Unfortunately, it rains a lot in Taiwan and Brian kept slipping in his slick soled tennis shoes.

That weekend we went on a shopping trip to sporting goods stores in Taichung. Our company driver took us to a central shopping center and left us. It was like being dropped into the full force of the north easterly winds of a hurricane, or a typhoon as they were called in the Far East.

Taichung was a bustling city of nearly 2 million people between the South China Sea and the central mountain range that stretched the length of the island. It had a vibrant, diverse economy of traditional businesses, small family run shops and factories, large industrial areas, and thriving commercial enterprises. Famous for its tea houses and pastry shops, the city was a major manufacturer of bicycles, sporting goods, and shoes. Our driver told us we would have no problem finding Brian a pair of track shoes.

The streets were crowded with trucks, autos, bicycles, motor cycles, and pedi-cabs. Crossing the streets, even at the intersections required a constant vigil because the traffic completely ignored the overhead signals. A red light meant the driver might have to slow a little, but stopping was out of the question.

The sidewalks in front of the many businesses were crowded with shoppers and vendors of clothing, watches, handbags, tee shirts, and other clothing items. As in most Asian countries the posted prices of items were never paid; bartering was a way of life. A rule of thumb I learned in Viet Nam was to offer half the asking price and then walk away. Usually the seller would pursue me and agree to my offer.

Brian and I went to a half dozen sporting goods stores but were unable to find track shoes that fit him. Later I called my son Alan in North Carolina. He found the right shoes and sent them to Brian, and he was able to continue on his high school track team.

Even though downtown Taichung was hectic and physically challenging, it was a safe place for teenagers like Brian. He and his friends often went there without adult supervision. Crime was noticeably scarce in Taiwan; particularly violent crime. During the three years I lived there, very few murders or robberies occurred, and most of those were attributed to gangs in Taipei. Taichung stayed in the eye of the typhoon.

The American compound where we lived was large and very comfortable. We had a two-bedroom apartment just down the street from a clubhouse with a swimming pool, grocery store, and dining facility. The stairs up to our apartment required a turn to the right to enter the living area. According to the Chinese concept of Feng Shui (wind-water) a ghost cannot turn to the right. Later I would learn much more about Feng Shui as it applied to our apartment and more about the Chinese ghost phenomenon.

The manager of the clubhouse was an interesting gentleman named Heinz Ouyang. Yes, as his name implies, he was of mixed race; his mother was German and his father was Chinese. I would get to know Heinz quite well, and he became a life-long friend. He would surprise me with a very unusual coincidence about my home town in Idaho, and I would help him write his biography about his family during the Second World War and the aftermath when he would become a fighter pilot ace in the conflict with mainland China as Chiang Kai-shek established his new country in Taiwan.

Unfortunately, both of those events were delayed by a near death experience I had soon after my assignment in the island. The hospital report:

TAICHUNG VETERANS GENERAL HOSPITAL, VACRS
Taichung, Taiwan, 407
Republic of China

Certificate of Diagnosis   Date: March 6, 1992
Name: Kenneth L. Miller, Sex: Male, Date of Birth: Aug. 4, 1939
Nationality: American
Diagnosis: 1. Fracture of Scapula, Left
2. Fracture of Clavicle, Left, Middle Third
3. Fracture of Ribs, 4th through 9th, Left
Remarks: 1. The patient was sent to our surgical emergency room on March 1, and was admitted to ward on March 2.
2. Figure-8 of splint fixation was done on March 5.
3. Discharged on March 6.
4. Follow-up at Orthopedics Clinic two weeks later.

I survived a week in a Chinese hospital, and what a week it was. How did I get there?

The previous Saturday morning I had looked out our apartment window and observed one of our neighbors, another American advisor, push a motor scooter out onto the curb. I went out and asked him if I could take it for a ride.

He handed me a helmet and said, "Be careful of the traffic, especially the gravel trucks. They'll run you off the road and keep on going."

How right he was. I had no sooner turned onto the road from the compound leading into Taichung when a huge gravel truck rumbled up behind me, blasted a raucous horn, and forced me onto the shoulder of the road. I hit a jagged piece of broken pavement and plunged down a steep embankment.

Gravel trucks were the official road warriors of Taiwan. They terrorized the highways and gave no quarter. Any driver or pedestrian with any sense gave them a wide right-of-way and stayed out of their thundering path. The gravel trucks were responsible for an innumerable amount of accidents, many of them with bloody and deathly consequences. And they seemed to be above the law, what there was of it, for no charges were ever made against the drivers or owners of the behemoth monsters.

One of my fellow American advisors had cut in front of a gravel truck in his small auto once and the truck driver tried to ram him off the road. My friend said he pulled into a petrol station and ran away on foot as the truck driver pursued him with a large cane knife. He was only able to escape because he was the fastest runner. When he returned to his car it was in shambles, the windows broken out and the tires slashed.

My experience with a gravel truck that day was even more disastrous. As I tumbled down the incline I hit my left shoulder and side on several large boulders, and wound up at the bottom with the motor scooter on top of me. I lay there stunned for a long time as heavy traffic thundered by above me.

When I was able to turn my head and look up, I saw several people gawking down at me and chattering in Chinese. But they soon disappeared, not wanting to get involved.

The Chinese believe if they assist someone who is injured, they will have a life-long responsibility to them and the maimed person's survivors if he dies. As a result, many of them avoid helping those who are in physical need.

I don't know how much time elapsed until I was finally able to push the scooter off with my right hand. My left arm and shoulder were painful and my ribs on that side hurt with each breath. I wasn't sure of the extent of my injuries, but I knew they were severe. Finally, I was able to stand up. I hollered as loud as I could for help, but the traffic drowned out my feeble attempts to call for assistance.

Somehow I was able to right the scooter with my right hand. Fortunately, the starter and accelerator was on the right side, and I mounted it and drove it down the ditch I was in before climbing the embankment and motoring unsteadily back into the American compound.

Unfortunately, the Veterans Hospital was the nearest one to our apartment so that is where I was taken. I ended up on a tiny metal gurney in the emergency ward with my feet hanging over one end and my head over the other. The ward, stretching nearly half the width of the hospital, was alive with the sounds and sights of hundreds of patients and staff. The clamor of moans, crying, and shouting flooded over me. Brian had accompanied me to the hospital and he stood near holding my right hand. I could tell he was distraught and feeling helpless.

Although there were curtained-off areas at the rear of the ward, most of it was one large open space. That space contained patients lying on gurneys, like me, slumped in wheel chairs, reclining on wooden benches, standing against the walls, and lying on the floor. A small staff of white-clad doctors and nurses were tending to the patients in a haphazard manner. They seemed to be responding to those who cried and screamed the loudest. Since I was suffering in silence, they ignored me.

I found out later no one wanted to treat me, an American. Their Chinese tradition of being responsible to my family if I died apparently included their medical profession. It didn't seem to apply to their treatment of other Chinese.

I certainly was not prepared for the madhouse I was in. Most of the other patients were men. The hospital, well named the Veterans Hospital, provided free service to anyone who had served in the military, even for a short time. It also received most of the traffic accident victims in the city who could not pay for medical care. The veterans and indigents came from far and near with their illnesses and injuries.

After lying on the hard gurney for a long time without care, I suddenly decided that I wasn't going to survive. So I thought, what the hell, and decided to observe the bedlam surrounding me.

One of the doctors, accompanied by a nurse, visited a line of patients sitting on chairs against one wall. The doctor had to shout to make himself heard over the high noise level in the room.

The first man in line was holding a bloody hand up to the side of his face. When the doctor removed his hand, the man's ear flopped loosely down, held in place by only a strand of skin. The nurse wet a sponge from a basin she carried and rinsed the man's head. When she finished, the doctor took a needle and thread from his pocket and quickly sewed on the man's ear without the aid of an anesthetic. The nurse held him, as he thrashed and screamed in agony, while the doctor finished his crude surgery.

The doctor wore a pair of surgical gloves, but I noticed he did not replace them when he went to the next patient; he simply wiped the blood and other bodily fluids off his hands using a dirty towel. Nor did the nurse change the water or disinfectant in the basin she carried. In a short time, the two ministered to nearly a dozen patients suffering from cuts and contusions.

When the doctor stopped in front of a patient with a major injury, a head wound or a broken bone, he ordered them to go to another part of the ward where other doctors were tending to those more severely injured. The banished patients who had a family member or a friend with them received assistance as they left, but those who were alone shuffled or crawled off aimlessly after the doctor shouted repeatedly at them to leave his area.

At the street entrance to the emergency ward, a steady stream of walking patients and others carried on stretchers by ambulance personnel filed through the doors. I was astonished at the large number of people entering the hospital.

I turned my head to a nurse standing near me who appeared to be near exhaustion. The young woman was bent over and touching her knees to relieve her sore back.

"What is happening; why so many patients?" I asked not expecting a reply.

For a moment, the nurse did not respond. Then she caught her breath and answered in fluent English, "Oh, what a terrible accident. A train ran into a loaded bus. Many are dead or severely injured."

Suddenly a commotion broke out near the rear of the ward. A tall, thin man, bare to the waist and wearing a bloody bandage on his head, burst out from one of the curtained rooms screaming loudly. He held a bottle of clear liquid above his head with one hand. A tube extending from his other wrist was attached to the bottle.

Following him, also shouting, was a young doctor, his stethoscope swinging wildly from his neck. But he could not catch up with the patient who began running while still holding the bottle high above his head. The doctor stopped chasing him as the man disappeared through the door leading to the street.

At that moment, one of the curtains parted and a nurse, pushing a narrow mobile bed in front of her, came out into the open area. On the bed, completely encased in a sheet, was a dead body. I watched as the nurse pushed the corpse past the curtained rooms and turned toward a door at the corner of the ward.

I was suddenly disoriented by the maelstrom swirling about me. I closed my eyes and struggled against the pain wracking my left side. Brian's grip on my hand finally brought me back to reality. When I recovered, the nurse I had spoken to earlier was bending over me, concern showing in her eyes.

"What are your injuries?" she asked.

"I don't know," I whispered. "They just brought me and my son in and left us here."

"My goodness," the nurse said. "I must find a doctor who speaks English."

Fortunately, the nurse was able to find an English speaking doctor and, at the insistence of my company, General Dynamics, he agreed to treat my injuries.

The Chinese hospital I was in was quite different from the ones I had visited in the U.S. When doctors or nurses came into my room to see me, I never saw them wash their hands. Sanitation gels were unheard of then, but I did worry about the spread of germs. Patients were not fed by the hospital staff, they had to depend on family and friends to bring them food.

Fortunately, the American advisors came together in my support. They brought me food and stayed with me to give Brian time to go home to sleep and go to school.

After I was sent home to recuperate, Barbara Thigpen, who was the wife of one of the other American advisors and a registered nurse, visited me daily and hastened my recovery.

Several weeks after the accident, I still couldn't raise my left arm to shoulder height. Barbara told me to stand under a hot shower and make a spider out of my left hand. Each day, she instructed, I should try to climb the spider a little higher on the shower wall using my fingers.

One day I was trying to walk the spider up the wall when I felt something give in my shoulder accompanied by a popping sound. Suddenly I was able to extend my arm high over my head. The spider had worked.

Our maid, assigned to us by AIDC, was very upset when I came home from the hospital. Looking around our apartment she said in halting English, "No good. No Feng Shui."

She proceeded to rectify the situation by reorganizing our furniture, placing a large mirror on the wall facing the front door (ghosts cannot stand to look at their reflection so they would not enter), and hanging pieces of aluminum foil on strings in our windows (again to frighten away ghosts). I don't know if our maid's Feng Shui efforts worked but both Brian and I made it through the rest of our Taiwan assignment without being injured.

I was assigned as the lead advisor to the AIDC Logistics Department under the supervision of a retired Republic of China (ROC) colonel, Ting Wang. The normal way Chinese listed their names was with the family name first and the birth given name second.

I was to learn that the Chinese were strong believers in the ghosts of departed people. Many of the families would give their newborn an official given name and also an alias. They felt that, if they called the child by the alias, the ghosts that roamed the countryside would be confused by the name and leave the child alone.

Ting Wang was a slender man with a vast amount of personal energy. My desk faced his in a small office. The first thing I noticed was that he smoked incessantly. I never saw him without a cigarette in his mouth or in his hand. His habit, which I did not share, encouraged his staff members to smoke in the office. As a result, I spent a lot of time out visiting other logistics personnel in their offices or in the hallways.

While Ting Wang was not a personable man. I wouldn't say he was aloof, but during the three years I worked with him, he never talked about his family and I rarely met them. He also had a constant hack and cough, which was consistent with most of the Chinese men I met. It seemed like every male over the teenage years were smokers. One of them told me that if they didn't they were considered sissies.

Ting's assistant, David Yuh, also a retired ROC colonel, was the direct opposite of him. David, who had received his pilot training in the United States, was very personable and engaging. He, his wife, his daughter, and his son were to become dear friends to me and Brian. Years later David retired from AIDC and moved to California. I visited him there and he has come to Fort Worth to see me.

One weekend, after I had recovered from my motor scooter accident, David and his family took me and Brian on a hike in a park nearby. We walked up an incline to a peak named Monkey Mountain through a myriad of trees and shrubbery.

The Acer Kawakamii Koidzumi is a maple tree native to Taiwan and Japan. The leaves do not have the deep lobes associated with American maples and are a rounded heart shape. They grow to nearly 70 feet tall providing vast areas of shade, which make them very popular for private homes and parks. The Acacia Confusa Merr is a thorny shrub with compound leaves made of a dozen smaller leaflets. The Merr grows to around 15 feet tall. Half inch fragrant yellow flowers grow in clusters on its branches.

Suddenly I was aware of a pale fog of pollution covering the valley below where we had started. Then something else hit me. Although a slight breeze rustled the hillside flora that was all I could hear.

Turning to David, I asked, "Why don't I hear anything? There should be lots of birds here. And if this is called Monkey Mountain, where are the monkeys?"

"There used to be lots of monkeys here," David replied. "But they have all died off."

"Died off! What killed them?"

David just shrugged and said off-handedly, "A virus or the pollution, I guess." Then he turned and continued up the hill devoid of any signs of bird or animal life.

Pollution, I was to learn very quickly, was the price Taiwan paid for its exalted position as one of the "Four Asian Tigers" of industry. In addition to the large and small manufacturing endeavors that flooded the island, it seemed like every family had their own private business operating out of their homes. I bought a set of handmade golf clubs from a family who also had a vegetable stand in the Taichung square.

I have seen some strange sites in Taiwan. Rice paddies tucked in and around office buildings and high rise apartments. I saw half naked boys leading water buffaloes through the water as they tended to the rice fields while trucks, buses, autos, and motor scooters surged by only a few feet away pouring undiluted exhaust smoke into the air.

Many of the country's businesses, including heavy manufacturing and coal burning power generators, also pumped polluted smoke through chimneys into the atmosphere. Unfortunately, they had the same cavalier attitude toward solid waste; they just poured it into the sewers emptying into the rivers and lakes. Tests showed that many of the waters no longer contained fish or plant life.

Not far from Taichung was a beautiful mountain lake called Sun Moon Lake. When I visited it one Saturday afternoon, I expected to see people crowded onto the smooth beaches and swimming and boating in the placid water. But there were very few people about, and no one swimming in the lake. I learned there was almost no fish or plant life in the water because of years of sewage pollution from bordering businesses.

Aside from that, I discovered that many Chinese avoid swimming in lakes or the ocean because of their fear of ghosts. They believe that the deceased spirits of bad people can dwell under the water in wait for unlucky bathing victims.

Once a year, in the early fall, they celebrate Ghost Month. During that time the wayward ghosts, especially males who committed crimes during their lives or females who died without giving birth to children, would rise from the waters and haunt the living. To placate the bad ghosts and celebrate the good memories of those who had lived an exemplary life, they would set out tables with food, drink, and money for them.

Before I left Taiwan, a new fad had arisen; ghost credit cards for use in the afterlife.

During Ghost Month one did not enter into business dealings, get married, or make expensive purchases like houses, automobiles, or furniture. One of our company advisors, who was setting up an apartment for him and his wife in Taipei, made the mistake of buying furniture for it during Ghost Month.

The furniture dealer tried to talk him into waiting, but the advisor was insistent. The truck delivering the furniture disappeared and was never seen again. When the advisor and his wife went to purchase replacements, she slipped in the rain and sprained her ankle. Finally, he saw the wisdom of delaying his furniture purchase and stayed in a hotel until Ghost Month was over. After that, everything went smoothly, the furniture was delivered safely, and he was able to move into the apartment.

At the end of Ghost Month, the Chinese had a national holiday with colorful fireworks, sumptuous feasts, and a strange ritual where they put rice cakes into swimming pools, lakes, rivers, and the ocean. The floating cakes would entice the roaming spirits to come down out of the air to eat them and be swallowed up by the waters where they would dwell until the following year's Ghost Month.

Returning to the issue of pollution: the area around Taichung was constantly covered by an unhealthy haze; a low brown cloud that hovered ominously overhead. Many days, when I went to and from work as we drove around the end of the airport runway beside AIDC, I couldn't see half way down the runway because of the smog.

We looked forward to typhoons buffeting the island because, at least for a few days, the bad air would be swept away in the storms.

On Saturday mornings the AIDC Chinese supervisors would get together at the work facility. They preferred to be without the American advisors so many of us would play golf at a local course.

One Saturday, when a typhoon was forecasted to strike the area, several of us motored to the course, jumped out, and hammered tee shots on the first hole with the increasing wind shrieking behind us. Each of us got two shots, with whoever hitting the longest and shortest balls having to buy a round of drinks at our club house.

That day, I had the honor of doing both. On my first swing on the 350-meter hole a gust unbalanced me and I topped the ball rolling it about ten feet. But on the second stroke, I hit the ball flush with my driver, and it sailed upward carried by the strong typhoon fore winds. As we watched through the falling rain, we saw the ball bound forward from the front of the green and roll up near the thrashing, bending flag stick. When we had all hit balls, we jumped in our car and hurried back to the American compound arriving just before the torrential rains and hundred miles an hour winds.

Before I arrived in Taiwan the government, concerned about criticism of its environment policies, hired an American advisor who had worked for the U.S. Environmental Protection Agency (EPA). Following his recommendations, they issued guidelines for handling air, water, and sewage pollutants with attendant fines for violators.

Shortly after that a report came out that the country's gross national product indicators, while not decreasing, had slowed in their rapid increase. The government immediately fired the American EPA advisor and rescinded its environmental guidelines. You don't mess with an "Asian Tiger."

Taiwan hospitals didn't record air pollution as a cause of death. It manifested itself through an increase in already prevalent heart and lung diseases. Millions of vehicles (most of them never checked for pollution control devices), diesel powered generators, coal plants, and uncontrolled manufacturing waste disposals pumped early death into the air around the clock and around the calendar.

I bought an old used car while there. When I took it to a pollution control examining garage, the attendant placed an instrument up the tail pipe to test the engine emissions. He shook his head sadly as he looked at the dial and told me in halting English it did not pass.

Then he smiled and held out his hand. I gave him some local currency as I had been cautioned to do by other American advisors.

He took a small powered drill and poked several holes near the end of the tail pipe. When he tested it again, the meter showed it passed, thanks to the fresh air drawn in through the holes, and I was on the road doing my part to add pollution to the smoggy skies.

One of the first challenges I faced as the logistics advisor for AIDC was understanding "Chinglish."

The Chinese written language, one of the oldest in the history of the world, hasn't changed significantly in thousands of years. There are many spoken dialects, in fact many areas within the country can't speak to one another, but they do have common written characters, which allow them to communicate. Their classical orthography (pictographs) is written in rectangular blocks in vertical columns read from the top to the bottom and right to left across the columns using dialectic characters representing descriptive words.

One example I learned was that a computer, which certainly did not exist thousands of years ago, was two characters: the first one signifying a bolt of lightning and the second one representing a human brain.

But in the modern world of computer technology, high performance aircraft, and complex weapons systems such a simple language would not suffice. Hence the rise of Chinglish. Our technical reports, when they were translated by the Taiwanese, were a mixture of English words and Chinese characters.

It is a good thing that the Chinese written language had some semblance of order because the spoken language was extremely difficult for Americans to learn because of the use of tones to distinguish words. An example is the two letter word "ma." With a high level pitch contour it means mother, with high rising it is hemp, with low falling-rising it is horse, with high falling it is scold, and with neutral it is question. So you have to be careful when you say "ma" to a Chinese. You could be calling them a mother or a horse.

Before I arrived in Taiwan, the supervisor of the AIDC American advisors, who had spent several years in country while trying earnestly to learn the language, attempted to give his farewell speech to the Chinese speaking in their language. When he finished, a Taiwanese dignitary sitting next to him leaned over and whispered to him, "Are you trying to speak Chinese?"

I have never been able to speak foreign languages well with my Idaho flat intonations. I did find something interesting in the simple word "ma" as I traveled the world as a sojourner. China is not the only country where it denotes mother. In diverse cultures around the globe from the Americas (north and south), Asia, the Polynesian Islands of the Pacific, and other countries "ma" is one of the first words new born children called their mother. Does it mean that all spoken languages have a common root going back over millenniums of time? I'm not an anthropologist, so I can't answer that. But I do find it interesting.

One of the tasks we American advisors had was to assist our Chinese counterparts write test procedures for their aircraft development. That's where Chinglish came forefront. We would write our recommendations in English and they would translate them into

Chinglish.

I wrote one recommendation for supporting the F-2 aircraft at the first air base that would receive them off the manufacturing line. After I submitted it to Colonel Ting, it was translated into Chinglish. Several years later I saw a copy of it that was re-translated into English. I absolutely did not recognize it as something I had written.

The Chinese, bless their hearts, tried their best to translate their own language into English for us Americans and other's from the west. But their best was often hilarious. Next to the Chinese characters over a roll of toilet paper in a men's bathroom in a Taipei hotel was the translation "Bumf Box," and on a restaurant menu was "Fried Enema," where they meant to say "Fried Sausage."

One evening at the American compound restaurant I was sitting with the manager Heinz Ouyang. I asked him how he got his name.

"My mother was German," he answered. "And my father was a Chinese doctor."

"Where are they now?" I asked.

"Both of them have passed on," he said. "My father died in China and my mother in the United States."

"Really," I said. "Where in the United States?"

Then he dropped a bomb shell on me. "Oh, nowhere you would know," he said. "A small town in Idaho. Bonners Ferry."

He took a photo out of his pocket and handed it to me. It showed him standing on the Bonners Ferry bridge with the town in the background.

For a long moment I couldn't speak. Bonners Ferry; that was my home town. "Okay," I said. "You better tell me your story. I grew up in Bonners Ferry, and I knew most of the people there."

Heinz told me the strange and tragic tale of his family. In 1940 his mother had gone to Germany to visit her family just before the Japanese invaded China. Heinz, his brother, and his father lost communication with her. They thought she had died during the Second World War. She, in turn, thought they had been killed by the Japanese since she couldn't get in contact with them.

Fleeing before the Japanese advance, Heinz, his father, and his brother, Botho, traveled through a large part of China. After the war, his father died and he migrated to Taiwan with Chiang Kai-shek's army.

Meanwhile, his mother married an American GI stationed in Germany and they moved to Arizona where he worked for the postal service. Years later they moved to Bonners Ferry, Idaho where he had an appliance repair shop across Main Street from the movie theater. I had walked by his shop many times when I was in high school on the way to the movie theatre or the library.

Heinz joined the ROC Air Force and in 1952 became a national hero when he shot down two Chinese mainland aircraft during an attempted invasion of Kai-shek's new territory.

Over the coming months, Heinz tape recorded his story, and I typed it out for him. He had it translated into Chinese for publication in Taiwan. We became close friends and played a lot of golf together at courses all over the island.

Suddenly, in the middle of the night in November of 1992, I received another one of those phone calls no one wants to receive. My brother, Bob, called to tell me Dad had passed away from a heart attack. It was like my world came to a sudden stop. My lifelong hero and the one who had given me my sojourner genes was no long with me.

I returned to Bonners Ferry for Dad's funeral service and burial at Grand View Cemetery next to Mom. It was a cold, wintry day, but one I remember vividly. All my surviving family was there including my son Alan. We huddled together in our grief and love for my father.

After the funeral we gathered at the house on Camp Nine Road. The memories of my childhood there washed over me. When I left to return to Taiwan it took me a long time to come to grips with the loss of the patriarch of our family.

A few weeks ago, while I was working on this memoir, I took Candy's elderly mother-in-law Johnelle to her doctor's appointment. When I pulled up to her house she was on her way to the car. I opened my door and started to get out.

"Oh, you don't need to get out," she said.

But I did. I opened the passenger door, assisted her while she sat, and adjusted the shoulder harness for her.

When we arrived at the doctor's office, I went around, opened her door and helped her out.

"You don't need to do that," she said. "No one I know opens my door. You don't have to."

"Yes I do," I responded.

"Why do you?" Johnelle asked.

"Because my father would do it. He wouldn't like it if I didn't."

Dad had an interesting way of responding to requests for advice. Many time over the years, while I was growing up in his household and later as an adult sojourner, I would ask his advice when I faced a dilemma.

He would always tell me, "I can't tell you what you should do. You have to make your own decision."

After thinking the situation over a moment, he would add, "Here is what I would do if I was in your place."

Then he would give me advice as if the situation applied to him. Invariably, if I did what he said he would do in my shoes, things would turn out okay. When I didn't, I found myself in a more complex mess. It took me many years to realize that Dad was the smartest and most perceptive person I ever met in my life.

But I had lost my wise counselor. Now I was on my own.

I really liked the Taiwanese I worked with at AIDC. They were courteous, friendly, respectful, and very curious. Many of them had spent time in the U.S. at AIDC's Fort Worth office so they had been exposed to some of our idiosyncrasies. But some of them had never left the island and their exposure to us had been in their English language courses and from watching American movies.

One day, a young woman came up to me in the hallway and told me about a movie she had seen the night before. Then she asked me, "Don't you Americans ever bathe before you go to bed?"

I wasn't sure what she meant, so I asked her where that idea came from.

"In the movies I've seen, I never saw anyone bathe before going to bed." Then she added shyly, "And they don't bathe before making love."

One of my fellow advisors, and a good friend, Rod Gilley, the son of Van Gilley who I had met in Turkey, told me a Taiwanese approached him once while he was with several people after seeing an American movie. The young man asked Rod, "What does 'f*** you' mean?"

Rod said he shushed the man and took him aside where he told him, "Don't use that word in public; it isn't nice."

"Why did they say it in the movie?" the man asked innocently.

Rod said he couldn't come up with a suitable answer.

I had the good fortune of working for a fine American advisor director, Rich Loman, while I was in Taichung. Rich had the three "P's" I feel all good supervisors must have: Professionalism, Proficiency, and Personality. After retiring from Lockheed, Rich and his wife Laura moved to Evergreen, Colorado. We have continued to maintain contact over the years. Each time one of my books is published I send them one of the first copies.

After Brian graduated from Morrison Academy he returned to the United States to attend college in Florida. Later he relocated to Fort Worth where he worked at the Guitar Center and pursued a career as a professional musician with several excellent bands including the Chris Watson Band.

Upon completing a three-year tour in Taiwan, I returned to the Logistics Department in Fort Worth and was assigned to the Japanese Program working out of an off-site facility. I was trading one Asian assignment for another one.

Chapter 19
Japan, Sorry Dad

Lockheed signed a contract with a Japanese company, Mitsubishi, to assist them in building a multi-role fighter aircraft for the Japanese Air Self Defense Force. The F-2, named Viper Zero, was to be a split in manufacturing between Japan and the USA. Production started in 1996 with the first aircraft to enter service in 2000. I joined the program working out of a high rise building outside the main Lockheed plant.

My first trip to Japan was an eye opener. After a night in Tokyo at the most expensive hotel I have ever stayed at, I took a high speed train to the manufacturing facility at Nagoya. And I mean a high speed train. Whooshing off at nearly 300 miles an hour on an earthbound vehicle was an exhilarating and frightening experience.

As I looked out the windows of the train, the landscape whizzed by so fast I couldn't make out individual buildings or streets. Yet it was amazingly smooth, like a jet aircraft at cruise speed only at the ground level.

When the overhead high definition screens at the Tokyo terminals said the train would leave at 10:02 am, it meant 10:02 am. And it arrived at exactly the time they said it would arrive in Nagoya. The efficiency was something I had ever seen before.

Nagoya, the home of Mitsubishi's manufacturing facility was the third largest city in Japan. Located on the Pacific coast of central Honshu, it was the origin of powerful warlords who unified Japan in the 17th century. It is known for unique local cuisine like *tebasaki* chicken wings, *uro* rice dumplings, and *kishimen* noodles in soy sauce.

The city is also the home of the ancient Nagoya Castle, which is famous for its golden carp (koi) and the Noritake factory, the home of fine chinaware.

Based on the Lockheed F-16 fighter aircraft, the F-2 was controversial for its excessive cost, more than four times what the F-16 cost in the United States. But the Japanese government wasn't too concerned about the price.

After the Second World War, when Japan was governed by the United States under Douglas MacArthur, their war making capability was completely shut down. For many years, their emerging national government forbid any development of ground or air military systems under an anti-war policy. Their brutal invasion of neighboring China and other Asian countries was still not forgiven generations after their sudden and ferocious attacks.

Then, early in the 1980's, Japan began to feel paranoid again, as if they felt threatened by other countries outside of the rising sun. The emerging economy and the build-up of arms by their huge neighbor, China, made them restless. A tiger was sharpening its claws just across the narrow ocean separating them.

When I attended the first F-2 meetings with Mitsubishi in Nagoya, an uneasy feeling came over me. The Japanese were not friendly and respectful like the Chinese in Taiwan. During my discussions with them, they never looked me in the eyes when they talked to me. I felt like they thought my representation of Lockheed was an intrusion to them, and they were only talking to me to fulfill contractual obligations.

But there was more to it than that. I felt like they were conducting something in secrecy behind my back. Perhaps Dad was right when he called them "sneaky bastards." Dad had passed on, but I sensed his presence beside me as I sat in the sumptuous board rooms of Mitsubishi trying to make sense of the shallow discussions swirling around me. Somehow, I knew all that glitters was not gold.

When I returned to Fort Worth my uneasiness didn't go away. After thinking about it for several weeks, I had a discussion with the Lockheed Japanese Program Director.

"You have too much imagination," he said. "The F-2 Program is on the up and up. And it is very lucrative for our company. We should make several hundred million dollars before it is over. Don't rock the boat."

I made several more trips to Japan, marveling over the high cost of hotels and restaurants in Tokyo and the efficiency and speed of the bullet trains, and quietly absorbing the bullshit from Mitsubishi about the aircraft program.

Then I couldn't take any more, and I submitted my retirement papers to Lockheed. After 19 years, a number of challenging assignments, millions of miles of travel, many lasting friendships, and some great experiences I decided to move on to other challenges.

Several years later I was told by another retired Lockheed person that Mitsubishi was in fact developing two aircraft; one under the Lockheed contract based on a defensive version of the F-16 and another one at the far side of their facility in a high security area as an offensive fighter aircraft with long range weapons capability (including air-to-air and air-to-ground missiles under development by Mitsubishi and other local contractors) that was forbidden by official national decree and not approved under the Lockheed contract.

Dad, as usual, was right, the Japanese, at least many of them I worked with, were sneaky bastards.

Dad was right about something else also. He knew what he was talking about when he told my sister to park her Japanese made Toyota off his property. I made the mistake of buying one of those from a friend of mine who was a Toyota dealer in Fort Worth.

I bought a brand new (I wonder where that term "brand new" came from. Toyota certainly wasn't a new brand, they had been manufactured in Japan since the Second World War and exported to the United States since the 1950's.) Camry top of the line, with all the bells and whistles autos came with in the 1990's, like a sliding moon roof, speed control, leather bucket seats, and blast your ears and make your hair stand up like a Mohawk stereo system.

As I left the dealer's showroom, I think I heard Dad roll over in his grave. I should have returned the car straight away, but I blithely motored on.

The Toyota then had a three year or 30,000-mile warranty. Mine didn't last the mileage limit though. Just after I passed the three year mark the air conditioner compressor went out, the radiator sprung a chronic leak, and the alternator needed to be replaced because it was eating batteries like a prehistoric monster eats small animals with short legs. But strangest of all, the paint had flaked and discolored like it had been sand blasted just after a few hundred birds had defecated on it. I had never seen anything like it.

I took the car back to the dealer. He looked at it, shook his head, and said, "I have never seen anything like it."

Then he added, "Unfortunately the warranty has run out. There is nothing we can do about it."

"Can I sell it back to you?" I asked hopefully.

"I couldn't offer you very much for it," he said ruefully. "It would cost me a couple of grand to fix it up and give it a new paint job. Have you been driving in sand storms?"

So I had the air conditioner, radiator, and alternator repaired by a local cut rate shade tree mechanic who added a cheap paint job, and then placed an ad in the Star Telegram. The day I watched the buyer of my Toyota top of the line Camry drive away, I'm sure I heard Dad sigh, roll back over, and relax.

Chapter 20
The Devil's Highway

Just before I retired from Lockheed I bought a Roadtrek 190 Class C motorhome built in Canada with a Chevrolet engine and chassis from the United States. What a beautiful machine it was. By reclining the four front seats, it could sleep six adults. With a double bed, built-in shower, marine toilet, microwave, two-burner gas stove, refrigerator, and lots of storage it was a pleasure to travel in.

Someone looked at it and said I was like a turtle carrying a shell around with me; I didn't need anything else.

On one of my first trips secure in my turtle shell, I drove from Fort Worth to Phoenix, Arizona to visit my son Mike and his family. I wanted to make several stops on the way: at the Four Corners Monument, where the states of Utah, Colorado, Arizona, and New Mexico come together at one point; at Monument Valley, which I had never visited; and at the Grand Canyon, which I had seen several times since I was a teenager.

Traveling in the northwestern part of New Mexico through towns like Blanco, Bloomfield, Farmington, and Upper Fruitland (I never saw Lower Fruitland but there weren't any upland or lowland in the area. It was all as flat as my mother's ironing board) wasn't very exciting. The Rocky Mountains were far away and a recent drought had turned the high plateau into a rolling sea of dusty brown wild grasses and drab weeds only occasionally interrupted by scrubby trees drooping along dry river beds in anticipation of nourishing rains that might never come.

One afternoon, after hours of motoring across the ugly landscape, I saw something on the horizon that looked out of character, a man-made structure that grew larger as I approached it.

When I could finally make out what it was, I thought I was seeing a mirage. Out in the middle of nowhere was a huge casino. Then I realized it was on a Navajo Indian reservation, which was not subject to state laws forbidding gambling establishments.

There were no casinos in my home state of Texas (actually my second home state, Idaho being the first). Tired of the constant raids by Comanches, in the 1880's the Texas legislature banished all Indian tribes (even the peaceful ones in the eastern part of the state) to Oklahoma and confiscated any property that might be considered a reservation. As a result, to lose their hard earned money to one-armed bandit slot machines and greedy gambling tables, Texans had to travel to Louisiana, Oklahoma, and, now I realized, out in the middle of nowhere in New Mexico.

I had lunch and lost several dollars' worth of quarters at one of the casino slot machines. As soon as I left it, an elderly lady, carrying jangling coins in a purple Crown Royal draw string bag, plopped down on my stool and began feeding quarters to the insatiable money eater that had reached into my pockets, removed all the change I had, and noisily devoured it.

I was surprised to see so many people there, it was like an oasis in the middle of the desert drawing visitors from all over who no longer liked their money and wanted to give it to the non-Indian financiers who bank rolled the gambling mecca.

As I watched the casino grow smaller in my van's rear view mirrors, I thought about a middle-aged couple I had overheard talking while the husband was getting cash out of an ATM machine.

"You can't do that," his distraught wife said as she tried to pull him away from the money dispenser. "It will come out of our checking account, and we won't be able to pay our house payment next month."

"Don't worry," the husband snapped. "The cards are turning in my favor now. With my luck, we won't have to worry about it."

After later research, I found out that the Indians, who gave up the ancient privacy of their reservation to allow millions of voracious gamblers from all over the world to descend like a plague of locusts on the gambling houses, received a very small percentage of the casino profits. Of course, it did provide paying jobs for some of them, but it also destroyed their self-worth and strained their family relationships. In 2011, the Navajo Gaming Enterprise reported that across the United States, Indian gaming centers (read that federally sanctioned casinos) brought in over $27 billion in revenue.

Yet about half of the Navajo nation is still unemployed. Many live without electricity and indoor plumbing on isolated dirt roads. Whatever minuscule amount the New Mexico casinos pay to the local Indians hasn't improved the overall quality of life a whit for most of them. In the areas where the casinos perch like carrion birds, compulsive gambling, alcoholism, drugs, crimes, and loss of culture has become rampant.

The Faustian tale of a troubled man making a pact with the devil is a recurring motif in Christian mythology. As Shakespeare wrote in *Merchant of Venice*,

"All that glitters is not gold.
Often have you heard that told:
Many a man his life has sold."

In my estimation, the Navajo tribes, like many others scattered throughout the United States, have sold their life, their very soul for the false security of income from spectacular casinos that rise out of the land like mirage oases in the deserts.

Nearing the border of Arizona, I turned north toward the Four Corners Monument. The first thing I noticed was the number of the highway: 666. An instant later a truck in front of me tossed up loose gravel with its tires and my windshield exploded in large cracks.

Did that really happen just because I pulled out onto a roadway called the Devil's Highway? Yes, it did. As my brother Charlie often said, "Truth is stranger than fiction."

I had to make a u-turn and cancel my trip to the Four Corners Monument. I spent two nights in a sleazy motel in the small town of Little Water, New Mexico (and I didn't make that up either) while a local garage had a windshield sent in from Santa Fe for my van.

I called the motel sleazy; actually it was worse than that. Built back in a time immemorial of crumbling adobe brick, splintery boards that must have been salvaged from pig sties, and windows that were last washed by the Civilian Conservation Corp during the great depression, by comparison it made the Bates Motel from the movie *Psycho* look like a 4-star resort.

The ancient black and white television didn't work, but that was okay because I was serenaded all night by a dripping faucet, the furtive scratching and scrambling of roaches, mice, and, I swear, rats big enough for Mickey Rooney to ride on them.

The only café, a greasy spoon behind a Texaco station, specialized in green chili. A New Mexico tradition, and I think required by law, they served green chili with every meal; with eggs for breakfast, on hamburgers for lunch, and as a side with chicken fried steaks for dinner. I asked the amply proportioned and height challenged waitress if I was to order ice cream for dessert would it come with green chili.

She popped her gum, wiped her hands on her filthy apron, and answered seriously, "Which ever ya want, Sweetie."

Several years later I read an article about New Mexico, tired of the negative connotations of the 666 number and the derogatory nickname of Devil's Highway, changing the road number to 491.

Unfortunately, they announced it ahead of time. They should have had hundreds of workers posted out in the middle of the night and at a one-time signal snatch down the 666 numbers and put up the 491 numbers. But in typical government bureaucracy lack of oversight, they gave the public over a month of warning, announcing it widely in newspaper articles and television broadcasts.

As a result, armies of scavengers descended on the highway signs with saws, hammers, and crow bars stealing the 666 signs as keepsakes for their living rooms and man caves. A number of them were apprehended by state police, but the authorities had to turn them loose because no one could put a value on the signs, and they didn't want to prosecute all the misdemeanor charges.

After getting my windshield replaced I continued on to Monument Valley. I had been wanting to visit there since I was a youngster enthralled by western movies set in the area. Characterized by a cluster of vast sandstone buttes, the largest reaching over 1,000 feet above the mile-high valley floor, it lies inside the Navajo Nation.

The floor is largely siltstone deposited by the meandering rivers that carved the valley after the last ice age covered most of the North American continent. The vivid red color comes from iron oxide and the darker blue-gray rocks in the valley get their color from manganese oxide.

Director John Ford used the location for a number of films, most of them starring my Dad's favorite actor John Wayne. Included among them was (I believe) the greatest western of all time *The Searchers*.

As I looked out at the buttes (including the famous "Mittens" thrusting upward into a nearly cloudless sky as if they were waiting for some giant to toss them a colossal baseball), I imagined the cavalry under the command of John Wayne wheeling across the sandy soil under a cloud of red dust as it approached the setting of the fort where *She Wore a Yellow Ribbon* was filmed.

The afternoon sun was setting on the western horizon snatching the vibrant red, purple, and blue colors from the valley and leaving it with varying shades of gray. The small RV Park at the Monument was full so I left and, with some trepidation, headed back to the Devil's Highway. I hoped I could drive down it to the nearest town without damaging my poor Roadtrek turtle shell again.

I've seen many natural wonders around the world during my sojourner days. Several of them stand above the others in their awe inspiring beauty. Among them were the cascading Niagara Falls in New York, the massive glaciers of Iceland, the beautiful Rhine River in Germany viewed from a castle high above, the roaring rapids of the Kootenai River in Montana, the boiling cauldrons and erupting geysers of Yellowstone Park, the unimaginably huge wasteland of the Outback in Australia, the cloudy peak of Table Mountain in South Africa, Mount Rainer thrusting its awesome snow clad summit above the clouds in the state of Washington, the revered Mount Fuji in Japan, the awesome spectacle of Angel Falls in Venezuela, the forbidding sawgrass marshlands of the Florida Everglades, the enticingly beautiful Lake Coeur d' Alene in Idaho, the historic beckoning white cliffs of Dover in England, and the tropical beauty of the Diamond Head Crater in Hawaii.

But none of them equaled the breath taking panorama of the Grand Canyon of Arizona.

The canyon is 277 miles long, up to 18 miles wide and attains a depth of over a mile. Nearly two billion years of Earth's geological history have been exposed as the Colorado River and its tributaries cut their channels through layer after layer of rock while the Colorado Plateau was uplifted.

While the specific geologic processes and timing that formed the Grand Canyon are the subject of debate by geologists, recent evidence suggests that the Colorado River established its course through the canyon at least 17 million years ago. Since that time, the river continued to erode and form the canyon to its present day configuration.

For thousands of years, the area has been continuously inhabited by Native Americans who built settlements within the canyon and its many caves. The Pueblo people consider the Grand Canyon ("Ongtupqa" in the Hopi language) a holy site, and even today make annual visits to it. To them it's like the *Haj* pilgrimage to Mecca for Moslems.

The first European known to have viewed the Grand Canyon was García López de Cárdenas from Spain, who arrived in 1540.

Major John Wesley Powell led the first expedition down the canyon. Gathering nine men, four boats, and food for 10 months, he set out on May 24 and completed the journey with many hardships through the Grand Canyon on August 13, 1869. In 1871 Powell first used the term "Grand Canyon"; previously it had been called the "Big Canyon."

As I sat on the south edge of the canyon with my feet hanging above thousands of feet of vast emptiness staring out at the varying colors of rock strata shimmering in the sun, I recalled the first time I had seen the Grand Canyon.

After I graduated from Bonners Ferry, Idaho high school in 1957, I worked for the U.S. Forest Service for the summer to save money to go to college that fall in Coeur d' Alene. Deciding that I needed a vacation before heading off to school, I set aside a few weeks to travel to Show Low, Arizona to visit my high school friend, Jim Morgan, who had moved there with his family. Jim's father had taken a position as the manager of a lumber mill in the small Apache Reservation town in the White Mountains.

I bought a round trip bus ticket on Greyhound and headed south. Unfortunately, in the Salt Lake City, Utah terminal I lost my ticket. I'm not sure if someone picked my pocket or I just mislaid it; but I couldn't find it. Since I had no record of the purchase (this was in the days before credit cards for people like me), I wasn't sure what to do.

I didn't have any checks with me since all my funds were in a savings account at the First National Bank of Bonners Ferry, Idaho. I could have used a pay phone and called Dad or Mom and have them wire some money to me at a local Western Union office, but I didn't want to do that. Counting my spending money, including some change, I found that I had $42.63 between me and destitution.

Checking the bus fares, I found I could buy a ticket to Spokane, Washington (a little over 700 miles from Salt Lake City) where my brother Charlie lived and have enough left to buy a box of saltine crackers. I figured I could get water for free.

So, what was the smart thing for me to do? Cancel my trip to Arizona and head back home? Call Dad and ask him for advice?

Well, no one has ever accused me of being real smart. I decided to continue on to Arizona rather than returning home to Idaho. Pulling on my backpack, which contained some extra clothes, toilet articles, an Arthur C. Clark science fiction novel, and a notebook, I walked south on the main highway, sticking my thumb out hoping for a ride. This was the first major sojourner decision in my life; ahead of me was an unknown adventure.

Hitchhiking was something I had done on a small scale around Boundary County, and it had been successful, so I figured it would work on a major roadway. This was late summer in 1957, just 12 years after the end of the Second World War. Many of the American GI's returning from the European and Asian theaters had made their way around the country at the end of a thumb so it was common to see hitchhikers like me. Mass murderers and road rage highway violence was far in the future.

I didn't have to walk far until a 48' Ford sedan, clattering and smoking with an elderly couple in it, stopped and picked me up. They graciously carried me almost a hundred miles before they had to turn off to their farm. As a parting gift, the woman handed me a small basket of apples.

My next ride was in a large 18-wheeler refrigerated truck. The driver, a pleasant tobacco chewing fellow with a bulbous nose and a protruding stomach, had served with the 8th Army in France and Germany. He had a penchant for telling dirty, and not very funny, jokes, which he laughed at himself when I didn't. He told me he was going to Flagstaff, Arizona.

As we approached the Grand Canyon area, he asked me if I had ever seen it.

"No," I answered. "Sure would like to."

"I'm not going there," he said. "But I can drop you off at the road going to the south rim. It's a sight to behold."

And so I received an unexpected and most welcome treat; I stood on the top of the Grand Canyon and watched the multi-colored hues of the rock formations stretching off for miles on either side shimmering and changing under the afternoon setting sun.

The truck driver was right; it was a sight to behold, and it happened because I lost my bus ticket in Salt Lake City. The life of a sojourner, I found out back then as a teenager, was filled with wondrous experiences.

The next trip in my Roadtrek van after my retirement from Lockheed was to attend the United States Golf Teachers Federation (USGTF) advanced instructor school in Port St. Lucie, Florida. They train and certify golf teaching professionals. Established in 1989, it is the largest organization of certified golf teaching professionals in the world.

I had signed up for a week long advanced training and certification program with lodging at a golf course hotel. In 1995, I had completed the basic USGTF course at Tapatio Springs in Texas, and I was looking forward to the follow-on school.

I started playing golf when I was an airman at McChord AFB near Tacoma, Washington. My first lessons came after the Air Force sent me to Washington State University to get my engineering degree. They provided me a house just off the first fairway of the college golf course. There I fell in love with the game and it became a life-long challenge to enjoy the sport and constantly improve.

Over the years, I took a number of lessons and bought many instructions tapes and books. My favorite was an illustrated book by Jack Nicklaus. I kept it for years and wore out many of the pages.

I had given lessons to others and really enjoyed it. I thought, now that I had the time, I would get certified as an advanced instructor and teach classes part time. It would be a way to give back to the game that had given me so much pleasure.

The day before I was to leave for the instruction school, I was lifting weights in the workout room at the apartment house where I lived. While doing a biceps curl with a light weight, I felt a sharp pain in my right shoulder. I had no idea what it was, but I cut my workout short.

The next morning, I woke up with terrible sinus pressure and a dull, nagging pain in my shoulder. Knowing I had to be in Port St. Lucia for the beginning of my golf school in two days, I strapped on my turtle shell and started out.

The next day, as I entered the Florida Panhandle, my sinus problem became unbearable. I stopped at the hospital on Eglin AFB where I was diagnosed with a full blown sinus infection and started on antibiotics.

Although my shoulder hurt, I didn't mention it to the Air Force doctor. I didn't want him to whisk me off to the operating room and remove my right arm. He appeared to be very young and I'm sure he would relish the experience. In light of what happened, not getting my shoulder examined turned out to be a mistake.

On the second day of the school we were scheduled to play a practice round at the hotel golf course. When I tried to hit warmup shots on the driving range, I felt a sharp pain knife through my shoulder. One of the instructors told me how to find a medical emergency clinic. After x-rays there a doctor told me I had a torn rotator cuff and would need surgery to repair it.

So ended my attempt to get an advanced golf instructor certification. In retrospect, my shoulder injury may have been a blessing in disguise. During my recovery, after an operation back home in Fort Worth, I happened to find several notebooks I had written in during my tour in Viet Nam in the early 1970's. As I read them, the vivid experiences of that momentous year came back to me, and an urge that had been festering inside of me burst to the surface. I wanted to write a novel based on that time. And so my third career was about to begin.

Chapter 21
Real Aussies Don't Drink Fosters

Mark Twain, the author of two of my favorite novels *Tom Sawyer* and *Huckleberry Finn*, once remarked at a dinner speech, "Outside of a dog, reading is man's best friend. Inside of a dog, it's too dark to read."

I would find a way to read inside of a dog if I had to. Let's see, I could light a match (which I have done to read something that had to be perused immediately), however the dog might not like the heat in his intestines and have a conniption fit. Or I could use a flashlight (another much used instrument, especially when I was sharing a bedroom with three or four of my brothers when I was a youngster in Idaho and ducked my head under the covers to read). But it would have to be a small flashlight. I don't think the dog would tolerate a big, long policeman's light along with me and a book inside of him.

Perhaps being a sojourner and an avid reader go hand in hand. I know my Dad was a reader. He kept a box of books beside his chair and it was always over flowing. He could read with a blizzard howling outside, us kids arguing and fighting like armies of Huns versus the Moors, Mom shouting at him to discipline us so she could fix supper, and sparks of burning embers shooting up from the grate above the basement wood furnace threatening to burn the house down in flames.

I'm like Dad, I can read anywhere (and I have). Stories, fiction and non-fiction, transport me to other places and times; some good and some not so good. I think my epic dreams are an adjunct to being a voracious reader and, as we'll see later, provided the basis for several of my novels. I've always been a writer also (the chic description now is author, as if just being a writer means you write advertisements, church flyers, or sports columns).

Over the years, I have written many short stories, newspaper articles, speeches, book reviews, letters, and published and un-published novels.

As I read the notes from my Air Force tour in Vietnam, the memories of that time flooded over me. On the first page of one of the small green notebooks I had scrawled a verse from the poem *The Naulahka* written by Rudyard Kipling:

Now it is not good for the Christian's health to hustle the Asian

> brown,
> For the Christian riles, and the Asian smiles and he weareth the
>   Christian down;
> At the end of the fight is a tombstone white with the name of
>   the late deceased,
> And the epitaph drear: "A Fool lies here who tried to hustle the
>   East."

At the end of the Southeast Asia fight over 50,000 tombstones white were laid out over the remains of Americans because we tried to hustle the Asian brown. Plus, several thousand servicemen still lay undiscovered in the mountains, lowlands, and the waters of that small and remote country.

But two other parts of that tragic conflict were never well addressed: over 2 million Asian men, women, and children were killed, and the role the United States forces played in trying to stop the perceived threat of the spread of communism was not approved of by the majority of fellow Americans even after the passage of over 40 years (a first in the history of our country where soldiers of war are normally held in the highest regards).

And so in the literary environment of a time that was unappreciative of, and even hostile to, articles, stories, and novels about the Southeast Asian Conflict I started writing my novel *Evening of Pale Sunshine*. The cover summary read:

> *Occasionally love awakens in us passions that transcend time and place and the loss of loved ones. Evening of Pale Sunshine is the story of such a love; a love between two people who think they have lost everything only to find they have so much to live for: with each other.*
>
> *Paul Hansen is a young military officer who has lost his wife and baby daughter to a violent criminal. Linh Than is a beautiful French-Vietnamese woman who has suffered the loss of her spouse and child. Brought together during a historical moment in time, they are separated by a disastrous war that threatens to destroy a sovereign nation and embarrass the United States.*
>
> *Assisted by a rag tag army consisting of a little orphan girl, a legless beggar, and an enemy spy Paul searches through a war torn city to rescue his love from her brutal captors on an Evening of Pale Sunshine.*

Writing is a strict taskmaster. When I wasn't working on the novel,

I was thinking and dreaming about it. Character development, dialogue, plot structure, settings, points of views, grammar, and spelling all had to be addressed as I built the story.

Over the previous years, I had developed a manuscript evaluation checklist that I put to good use. One thing that helped me was a suggestion I had read in a *Writer's Digest* magazine article to develop each chapter like a scene in a movie.

In the last paragraph of *Huckleberry Finn*, Mark Twain wrote, "...if I'd a knowed what a trouble it was to make a book I wouldn't have tackled it, and ain't a-going to no more."

I knew going into *Evening of Pale Sunshine* what a trouble it would be, but it became a labor of love, and I was to go on and write a number of additional books including this memoir.

After working on the manuscript for several months (which included researching, writing, editing, re-writing, and repeating the cycle over and over), I decided to take a break and travel to Australia to visit my brother Joe and his family: Alice, Joel, and Kaylin.

I guess my feet were getting restless, which is a symptom of a chronic sojourner. I am reminded of one of the songs on Frank Sinatra's great album *A Man Alone* with lyrics written by the wonderful poet and songwriter Rod McKuen. In *Lonesome Cities*, Frank sings "There's a few more lonesome cities that I'd like to see while the wine of wandering is still inside of me." The wine of wandering was still inside of me.

You have to really want to travel to wander to Australia, you can't just step across the street, hop in a bus, transfer to an airplane, and be there. The first leg for me was to fly over a thousand miles from the Dallas-Fort Worth airport to Los Angeles. Then came a month and a half flight (well actually about 14 hours in a crowded coach section next to a family with a colicky baby and a rambunctious six-year-old boy who had to climb over me 22 times to go to the bathroom) to Sydney.

Don't get me wrong, I love children, especially those who are disciplined. This youngster was not. He kept bouncing up and down in the seat next to me like a kangaroo on uppers and spilled his drinks on me several times. I wished I had a tube of Gorilla Glue so I could slather some on his pants and stick him to his seat permanently.

Somewhere over the Pacific Ocean I lost a day. Yes, I lost a day. When I left California it was actually a day later in Australia. After all my years of traveling, I had learned not to worry about the lost time; I would get the day back when I returned to the United States. With my training in science and engineering I understood the necessity for time zones. If we didn't have them when it was 12pm noon in New York city and everyone was taking a mid-day lunch break, it would be 12 pm noon in Taipei, Taiwan but everyone (with the exception of night workers and marauding gang members) would be fast asleep under the polluted non-starry sky.

I remember listening to the Cajun humorist Justin Wilson on the radio years ago telling a story about flying. He was in the Atlanta, Georgia airport (Eastern time zone) and about to board an airplane to Birmingham, Alabama (Central time zone). At the check in counter, he asked the clerk what time the plane left.

"Quite soon, sir," the clerk answered. "At 9:30 am."

"What time do it get to Birmingham?" Justin asked.

"It's a short flight, sir. It gets in at 9:20 am."

"Well," Justin demanded. "Give me my money back. I don't want to ride on no airplane that arrives before it leaves."

Sydney is a fascinating city, and I didn't notice the flipping of the calendar. It was a great place to stop for a day or two and let my body catch up on the diurnal time changes and get back to a normal circadian rhythm. And it gave me time to get the soda stains the pleasant little tyke from the airplane deposited on me out of my clothes.

The world famous Opera House and its serrated clam shell roof, it looked like a flock of prehistoric female pterosaurs (36 foot winged lizards) dropped their amniotic hard shelled eggs from high in the sky and they broke up haphazardly atop the Opera House. It gleamed an opalescent white in the bright sunlit sky against the background of the dark blue bay next to the massive Harbour Bridge.

Sydney was founded on January 26, 1788 (Australia Day) by Captain Arthur Phillip who sailed from England with some fifteen hundred souls, most of them minor criminals sentenced to transportation to a remote island that was thousands of miles away. Those felons would be the first of many more sent to Australia over the coming years to provide the heritage that would populate the country and subjugate the Aborigines (those that survived the foreign invasion) until the mid-20th century.

Here I was in Sydney on the east coast. Was I near to my brother and his family? No, not even close. Australia was big; no it was huge, humongous, and gigantic. It was as large as the continental United States, but it only had the population of the state of Texas where I was from. Where did those few people live? Most of them, with the exemption of a scattering of Aborigines, sheep farmers, miners, and some wandering souls who weren't sure where they were, resided around the periphery of the island continent near the oceans surrounding it.

The vast interior, called the Outback, was too arid and hot to support life other than poisonous snakes, lizards, ants, and a few other scuttling earthbound and flying creatures. Camels were brought into Australia in the 19th century as pack animals in the dry interior. Unfortunately, their human handlers couldn't stand the austere conditions and left the wobbly legged animals (horses designed by a committee of blind government employees?), to fend for themselves. No one knows how many camels survived, but the estimates (Who is going out in that baked desert to count them?) suggest many thousands. Hard scrabble plant life sucked thirstily for nearly non-existent moisture in the sandy, rocky soil as spurious dust devils swirled across the landscape mostly unobserved by human eyes.

As I flew the nearly three thousand miles across the Outback from Sydney to Perth and stared out the window at the flat, colorless land below, I recalled reading an article in the magazine *Popular Science* by an environmental scientist who predicted that one day we will be able to control the weather and send the rain fronts that stall on the shores of Australia out into the Outback. When that happens, he wrote, hundreds of millions of acres of fertile farm land will be created turning the country into the bread basket of the world.

How long was the flight across Australia? I had at least six meals, which were quite good thanks to Qantas' great kitchen and friendly stewardesses—they weren't called flight attendants then, re-read *Grapes of Wrath* by John Steinbeck, read *Allan Quatermain* by H. Rider Haggard, perused the airline magazine several times, worked two American crossword puzzles (The ones from Australia were Greek to me—how did a car hood become a bonnet? I thought that was something my mother put on her head when she went outside to work in the garden.), had eight or ten or twelve glasses of Southeastern Australia wine, sipped a half dozen bottles of water, dozed three or four times, and made about eight trips to the restroom.

There were times when I wished I had that rambunctious lad from my trans-Pacific flight to liven things up. Not really; I did want to arrive at the airport with clean slacks and a gentle temperament.

Perth was a refreshing respite from the austere, featureless Outback. A large, modern city and the capital of West Australia, which is a large as California, Oregon, and Washington together, one of Perth's greatest attractions was the beautiful King's Park. I have a photograph on the wall my nephew Joel took of me, Joe, Alice, and Kaylin on a park overlook with the city outlined in the background.

Several years after my first visit to see Joe, my sister Carole and I returned to see him. It was just before the Christmas holidays. Kind of strange, it was the middle of the summer, not the winter time I was used to for that holiday.

I remember reading in the Perth newspaper that a murder had been committed for the first time that year by a hand gun. Wow! We are talking late in December in a city of a million inhabitants. In my home town of Fort Worth, murders were almost a daily occurrence; certainly weekly. And I just heard on the television news that in the year of 2015 in the city of Chicago alone nearly 1,400 people were shot; a dubious record pace.

Why is Australia so murder free?

In April 29, 1996, 35 people were killed and 23 were wounded when Martin Bryant, a 28-year-old man with intellectual disabilities, opened fire in Port Arthur, Tasmania, a former penal colony and tourist destination. After eating lunch at a l, Bryant pulled out a semi-automatic rifle and opened fire, killing 20 people and wounding 12. He then walked to his car, killing several people in the parking lot, and drove off. Up the road he stopped and killed a young mother and her two daughters, ages 6 and 3. Next he hijacked a BMW, killing four people inside, shot the female passenger in a Toyota, and took her boyfriend hostage.

After shooting at several people along the highway, he holed up in a cottage, dragging his hostage inside. Following an overnight standoff with police, Bryant set the cottage on fire and ran out. The hostage and the cottage owners were dead.

The massacre shocked and horrified Australians, and in just 12 days the government proposed and passed the National Firearms Agreement (NFA) and Buyback Program. The new gun laws included a ban on many types of semi-automatic, self-loading rifles and shotguns. Each gun required a separate permit with a 28-day waiting period, and Australia created a national firearms registration system. Guns could only be sold by licensed firearms dealers, and limits were placed on the amount of ammunition that could be sold.

Firearm owners had to be 18, complete a safety course, and have a genuine reason for owning a gun, such as sport shooting, hunting, or occupational requirements (personal protection did not count as a legitimate reason). Licenses expired every five years, and could be revoked if police found reliable evidence of a mental or physical condition which would render the applicant unsuitable for owning, possessing, or using a firearm.

The new laws also included a national gun buyback program for newly prohibited weapons. The program cost $230 million, which was raised through a small health insurance tax increase, and ultimately more than 700,000 firearms were purchased by the government or voluntarily handed in.

President Obama and other gun control advocates often say that Australia has had no mass shootings in the past 19 years. That depends on your definition of mass shooting. The Australian Institute of Criminology describes it as a shooting in which four or more people are fatally shot by a single gunman. In 2002 two people were killed and five were injured in a shooting at Melbourne's Monash University; in 2011 three people were killed and three were wounded in the Hectorville siege; and last year three people (including the gunman) were killed in a Sydney hostage crisis. In the 18 years prior to the Port Arthur massacre, 112 people were killed in 13 mass shootings in Australia.

Even that is amazing; 112 murdered in 18 years in an entire country. Tell that to the gun's rights advocates in the United States.

Some argue that Australia's homicide rate was already declining before the NFA was implemented in 1996. But in 2012 a study by Australian National University concluded that in the decade after the law was introduced, the firearm homicide rate dropped by 59 percent and the firearm suicide rate fell by 65 percent, with no corresponding increase in homicides and suicides committed without guns.

In the United States in 2014, the Federal Bureau of Investigation (FBI) reported there were 14,249 murders. Would a national policy like Australia's work in our country? Sad to say, no it would never get off the ground. Our society of over 300 million people is too diverse ethnically, religiously, and philosophically for us to pass such strict gun control laws and get the majority of citizens to support them.

There is a curious foible (weakness or eccentricity) in the human character. We might have a belief in something but it takes someone with an opposite view to solidify that belief in our minds and raise our awareness, make us outspoken, and even violently antagonistic towards those taking the opposing viewpoint. Pro and anti gun advocates (especially the former who are backed by multi-billion dollar industries willing to buy the support of our elected representatives) have taken opposing sides of such magnitude they will never reach agreement.

It won't matter how many mass murders or accidental shootings take place in this country, our congress is reluctant to take any legal steps to curtail gun ownership. We are destined to live in a society where violence and the proliferation of weapons will be a way of life.

The 2nd Amendment to our main guiding document the *Constitution* that established us a sovereign nation separate from England in the 18th century gives all of us the right to bear arms. As ratified by the States and authenticated by Thomas Jefferson, then Secretary of State, it states simply, "A well regulated militia being necessary to the security of a free state, the right of the people to keep and bear arms shall not be infringed."

Hmm! What do you suppose our founding fathers meant by the term "well regulated?" Do you think they meant it was okay for me as a private citizen to own automatic weapons with high capacity magazines, hand grenades, explosive vests, armor piercing bullets, and shoulder fired missiles? Of course these arms were not available when the Constitution was written, but if the writers had been able to see into the future to today with the proliferation of mass killings of our own citizens, which have little or nothing to do with "the security of a free state," would they have defined "arms" more carefully?

(Note: I want to give credit for the rest of my comments on gun control to an article in the New York Times on December 2, 2015 by Nicholas Kristof titled *On Guns, We're Not Even Trying*.)

So far by early December of 2015, the United States had averaged more than one mass shooting a day, according to the Shooting Tracker website, counting cases of four or more people shot. Just in the last four years, more people have died in the United States from guns (including suicides and accidents) than Americans have died in the wars in Korea, Vietnam, Afghanistan, and Iraq combined. When one person dies in America every 16 minutes from a gun, we urgently need to discuss remedies without reacting in anger.

Perhaps we need to recall one of Mark Twain's sayings, "When angry, count to four; when very angry, swear."

Democrats, including President Barak Obama, emphasize the need to address America's problems with guns. Republicans talk about the need to address mental health. Both are right. We need a new public health approach based not on eliminating guns (that simply won't happen in a land awash with 300 million guns) but on reducing the carnage they cause.

We routinely construct policies that reduce the toll of deadly products around us. That's what we do with cars (driver's licenses, seatbelts, and guard rails). It's what we do with swimming pools (fences, childproof gates, pool covers). It's what we do with toy guns (orange tips). It's what we should do with real guns.

What we should focus on is curbing access to guns among people who present the greatest risk. An imperative first step is universal background checks to acquire a gun. A new Harvard research suggests that about 40 percent of guns in America are acquired without a background check.

It's perfectly legal even for people on the terrorism watch list to buy guns in the United States. More than 2,000 terrorism suspects did indeed purchase guns in the United States between 2004 and 2014. Democrats have repeatedly proposed closing that loophole, but the National Rifle Association and its Republican allies have blocked those efforts, so it's still legal.

While Republicans in Congress resist the most basic steps to curb gun access by violent offenders, the public is much more reasonable. Even among gun owners, 85 percent approve of universal background checks, according to a poll this year.

Likewise, an overwhelming share of gun owners support cracking down on firearms dealers who are careless or lose track of guns. Majorities of gun owners also favor banning people under 21 from having a handgun and requiring that guns be locked up at home.

These are steps that are, tragically, blocked by the National Rifle Association (N.R.A.) and its allies. The N.R.A. supported the first major federal gun law in 1934 and ultimately backed the 1968 Gun Control Act. But in recent years, the N.R.A. has turned into an extremist lobby that opposes even steps overwhelmingly backed by gun owners.

As for mental health, Republicans are right that it is sometimes related to gun violence. But it's also true budget cuts have reduced mental health services. We need better mental health services just as we need universal background checks.

When we tackled drunken driving, we took steps like raising the drinking age to 21 and cracking down on offenders. That didn't eliminate drunken driving, but it saved thousands of lives.

But as Mark Twain said, "We have the best government that money can buy." I guess we just have to buy representatives more interested in the welfare of the majority of us.

President Ronald Reagan wrote in a 1991 New York Times article, "If tighter gun regulations were to result in a reduction of only 10 or 15 percent of the gun violence numbers (and it could be a good deal greater), it would be well worth making it the law of the land."

Joe, one of my favorite siblings, (strange to say that, but in a family as large as ours, cliques were formed for survival in the children wars that broke out when cabin fever terminally infected us during the long, dark, cold, and snowy winter nights and the lengthy evenings during the summers when the sun hung suspended in the western sky until midnight approached with no television in the house to divert us from our conflicts) lived south of Perth near the seaside community of Bunbury.

He worked at an aluminum processing plant and he and Alice owned a plant nursery consisting of a myriad of flowers and plants that I had never seen before and several resident kangaroos. According to David Attenborough's, *The Private Life of Plants*, Southwestern Australia "contains no less than twelve thousand different plant species and 87 percent of them grow nowhere else in the world."

I fell in love with the Australians (or Aussies as they called each other) immediately. They were hard working, friendly, and laid back. Each day while I was in Bunbury, one of the neighbors invited us out to a backyard barby (bar-b-que). Local beer (Foster's *"Australian for beer"* was not served, that was from the Southeast and thousands of miles away and culturally remote), great food, and pleasant conversation was the order of the evenings.

I decided I could live in Western Australia straight away if my family (sons and grandchildren) weren't so far away above the equator and east of the Pacific Ocean. It kind of reminded me of what the American frontier might have been like in the late 1800's with a few modern conveniences like motor cars, indoor plumbing, electricity, and cold beer.

Joe and his family took me on a visit to the great Jarrah and Karri forests of the southwest peninsula. The Karris are Australia's sequoias. Over 250 feet tall they fatten out to up to 50 feet in circumference at the base. The Valley of the Giants, as it was named, had an elevated walkway that allowed us to soar over a hundred feet above the forest floor as we strolled among the giant trees.

Later, while we were driving around Bunbury (driving on the left side by the way, which is quite un-nerving for an American), near the waterfront we saw huge piles of wood chips awaiting loading onto ocean going vessels. Joe told me they were from the Karris trees; one of Australia's major export items.

I thought it rather strange at the time; they were making chips out of those beautiful, stately trees that must take centuries to mature to send to countries like China and Sri Lanka where they were turned into computer desks, tables, and bed head boards for sale by cut-rate furniture stores in Europe and the United States.

We continued our outing through the Margaret River area where we stopped several times for wine tastings at the local vineyards. I was reminded of the Napa Valley area of central California; rolling verdant hillsides, sprawling estate buildings, and pleasant spacious cafes and wine display areas.

Then, down at the southwest corner of the country, we came upon one of the most awesome sights I have ever seen. At the confluence of the Indian Ocean and the Southern Ocean above Antarctica high cliffs overlooking the tumultuous seas, we could see fisherman, clad in weatherproof overcoats and tethered by ropes, casting with long poles out over the precipices into the face of the green, threshing waters.

"What are they doing?" I asked Joe incredulously.

"Fishing," he shouted above the roar of the ocean. "Every year several are pulled over the cliffs and drown."

My God! I thought. I don't think I would ever be hungry enough for fish to risk my life and sanity flinging a two-handed pole out over an abyss that threatened to suck me into it and swirl my frozen body to the South Pole where the Emperor Penguins would have to waddle around my icy corpse to dive into the waters for krill. My respect for the Aussies just went up ten-fold.

After returning to Fort Worth, I continued working on my novel, *Evening of Pale Sunshine*. I was about to learn "what a trouble it was to make a book," as Mark Twain wrote.

Chapter 22
A Sense of Time and Place

After completing what I thought was a final draft of my novel, I had it reviewed by a local editor. Then I bought a copy of *Writer's Market* for addresses of fiction agents and publishers and guidelines for submitting book proposals, which included a cover letter, a short synopsis, and the first three chapters of *Evening of Pale Sunshine.*

I made copies of the proposal and sent them to various New York City agents. The days of internet book developers who could work out of offices and homes in Podunk, Iowa or Anywhere USA was still in the future. Amazon was just a massive river in South America and Kindle and Nook were daydreams of teenagers suffering from acne with visions of sugar plums dancing in their heads. New York was still the place where publishing was king and the slippery slope to the *New York Times* bestseller lists, which led to numerous sales and the potential for Hollywood movie productions.

Of the sixteen proposals I sent out, I received two responses. Several others were returned in the SASE (Self Addressed Stamped Envelope) I had included. I could tell they had never been opened.

The first response was from an editor of a small press in New York City. He had hand scrawled a note over my cover letter that said, "Your wasting your time trying to publish a book about Vietnam. What the hell are you thinking? Nobody is going to read it."

Okay, I thought. I really don't want to work with a publisher who is stupid enough to write "Your" instead of "You're." And I thought my story was good enough that a lot of people would like to read it.

The second response was quite interesting. It was a personal three-page letter from one of the major New York literary agents. It was apparent he had read my entire proposal. He said he was impressed with my writing ability and character developments. Then he dropped a bomb on me.

"I think you have a rare talent for writing; however, the reading public is not yet ready to accept stories about such an unpopular war. My aunt was at Kent State protesting against our involvement in Vietnam when the National Guard opened fire on her and her friends. She was fortunate to survive. There is no way I could sell your novel to a publisher. I suggest you change the time and the setting of your story and re-submit it to me."

Whoa! That's like telling Margaret Mitchell she was a good writer but she shouldn't use the Civil War and Georgia as the time and setting for *Gone with the Wind*. Why not set it during America's industrial revolution of the 1950's with the steel mills of Pittsburg as a background. Or how about informing John Steinbeck that the dust bowl of the 1930's was too depressing for readers and he should set *Grapes of Wrath* in Miami Beach during a spring break of the 1960's.

I believe every story has its own unique sense of time and place. *Evening of Pale Sunshine* took place in the early 1970's in Vietnam as Secretary of State Henry Kissinger's *Peace with Honor* proposals were being scoffed at by the North Vietnamese who were not pressured by time constraints; they could wait for centuries if they had to.

After receiving a pile of rejections from agents all over the United States, I formed my own publishing company, KLM Literary Services. In addition to my novel, I published short stories and poetry from other authors in newsletters and internet outlets that were just becoming available.

I joined the Friends of the Fort Worth Library, a great organization headed by Bunny Gardner. We started a monthly book forum, and over the ensuing years I hosted a number of local authors as they presented their writings to our group.

It was a great venue for me to make book store contacts in the area. The manager of a Fort Worth Barnes and Noble invited me to her store for a book signing. I also spoke at several public organizations like the Fort Worth Model "A" Club and Lockheed's Retirement Organization.

In time, sales of *Evening of Pale Sunshine* grew and it became almost a cult favorite. When Amazon increased their internet book sales, they put it on their site as did Barnes and Noble. I received several great reviews on the book:

"BRAVO! This epic novel captured the sights, sounds, and smells of Asia and the culture and religious beliefs of the people." John Gilbert, Lt. Colonel, Infantry (Ret.).

"An excellent novel with a mixture of human interest and history. I am working on translation into Chinese." Liu, Kuan-Sheng, Taipei, Taiwan, Republic of China.

Even today, sixteen years after it was published I still get orders for the book. And, I guess I have come full circle as an author. A year or so ago I saw my novel on a Half Priced Book Stores bargain shelf for a dollar. I was tempted to buy it, but I decided to leave it in hopes someone would snatch it up and enjoy it.

One afternoon I met my friend John Gilbert for a drink at a local restaurant. John, a retired soldier, worked for the government in Saigon, Vietnam in May of 1975 when the North Vietnamese encircled the city. He was one of the last Americans to be evacuated by helicopter before the South surrendered.

John had maintained contact with a number of Vietnamese who had fled the country before and after the surrender. On this day, he told me an interesting story about a young Vietnamese man he knew who now lived in California.

The son of an American serviceman (who had left the country several years before) and a Vietnamese woman, as a youngster he had become separated from his mother when the North invaded. He became a "Bui Doi" a "leaf in the wind." Ostracized by his countrymen because of his father, he was denied schooling, medical care, and foster homes. Living in the streets like a feral dog, he foraged for food in garbage dumps and in the alleys behind restaurants.

Since there were no official communications between the United States and the newly united Vietnam, a council of world churches sponsored "Operation Babylift" in 1975 when 3,000 Vietnamese children of American GI's were airlifted through Thailand to the United States to be re-united with their fathers. John's young friend was one of those fortunate children.

That night I had a vivid dream about a young boy who was scrounging through the streets of Saigon under pale street lights. He looked up at me, and I could see he was disfigured, a deep gash obscuring one of his eyes. As I looked at him, tears of pain and anguish seeped down from his stricken eye and ran through the dust on his cheek.

From that dream was born my second novel, *Weep Without Tears*. It was a historical novel set in the turbulent post-war times of the 1970's. Epic in scope, it is a stirring adventure story of love, faith, and courage in the face of persecution and impending death. An exhilarating tale of a courageous young orphan boy, a man fighting for his life, and the woman who will unite them at the risk of losing the one she loves. The title comes from a Vietnamese expression by a woman who is separated from her loved one, "When you are gone, to smile is to weep without tears."

I tied it into my first novel, *Evening of Pale Sunshine*, as the boy became the child of Paul Hansen (who was recovering from a serious head wound) and Linh Than the boy's mother. I introduced a new character, Catherine Knight who would nurse Paul back to health.

Published by iUniverse, it was distributed to all the major internet book print suppliers and e-book sellers, Amazon, Barnes and Noble,

Kindle and Nook. Strangely, it also began showing up on a growing number of internet book stores all over the world. I found copies of it for sale all over the United States and in England, Australia, and other countries.

An advance summary of *Weep Without Tears* was the winner of a Lu Spurlock Black Gold Writing Award for an outstanding novel at the Fourth Annual Texans Writing to the World Writer's Conference. But before I could publish the book, several things happened that impacted my life; in fact, many lives in my family and country were touched.

On September 11, 2001 (9-11) a series of coordinated terrorist suicide attacks were committed by the Islamic group al-Qaeda on the United States.

Four passenger airliners, which all departed from airports on the U.S. East Coast bound for California, were hijacked by 19 al-Qaeda terrorists to be flown into buildings. Two of the planes, American Airlines Flight 11 and United Airlines Flight 175, crashed into the North and South towers, respectively, of the World Trade Center complex in New York City.

Within an hour and 42 minutes, both 110-story towers collapsed, with debris and the resulting fires causing partial or complete collapse of all other buildings in the World Trade Center complex, including the 47-story 7 World Trade Center tower, as well as significant damage to ten other large surrounding structures.

A third plane, American Airlines Flight 77, was crashed into the Pentagon (the headquarters of the United States Department of Defense) in Arlington County, Virginia, leading to a partial collapse in the Pentagon's western side. The fourth plane, United Airlines Flight 93, initially was steered toward Washington, D.C., but crashed into a field near Shanksville, Pennsylvania, after its passengers tried to overcome the hijackers.

In total, the attacks claimed the lives of 2,996 people (including the 19 hijackers) and caused at least $10 billion in property and infrastructure damage and $3 trillion in total costs. It was the deadliest incident for firefighters and law enforcement officers in the history of the United States, with 343 and 72 killed respectively.

I normally didn't watch television in the mornings, but for some reason I had my set on that day. As I walked by it, I stopped in surprise to see smoke pouring from the first Trade Center Tower, and soon after watched as the second airplane smashed into another tower. For a moment I thought I was watching a Hollywood disaster movie. But as I listened to the excited news announcers, I realized our country was under attack.

I immediately thought of my Dad witnessing the dastardly Japanese attack on Pearl Harbor on the 7th of December, 1941, almost 60 years before. On that day, we had no idea where the attack came from or if it was just the first of many to strike our country. On 9-11, we had the same fears. How had the attacks happened, and were they over with?

Immediately, air traffic all over the United States, and to and from foreign countries, was terminated, the active and reserve military forces were put on alert, and the President of the United States, George Bush, who was out of Washington D.C., was sequestered in Air Force One aloft on an un-announced flight pattern.

Following the attacks, President Bush's approval rating soared to 90%. On September 20, 2001, he addressed the nation and a joint session of the United States Congress regarding the events of September 11 and the subsequent nine days of rescue and recovery efforts, and described his intended response to the attacks.

In the largest restructuring of the U.S. government in contemporary history, the United States enacted the Homeland Security Act of 2002, creating the Department of Homeland Security. Congress also passed the Patriot Act, saying it would help detect and prosecute terrorism and other crimes. Civil liberties groups have criticized the Act, saying it allows law enforcement to invade the privacy of citizens and that it eliminates judicial oversight of law enforcement and domestic intelligence.

In an effort to effectively combat future acts of terrorism, the National Security Agency (NSA) was given broad powers. NSA started warrantless surveillance of telecommunications, which was sometimes criticized since it permitted the agency "to eavesdrop on telephone and e-mail communications between the United States and people overseas without a warrant."

On October 7, 2001, the War in Afghanistan began when U.S. and British forces initiated aerial bombing campaigns targeting Taliban and al-Qaeda camps, then later invaded Afghanistan with ground troops of the Special Forces. This eventually led to the overthrow of the Taliban rule of Afghanistan on December 9, 2001.

Unfortunately, the conflict in Afghanistan between the insurgents (now joined by ISIS) and the Afghan forces backed by NATO is ongoing.

As time passed, the U.S. went into an extended period of mourning because of 9-11. The loss of life and the feeling of invincibility as a country was difficult to recover from. But as the mythical bird Phoenix in Greek mythology regenerated and was reborn from the ashes of the flames that destroyed it, so too would the World Trade Center.

An eight-acre Memorial consisting of two reflecting pools, each nearly an acre in size, featuring the largest manmade waterfalls in North America, was constructed on the site. The pools lie within the footprints of where the Twin Towers once stood, and the names of those who perished in 2001 are inscribed on bronze parapets surrounding the pools. The plaza was officially dedicated on September 11, 2011—the tenth anniversary of the attacks. Towering above the memorial, at a symbolic 1,776 feet tall, the architectural and engineering marvel of the One World Trade Center is a symbol of renewal, hope, and the unquenchable spirit of Americans.

Then, not long after 9-11, something happened that would forever change my family's view of their own sense of time and place. Finally, we were to learn the truth about our parent's heritage, and discover relatives that we had no idea ever existed.

Chapter 23
Rule of 72, Sorry Dad, Sorry Mom

My sister Carole, who worked for the U.S Forest Service was transferred from Washington D.C. to an office at the Federal Center in Fort Worth, Texas as part of the department's attempt to de-centralize their operations.

She called me one day in 2002 to tell me the Census Bureau had released the 1930 census on microfiche to the public and they had an outlet near her office. By law individual census records are sealed for 72 years, a number chosen in 1952 as slightly higher than the average female life expectancy at the time.

At first, her call didn't excite me very much. Both my Dad and Mom had told us children they were born in Wyoming and had no living relatives. Several times over the years, during my travels through Wyoming, I had stopped at small towns, near where my parents had lived, to try to find evidence of their families. Dad had said both of his parents had died when he was a child, so I visited the local cemeteries to see if I could find their graves. But I was never successful.

So I wasn't too anxious to stare through a microfiche lens at dim photos of hand scribed census entries from decades earlier. And where would I start? Wyoming I guess.

The Fifteenth United States Census, conducted by the Census Bureau on April 1, 1930, determined the resident population of the United States to be 122,775,046. Dad might have filled out a census report that year. That actually stirred me into action. After all, I was retired and had lots of time, right?

When people asked me what I did during my retired days, I would respond: I don't do anything, and I don't start that until ten in the morning. Or, every day is Saturday, except Sunday when the big, thick paper comes.

Actually I kept busy researching, writing, corresponding, and playing golf. I was using email; although Facebook, Twitter, Instagram, and other internet people contact methods were still in the embryo stage. I was a member of the Friends of the Fort Worth Library, the Westerners Historical Association, and I played golf at the Lockheed Squaw Creek Course with friends from my corporate days.

When Carole called, I asked my sister Louise, who lived nearby in Fort Worth, to go to the Federal Center to help me research our family history.

Louise is another of those strange coincidences that linked Fort Worth with our sibling home town of Bonners Ferry, Idaho. At one time or another I, Carole, Louise, John, and Lavina lived here. That is five out of the 17 children of Charles and Ruth Miller. And John and Lavina died in the city. Louise moved here from California and Washington with her husband after her daughter, Robyn and her husband Tim, who was a Texas native, located nearby.

If you ever have the opportunity to search for information on microfiche, don't bother. There is an old wife's tale that excessive masturbation will make you go blind. I don't know about that; it was kind of hard to do in a small house in Idaho closely quartered with half a hundred brothers, sisters, parents, dogs, and snow drifts (And no that's not the reason I started wearing glasses at the age of twelve; it was due to reading under the covers with a flashlight).

But I will say that staring into a microfiche lens while cranking a small round handle as you try to make sense of obscure photo copies of thousands of pages of hand scribed census reports will make your eyes cross and go out of focus in a New York second.

We started with the reports for Converse County in Wyoming where Dad and Mom lived during the 1930's. One of the problems with microfiche documents, unlike today's internet searches, is that you had no way to narrow the search. Now you can go to Ancestry, type in Wyoming 1930 census for the Charles Miller Family and, zap, you would be staring at it Dad's entry straight away.

But with microfiche we had to review hundreds of pages of census entries before we came across Sheet Number 2B, Enumeration District 5-8, and Supervisor's District 3. I almost missed it. My eyes were so tired and bleary that I actually scrolled on down past Dad's entry before my brain said, "Stop," and I backed up to it.

There it was starting on line 7, *Miller, Chas C. Age 24, Occupation Laborer, Industry Ditch Rider.* Head of a family that included *Wife, Ruth, Age 22,* and two daughters *Opal (Eileen) 1 ½ years old* and *Verna Lee (Penny) ½ years old.* Over the years whenever Dad would write me a letter, he would always sign it *Your Dad, Chas C. Miller* so I recognized his signature on the report.

Then something rather strange stared out at us, under the entries for *Place of Birth of persons and parents* was written *Illinois* for both Dad and Mom.

Whoa! Both of them said they were born in Wyoming. And, although they never mentioned their parents directly, the family lore was that their parents were also from Wyoming. Louise and I looked at each other in astonishment. Where the hell did Illinois come from?

We decided to put our eyeballs back in and call it a day. That evening I called my brother, Bob, who lived in Noxon, Montana. He had helped administer Dad's will after he passed away ten years before. I told him what I and Louise had found in the census report. He put me on hold and in a few minutes told me he had looked at our parent's death certificates again.

"I never noticed this before, but both of them named their parents," Bob said. "Mom's father was Edward S. Bishop and Dad's was Carl Calvin Miller. I guess from what you found out from the census they were from Illinois."

Okay, now we knew the names of our paternal and maternal grandfathers. And we knew they were from Illinois. But where in that state? In 1930, 7,630,654 souls dwelled within the borders of Illinois, at least those that were enumerated on the census reports.

The Federal Center had hundreds of large reels of microfiche information and I was sure somewhere among the kazillions of census entries were our forefathers. Unless, of course, they didn't fill out the report. It was required by a national law, but they didn't assassinate non-participants (at least I never heard of government troops rounding up recalcitrant folks, blind-folding them, and shooting them against a wall because they refused to jot down their names and family information).

Reviewing all the Illinois entrants for our grandparents, since we had no idea of what county, city, or township they were from, would take the rest of my life expectancy plus a few years and a whole lot more eyeballs than just mine and Louise's. I discussed the dilemma with her and we decided to save our sanity and not plunge back into the microfiche morass.

By this time, information on the internet was more readily available, so I researched genealogy groups in Illinois with the hope they could help us. I sent out a number of letters and e-mails, and I called several of the organizations without positive news.

Then, several weeks later, I received an e-mail from an angel disguised as a gracious lady from Peoria, Illinois, Judi Goodwin. She said she was also researching the Miller family, but didn't think it was my father's family. She said she would try to find out information for me.

Did she ever, her next e-mail opened the door to my mother's family, the Bishops. Judi had found several entries in a funeral home book in Cuba, Illinois about the Edward Bishop clan. His death notice listed the names of his children, which included a Ruth Bernard. Who would that be? My mother's name was Ruth Irene Bishop (Miller after she married my father).

Using the information Judi sent, Louise and I made a phone call to the son of one of Edward's daughters, Edith. The door to our past, which was slightly ajar, was now pushed wide open by Max Mayberry, the mayor of Bryant, Illinois. He told us the Ruth Bernard from the funeral book entry was in fact our mother. Bernard was the name of her first husband.

Quoting my brother Charlie again, "Truth is stranger than fiction." Here is the story.

In 1926 my mother, Ruth Irene Bishop, of Cuba, Illinois married a young man named James Bernard. She was 19 years old at the time. Family lore said she worked in Chicago and owned a Model A automobile, which she commuted in. Several reports also stated that James Bernard was a heavy drinker and an abusive husband.

During my first meeting with our newly discovered family in Illinois in 2002, I actually talked with a high school mate of my mother, Emma Cline, and another woman who worked at a bar James frequented. Both related to me that James was a savage drunk prone to fighting and physically abused Ruth.

Then one momentous night in 1927, Ruth met a handsome young man named Cecil Hugho Miller who was only 18 years old, two years her junior. There was magic in the air that spring night as the two walked around the grounds of the Sailors and Soldiers Annual Fair in Cuba, Illinois with a bandstand group playing popular music like *Ain't She Sweet* by Jack Yellen, *High Hat* by Ira Gershwin, *Girl of My Dreams* by Sunny Clapp, and *Blue Skies* by Irving Berlin.

Before the night sky paled into dawn, a romance had blossomed that would last over 60 years and produce 17 children. Ruth and Cecil Hugho (who would change his name to Charles Calvin) fell in love. But it would be a difficult love for them to consummate.

When James Bernard heard about Ruth and Cecil walking around the fairgrounds hand-in-hand, he got drunk and went berserk. Snatching up his shotgun, he went in search of the young lovers, murder on his mind.

Cecil and Ruth jumped in her Model A and they went by his brother Leonard's house. They borrowed some clothes and a small amount of money from Leonard and his wife and disappeared without ever saying goodbye to her family or his.

Where did they go? No one in Illinois was ever to find out until 2002 when Louise and I made contact with them. Ruth's family thought she had died, in fact there was rumors that James Bernard had killed both of them and dumped their bodies in the Illinois River.

One of Ruth's sisters, Edna, tried to get on the popular television program of the 1950's and 1960's, *Queen for A Day* so she could send out a plea to Ruth to contact her family. Until the day she died, Edna never gave up believing that Ruth was still alive.

Actually she was, but Ruth was on her own private journey with Cecil (Charles) that took her to Wyoming and then throughout the western states until they settled in Bonners Ferry, Idaho and she passed away with her large family by her bedside in 1989.

Why didn't Dad and Mom ever contact their family? And why didn't they ever share their secret with us children? Those questions were never answered as my parents took their vow of secrecy to their graves.

I remember as a child wondering if I had grandparents, uncles, aunts, or cousins. When I would innocently ask either of my parents about it, their response was always the same, "That's not important. What is important is our family now."

Well, in 2002, the importance of our family grew very large when we made contact with our Illinois relatives and went to visit them. I'm sorry that Aunt Edna, who had died many years before, never realized her lifelong dream of seeing her sister Ruth again.

In 2004, we had a Miller/Bishop family reunion at the Twin Rivers Resort near Bonners Ferry, Idaho. Many of our Illinois relatives attended and years of secrecy was torn asunder as we reached out to each other.

Now it was time to get back to my third career, writing historical novels, and visiting a few more lonesome cities while the wine of wandering was still inside of me.

Chapter 24
What's Under the Kilt

While finishing my second novel *Weep Without Tears* I continued researching family history. Searching for my heritage became an obsession of mine. I opened an account with the Ancestry web site and discovered family history on my father's side (Miller) back to the 14th century in Switzerland and Germany and on my mother's side (Bishop) back to the 16th century.

A wealth of information was available in documents like census reports, birth and death records, newspaper articles, military rolls, and from other researchers whose family trees dovetailed with my *Miller Family Tree*. When I looked at one of my family members (my 1st great grandfather John H. Miller for example) if other researchers also included him in their family tree or a document included him, a green leaf would be displayed. I could click on it and view the inputs: information, photos, documents, etc. Then I could select information, verify it, and transfer it to my tree.

For instance, I found John (who was born in Illinois in 1853 and died there in 1930) listed in census reports from 1860, 1870, 1880, and 1900, and I was able to download and copy those documents onto the *Miller Family Tree*. I also saw his name in an Illinois Marriage License Registry and on several other researcher's family trees.

An interesting fact came to light as I looked at John's profile. I had always wondered where Mom and Dad came up with us children's names. Let's see, 17 children would require 34 first and middle names (except for my brother John who only had the letter E as a middle name). Did they just make up the names late at night after reading the *Saturday Evening Post* while we were all sleeplessly awaiting the next child to be hatched at home?

I don't think any of us were born in a hospital. I was told Mom gave birth to me in a small house built on the back of Dad's truck in Utah with several of my older sisters as midwifes, and probably being observed by the rest of the family and a passel of neighbors over the jumble of sleeping bags and blankets.

It would have been like a sideshow at a county fair with the barker shouting, "Come see a live birth. For the price of only one thin dime, see a child being born."

It's a good thing we weren't Mormons, I suppose. Brigham Young wouldn't have approved of such a scene in his state. Of course Mr. Young had 55 wives and 56 children (one of the wives must have given him two conjugal visits), so he probably saw a few births in his lifetime.

Great grandfather John had three sons and one daughter. The boys were named John Jr., Robert, and Carl Calvin. Ahah! Two of my brothers were named John and Robert, and my Dad took his father Carl's middle name, Calvin, for his own after he fled Illinois just in front of a shotgun.

During further genealogy research I found out that one of my sisters, Lavina, was named after my Dad's mother. I was named for a relative of Mom's, and so on. My parents weren't as imaginative as I had thought; they used names of their family members, family they never intended to contact or for us to find out about. Maybe that was their way of remembering their families; naming us children after them. Interesting coping mechanism!

Searching further back in the Miller family, I discovered that they immigrated to the United States from Germany in the early 1700's (while it was still a crown colony of Great Britain), and they Americanized their name from Mueller to Miller. Eventually they migrated from the East Coast to Illinois. Then thanks to my Dad's sojourner ways, we landed in North Idaho; scattering from there to places throughout the West, to Texas, and on to Australia where Joe started a new branch of the Miller family tree (actually it turned into a family forest with almost 1,200 members listed).

Just to illustrate how tenuous our individual grasp on life is, my 12th great grandfather, Kiklaus Mueller who was born in 1480 in Aargan, Switzerland, had a son named Adam with his wife Rosina in 1530. Rosina died during the childbirth. Somehow Adam survived the birth to continue the Mueller (Miller) family line. Had he succumbed (which was not a rare occurrence in the 15th century) I and my family would not exist.

As my son, Mike said, "The Black Death (bubonic plague) that swept through Europe about that time killed almost a third of all Europeans. If it had taken any of our male ancestors, we wouldn't be here today."

My daughter-in-law Jennifer, Mike's wife, knew she had a Scottish heritage, but she didn't know much about her ancestors. I was able to research her family back to Luss, Scotland on the shores of Loch Loman in the 13th century. Her 21st great-grandfather, Knight Sir Humphrey the 4th Lord of Colquhoun, was born in Dumbarton, Scotland in 1280.

An interesting event happened on September 24, 1439 when Sir John Colquhoun and his brother, Patrick, were slain by Highland Marauders at their castle home. Fortunately, John's son Malcolm (perhaps he hid in a fireplace) lived through the terrorist attack to carry on the family genes that survived down through the ages until Jennifer was born.

We visited Jennifer's ancestral home on the shores of Loch Loman in 2003. The ancient Colquhoun Castle had deteriorated over the centuries until there only remained part of one wall with a large open window.

One of the estate employees gave me a copy of a short story he had written about the Loch Loman area. We had just come from a stop at a local store that sold Scottish memorabilia including family crests, swords, and plaid kilts. I just had to ask him what they wore under the kilts.

He smiled at me and said with a gravely, rolling burr, "Ye are not supposed to know."

His story, titled *The Curse of Talorgen*, was an interesting tale about the legends and myths that abound in the ancient Scottish land. I still have a copy of it. When I read it, I'm taken back to a time when the highland clans were fierce rivals for land, wildlife, and women.

The story of a Scottish clan, *The Curse of Talorgen*, was about an elder, Talorgen, whose people lived in the area many centuries before where the remains of the Colquhoun Castle now stands on the shore of Loch Loman. Fearing Viking invaders, Talorgen assigned his son, Angus, as a lookout to alert the village if they were attacked so they could escape into the deep woods. But Angus left his post and dallied with a clan woman and the Vikings were able to come ashore to murder, pillage, rape, and kidnap women and children.

Talorgen, who survived the attack was livid. He called upon the gods to curse his son and banish him to his lookout post to keep watch until the women and children were returned, even if it took forever. Forever is a long time, and it has taken longer than that.

Angus still patrols the shores of the loch looking for the missing clan members at the site that became known as "Black Point" (Ross Dhu in Scottish). It is reported that on still, dark nights his footsteps can be heard as he patrols Ross Dhu. And if you look carefully at a certain tree near the water, you can see the outline of Angus' tormented face in the trunk as he stares across Loch Loman.

The Colquhoun estate, a huge sprawling acreage, is near the Loch Loman Golf Club where they play the annual Scottish Open. The estate includes vast gardens, shoreline guest quarters, and a multistory main building containing a library, hotel rooms, and a restaurant. Not surprisingly, the great house is called Ross Dhu (Black Point).

We had several delightful dinners at Ross Dhu. I was introduced to "haggis" there for the first time. For you non-gourmets who have never tasted the Scottish traditional food, you are in for a surprise; whether good, bad, or yuck, I leave to you to decide. Haggis is described as a savory pudding containing sheep's pluck (heart, liver and lungs); minced with onion, oatmeal, suet, spices, and salt, mixed with stock, traditionally encased in the animal's stomach. According to the 2001 English edition of the *Larousse Gastronomique*: "Although its description is not immediately appealing, haggis has an excellent nutty texture and delicious savory flavor."

Hmm. I wonder how much the Scottish Chamber of Commerce had to pay that chef to say it has a delicious savory flavor.

It is believed that food similar to haggis, a perishable offal cooked inside an animal's stomach, available after a hunt was eaten from ancient times. Although the name "haggis" was first used in England c. 1430, the dish came to be considered traditionally Scottish, even the national dish, as a result of Scots poet Robert Burns' poem *Address to a Haggis* of 1787. Haggis is traditionally served with "tatties" (potatoes), boiled and mashed separately, and a dram (a glass of Scotch whisky), especially as the main course of a Burns supper.

I think the name for haggis came from the sound you make when you throw up, *haggis*. It took more than one dram of whiskey for me to choke some of it down at Ross Dhu, and I've eaten strange culinary concoctions all over the world.

Close by Colquhoun Castle nestles the quaint little town of Luss. Saint Kessog brought Christianity to Luss at some uncertain date in the 'Dark Ages'. A number of early medieval monuments survive in the present churchyard, including cross-slabs which may date to as early as the 7th century AD. A well preserved medieval effigy of a bishop is displayed within the church.

The present Church of Scotland place of worship was built in 1875 by Sir James Colquhoun (one of my daughter-in-law Jennifer's ancestors), in memory of his father who had drowned in Loch Loman in December 1873.

Several centuries ago, the two main clans near Luss were the Colquhouns and the McGregors. They were sworn enemies, often fighting over lost sheep, wayward woman, and ancient perceived personal slights.

They did, however, agree on one thing. Sunday was a day for

worship at the Luss church. Since there was only one service scheduled, they both had to attend at the same time. In a rare spirit of détente, they would pile their weapons outside: broad swords, dirks (long stabbing knifes), halbards (a combination of a sword and an axe), and Claymores (great swords up to five feet long–curiously, the land mines used in modern warfare are also called Claymores).

With Colquhouns on one side and McGregors on the other, the service, often covering the subject of good will toward man and turn the other cheek kind of admonitions, would be conducted. Afterward, the clans would pick up their deadly arms designed for slaughtering human beings not for hunting. I guess there was no government arms control even back in medieval Scotland.

Then they would go back to their respective clandoms to plan continued wars against each other, many commencing on the day following the fire and brimstone preaching.

During one of their wars (never on a Sunday) in the 14th century, the two clans came together in pitched battle in a nearby valley. The sounds of the scuffle carried up the glen and through the windows of a Colquhoun school room. The teacher snatched up all the students and they ran to a hill overlooking the thunderous conflict. I think she wanted to see what the men wore under their kilts.

A few of the McGregors, noticing the onlookers, charged up the hill and slew (ancient word for killed) a number of the defenseless Colquhoun children.

Word of the atrocity reached the ears of the King of England almost immediately. This was in the days before CNN news, the internet, and Facebook, so the information must have been carried by fleet runners because few horses were available. The pontiff didn't send soldiers after the McGregors to exact an eye for an eye by whacking some of their young ones, and he didn't fine them or increase their already oppressive taxation; he issued a resounding edict against them. He took their clan, their family, name away from them. Yes, he did. He proclaimed that the name of McGregor would no longer resound throughout the kingdom.

I can just picture what impact that would have. Suppose many years later, a young woman from the clan once known as McGregor, went into the general store in Luss to order haggis for her upcoming bridal dinner. She was about to marry Malcolm, a sturdy lad with a strong constitution who could eat haggis without throwing up.

When the butcher asked her name, she replied, "Fiona."

"Aye, lass," he said as he jotted down her order with a goose quill pen. "What be ye clan name?"

"Clan?" Fiona responded in consternation.

"Aye, ye ken (know). Ye family name."

Fiona thought for a moment and then said, "What is a family name?"

Several centuries after the student massacre, clan elders petitioned the seated English king for restatement of their name. It was granted and McGregor once again was able to be bestowed on family members.

But I think the curse from the student massacre taints them even today. Among the many Scotch whiskeys available throughout the world (and only that actually distilled in Scotland can be labeled as Scotch), the absolute worst is the McGregor brand. It is so bad and so cheap, only Democrats, those named McGregor, and the homeless buy it. (Apologies to my old Lockheed Martin co-worker and friend Don McGregor and the homeless.)

While in Scotland, we traveled through much of the country, visiting the William Wallace (Braveheart) Monument and the city of Edinburg with its fantastic hillside castle. Then we rode a train back to London where we spent a few days touring the city before returning home.

Jennifer's Scottish family name Colquhoun reflected the area where they lived on land bequeathed to Sir Humphrey by the King of England. When her family immigrated to the United States in the early 1800's, they Americanized their name to Calhoun.

I can imagine overhearing a sweating, overworked immigration official at Ellis Island in New York City gazing apprehensively out over the noisy, squalid crowd of emigrants shoving their way up to the counter. "What you say your name is? Mueller and Colquhoun heh? Can't have that here. Hard to pronunciate. Let's make that Miller and Calhoun. What do you say?"

The publishing house, iUniverse, accepted my novel, *Weep Without Tears* for publication in 2004. They assigned an agent and editor to work with me on the final draft. After publication, they marketed it with Amazon, Barnes and Noble, and other internet print book sellers and made it available as an e-book on Nook and Kindle.

As part of the marketing effort, I reached out to readers on Twitter, Facebook, e-mail, and other web sources. In addition, I had book signings and presentations at the Fort Worth Library, several local book stores, and other organizations.

The book marketing business was a demanding one; but I enjoyed it. Both Fort Worth, Texas and my old home town of Bonners Ferry, Idaho put the book on their library shelves for local readers. A recent check of the computers at the Fort Worth Library shows *Weep Without Tears* and my later book, *Return to the Bosque*, are still available at many of their branch libraries.

The next year, 2005, was to become a most difficult one for me and all three of my sons, thanks to Mother Nature.

Chapter 25
Katrina Was No Lady

The 2005 Atlantic hurricane season was the most active Atlantic hurricane season in recorded history, shattering numerous records. The impact was widespread with almost 4,000 deaths and damage of $160 billion. The most catastrophic effects of the season were felt on the United States Gulf Coast, where a 30 foot storm surge from Hurricane Katrina caused devastating flooding that destroyed many structures on the Mississippi coastline, and subsequent levee failures in New Orleans, Louisiana caused by the storm crippled the city.

The season officially began on June 1, 2005, and lasted until November 30. A record twenty eight tropical and subtropical storms formed, and a record fifteen became hurricanes. Of these, a record seven strengthened into major hurricanes, a record tying five became Category 4 hurricanes and a record four reached Category 5 strength, the highest categorization for hurricanes on the Saffir-Simpson Hurricane Scale. Among these Category 5 storms were hurricanes Katrina and Wilma. That year was also notable because the list of storm names was used up and six Greek letter names had to be used.

The first of the hurricanes to directly affect members of my family was Irene (coincidentally the same as my mother's middle name). Although it didn't make a direct hit on Morehead City, North Carolina where my son Alan lives, its western eye wall swirled into the Outer Banks and the mainland on the 15th of August causing wide spread damage from tidal surges, torrential rains, and gale force winds. Fortunately, except for some minor flooding, roof and tree damage, Alan and his family survived the storm.

But the worst was yet to come. Hurricane Katrina originated over the Bahamas on August 23rd from the interaction between a tropical wave and the remnants of Tropical Depression Ten. Early the following day, the new depression intensified into Tropical Storm Katrina. The cyclone headed generally westward toward Florida and strengthened into a hurricane only two hours before making land on August 25. After very briefly weakening to a tropical storm, Katrina emerged into the Gulf of Mexico on August 26 and began to rapidly pick up in intensity.

The storm strengthened to a Category 5 hurricane over the warm waters of the Gulf of Mexico, but weakened before making its second landfall as a Category 3 hurricane on August 29 in southeast Louisiana. After moving over Louisiana, it made its third landfall near the Louisiana–Mississippi border with 120 mph sustained winds, massive storm surges, torrential rains, and scattered tornadoes.

As the huge hurricane ravaged the Gulf Coast area, my son Mike and his family who lived in Houston joined a stream of refugees fleeing the area along with millions of others.

Unfortunately, many did not leave the pending destruction and the loss of property and lives soared, compounded by the breaking of levees near New Orleans, which caused wide spread flooding. Over 1,800 fatalities were reported from the hurricane with the gentle feminine Dutch name of Katrina. It would become the third most destructive natural disaster ever in the United States behind only the Galveston Hurricane of 1900 and Hurricane Camille of 1969.

Most of the news coverage from Katrina was allotted to New Orleans when the mayor went on national television pleading for assistance with scenes of dead bodies in the streets and refugees crowding the Super Dome behind him as the flood waters continued to pour into the city.

The Gulf coast of Mississippi suffered massive damage from Hurricane Katrina on August 29, leaving 238 people dead, 67 missing, and billions of dollars in damage: bridges, barges, boats, piers, houses and cars were washed inland. The eye wall passed over the cities of Bay St. Louis and Waveland with sustained winds over 120 mph.

The Dutch lady's powerful right-front quadrant stormed over the Mississippi coast, causing a powerful 27 foot storm surge, which penetrated 6 miles inland in many areas and up to 12 miles inland along bays and rivers; in some areas, the surge crossed Interstate 10 for several miles. More than half of the 13 casinos in the state, which were floated on barges to comply with Mississippi land based gambling laws, were washed hundreds of yards inland by waves.

Unfortunately, the water surge, high winds, and heavy rains stormed across the low lying area of East Biloxi, Mississippi where my daughter-in-law Laura's parents lived. Since the spit of land stuck out like a sore thumb surrounded by the raging waters of the Gulf of Mexico to the south, and the Back Bay of Biloxi to the east and north, the storm surge swept south to north destroying buildings and people; then it reversed and tore north to south crumbling and splintering homes, automobiles, trees, and the few unfortunates who managed to survive the first sweep of destruction.

Even before the hurricane ripped into the mainland, all

communication with the Mississippi coast was cut off. The frantic efforts by Brian and Laura to contact her family was fruitless. Even calling emergency agencies like the Red Cross, Federal Emergency Management Agency (FEMA), and local police departments and news stations provided no information on the fate of Laura's parents or her brothers.

Several days after Miss Katrina lifted her skirts and went ashore in Mississippi uninvited, and with no contact with Laura's family we decided to load up my Roadtrek van and go find out what was going on. Stuffing it full of bottled water, canned goods, and other items we headed east to Jackson, Mississippi, knowing that taking the southern route through Houston and New Orleans would be impossible.

Lady Katrina had slashed up the entire state, and afterwards, all 82 counties in Mississippi were declared disaster areas for federal assistance. We turned south from Jackson on US Highway 49, planning to go through Hatttiesburg and then on to the coastal town of Gulfport; hoping we could make our way on to Biloxi.

Even though we were over a hundred miles from where Katrina made landfall, we could already see evidence of the massive destruction: downed power lines, ripped billboards, trees uprooted, carports torn off, and the muddy aftermath of the flooding.

Getting low on fuel, we looked for a station along the highway. For miles, all we saw were signs that gas was not available. Finally, just as we were getting close to driving on fumes, we saw a Texaco station that was open. I was able to buy 20 gallons of supreme (which was the only octane they had), and when I went inside to pay I was astounded at the price. It was over twice the cost advertised on the sign outside.

I asked the attendant why they were charging so much.

"Cause we can," he grinned at me through tobacco blackened teeth. "You lucky," he added. "We the only station around still with gas."

I had no choice but to pay the exorbitant price. Several months later I saw a newspaper article where the Attorney General of the state of Mississippi had filed charges against a number of businesses who were gouging the public after the hurricane. One of those listed was the station where I had paid so much. I imagined that grinning idiot at the cash register looking for another job to pay for his chewing tobacco after his boss had to pay stiff fines for his greed.

Interstate 10 was open just north of Gulfport and we were able to take it east to D'Iberville and then go south into Biloxi on Spur 110. The devastation on both sides of the highway was overwhelming as we neared the downtown area. Downed trees, overturned cars and trucks, buildings that looked like they had been exploded from within by high yield incendiary bombs dropped through their roofs, downed power lines everywhere, and trash of all kinds strewn around gave the landscape an eerie and ominous atmosphere. The few vehicles that were moving on the side streets were fire trucks, police cars, and ambulances with flashing emergency lights and screaming sirens.

Just before entering the center of Biloxi, we came up on a police road block. As we waited in line, we could see the authorities turning most of the vehicles in front of us around and sending them back north. When we finally reached the cordon manned by a half dozen police officers, one of them came up to my window and asked me why we were there.

I handed him my driver's license and told them we wanted to find Laura's family. She had had no contact with them since the hurricane.

I could see the anxiety on the policeman's face as he asked her where her parents lived. When she told him, he shook his head and said, "That area took the worst of it. All the homes there have been destroyed. I'm sorry."

"Maybe they got out," Laura said with deep concern in her voice. "Maybe they went to a shelter."

The policeman dipped his head for a moment, and then he looked up past me at the interior of the van, which was piled high with bottles of water, canned goods, and other items.

"I see you have supplies with you," he said. "That's good. The local water in undrinkable. I'm going to let you go on. There are some emergency shelters—tents mostly—set up near the beach. Check there for your parents. And good luck."

As we drove down Howard Avenue, I was reminded of the Atlanta street scenes in the Civil War movie *Gone With The Wind* when General Sherman was attacking the city: rampant devastation, people wandering aimlessly seeking solace and personal care, and the frantic efforts of relief organizations to bring some semblance of order to the confusion.

After visiting several of the emergency locations without success, Laura said her parents might have taken refuge in her uncle's boat shop, which was just north of the beach area.

And she was right; that is where we found Laura's parents. The sight of her and her mother hugging each other with tears in their eyes was overwhelming. Her parents had moved into the second floor of the boat shop just before Katrina stormed ashore and destroyed their home.

The next day I heard a sound outside the boat house. It was a fire truck delivering water and food to the devastated areas of Biloxi. As I approached it, I could see PFD in large letters on the side, and below that the words *Pittsburg Fire Department.*

Not only is Texas a large state, but it has thousands of cities, towns, and villages in it, some of them with just a few buildings at a remote railroad crossing. But all of them have names given to them by somebody, sometime, for some reason. Some have rather strange names that make you wonder what the town fathers were drinking when they came up with names like Old Glory, Turkey, Telephone, Happy, Utopia, and (my favorite) Lazbuddie. Some are named after countries like China, Holland, and Italy; others after cities like Paris, Athens, Palestine, Detroit, Atlanta, Memphis, Cleveland, and (I had heard of it before) Pittsburg.

It surprised me to see a fire truck all the way from Pittsburg, which is in east Texas. I commented to one of the firemen they must have driven several hundred miles to get to Biloxi.

"No," said the big strapping lad passing out water and sack lunches to a crowd who had swarmed around the truck. "We drove over a thousand miles from Pennsylvania."

"Wow!" I said. "What are you doing so far down here?"

"We took vacation to come help our brothers," he said motioning at one of the other firemen passing out food.

I could see a patch on the other man's shirt that was printed with *Biloxi Fire Department.*

As I drove around Biloxi the next few days awed by the massive damage, I saw no sign of FEMA, the Red Cross, or the Salvation Army. The emergency shelters were managed by church groups and private organizations. The eyes and ears of the United States was mostly pointed to the west, to New Orleans where refugees were still abandoned at the Super Dome and the mayor was ranting and raving on national television.

Electrical crews from all over the United States were working frantically to restore power to those homes and businesses that weren't structurally damaged. Laura's parents were able to turn on the lights in the boat shop where they were living. Local radio and television networks had come back on air soon after Katrina passed using emergency generators, and they announced that those who had lived in East Biloxi, where the destruction was worst, could make one last visit to what was left of their homes before the area was closed for safety reasons: exposed power lines, leaking gas mains, and the danger of wide spread fires.

Brian, Laura, her mother, her sister-in-law (with her baby daughter), and I jumped in my van and headed toward her parents' address. Well, it was no longer an address, because most of the road signs had been destroyed and it was difficult to tell where we were.

Somehow Laura's mother was able to navigate us through the congested streets and find her home, at least what was left of it, which wasn't much. An area of about 12 square blocks was destroyed, houses were ripped from their foundations and torn into small pieces, vehicles were strewn here and there (one car was hanging from the forked branch of a tree), and bricks, boards, and household items covered the entire area. It looked like a powerful atomic bomb had exploded a few thousand feet over the houses causing almost total destruction.

Laura's mother walked carefully through the wreckage of what had been her home for many years. The roof and walls (exterior and interior) were gone as if snatched up by some malicious giant's hand and flung away in anger. She found a few family photos and mementos and picked them up. Then when she came to the corner of what had been her kitchen and saw the shards of her china dishes, she broke down in tears and couldn't go any further.

We got back in the van and were driving away from the destroyed house when I looked over to see part of the outer wall of a house leaning toward the road. At one time it had a glass window, but Katrina had claimed that in her fury. I was surprised to see a cat sitting in the open window frame.

Laura is a cat lover. Over the years, she has probably rescued more wayward cats than the SPCA of Seattle. When she saw the cat in the window, we had to stop. As Laura and I approached the animal it didn't move. Then we discovered the cat was dead. Whether it had died in the window frame or someone placed it there after its death, we couldn't tell.

We left the cat there in its final resting place as a tribute to the death and destruction surrounding it. That relatively small housing area had suffered dozens of fatalities when the inhabitants (many of them neighbors and friends of Laura's parents), refused to leave their homes for emergency shelters when the hurricane sirens began blaring that fateful night.

An untold number of pets, besides the cat we saw, also died from Katrina. Strays were rounded up for months by relief organizations and many of them returned to their grateful owners. One dog that was missing for nearly a year was located over a hundred miles north of Biloxi and identified at a pet shelter from an ear chip.

We stayed with Laura's parents for several days watching Biloxi slowly come back to life. One of the first businesses to open was a hastily refurbished casino eager to take a large share of the wages from the thousands of temporary workers pouring into the area on local, state, and national contracts when billions of dollars of disastrous relief funds became available.

Finally, the day came when we had to say goodbye to Laura's family to return to our homes in Texas. It was time to put the year of the hurricanes, 2005, behind us and move on.

Chapter 26
Return to the Bosque

The history of Fort Worth and Texas became a deep interest of mine. In addition to continuing my volunteer work with the Friends of the Fort Worth Library, I became active with the Westerners Historical Society. The Westerners met monthly with interesting guest speakers who made presentations about local and state historical issues.

When most people think of the history of Texas, it starts and ends with the Alamo (Davy Crockett, Sam Bowie, and all the poor souls who died fighting the army of the Mexican General Santa Anna). While that is certainly a milestone event, it is by no means the whole story of the second largest state in the United States.

One of the best narratives of the history of Texas is the novel *Texas* written by a favorite author of mine, James Michener. He also wrote the definitive historical novel about the state where I lived for three years, *Hawaii*. T. R. Fehrenbach's non-fiction book *Lone Star: A History of Texas and The Texans* is also a very readable work on the state.

My first secretary when I went to work for General Dynamics in 1978 gave me a bumper sticker to put on my car. It read *I Wasn't Born In Texas But I Got Here As Soon As I Could*. I never gave much thought back then to staying in Texas, but except for a three year tour in Taiwan that is exactly what I have done.

In March, a few months after I retired from Lockheed Martin in 1998, I called my sister Eileen who lived near Pend Oreille Lake in north Idaho. She told me now that I was retired I should move back to Idaho.

Eileen is a positive person and always sounds upbeat. But that day, she seemed unusually enthusiastic about something. "Why are you so happy today?" I asked her.

"I can see my car," she responded.

"What do you mean, you can see your car?" I asked.

"We've had a lot of snow this winter, and my car was buried out in the driveway," she said. "It has melted down a little and I can see my car for the first time in months."

"Okay," I said. "And you want me to move up there?"

We occasionally get some snow here in Fort Worth, but I've never seen it get deep enough to cover up a car.

One night after researching the history of the Comanche Indians (the lords of the plains areas of northwest Texas and parts of New Mexico until the late 1880's), I had one of my epic dreams with color, sound, smells, action, and emotions.

In the dream I saw a woman standing in a small family cemetery looking down at the grave of her mother. The small plot was on a hill overlooking a tree lined river. A gentle wind stirred the grass around the graves and the cry of a lone water fowl warbled up from the river bank and disappeared into the sky graying into nightfall.

When I awoke, the dream was still vivid in my mind. I wrote it down in a notebook and went on about my day. But the vision of the lonely woman at the graveside haunted me. That night she re-appeared in my dream. This time she was looking down at a headstone that had her father's name on it (it was Robert C. Parker), but while it was inscribed with his date of birth, 16 June 1821, his death date was missing. I was aware of the ripple of the river below and could hear the woman as she spoke over the grave.

Serial dreams, according to psychologists and psychiatrists are very rare, but I have them frequently. Over the ensuing nights the woman re-entered my dreams and her story became clearer to me. Also, the name of the river came to my mind and was entered in my notes: Bosque River.

I had never heard of that river, and I didn't know where it was. Years ago I had visited the mountainous Basque region that spans the westernmost Pyrenees in adjacent parts of northern Spain and southwestern France, and I wondered if there was any connection.

So I looked it up on Google Earth and discovered it is a real waterway. The Bosque River, named by early Spanish explorers, is a 115 mile long river in Central Texas fed by four primary branches. Bosque is the Spanish name for forests found along the flood plains of streams and river banks in the southwestern United States.

The main branch of the river flows into the city of Waco and joins the Brazos River where it is dammed to form Lake Waco with eventual flow into the Gulf of Mexico. The Middle Bosque River adjoins the Prairie Chapel Ranch home of former President George W. Bush northwest of Crawford, Texas.

As I traced the river's flow I think I located the exact site where the Parker Ranch probably existed in 1856 at the start of my novel. Just off the present Farm-to-Market road 3310 between the small town of Clifton and the city of Waco, I saw evidence that a homestead had once stood on a hill overlooking the Bosque River. I was amazed at the coincidence between my dreams and a location that did actually exist but I had no knowledge of.

And so, I began writing my dream story. The back cover summary reads:

To protect her family, Sarah Whitman is forced to kill two intruders at her ranch who are fleeing from the law after a government robbery. Those murders haunt her as she searches for her missing husband in the raw frontier town of Fort Worth, Texas during the post-Civil War era.

Accompanied by her teenage daughter, infant son, and their pet dog, Sarah is aided in her quest by a saloon madam, a Shakespeare quoting newspaper owner, a young deputy marshal, an alcoholic attorney, and, through it all, the memories of her deceased father. Hounding her every move is a private investigator, Jack Kilpatrick, who suspects Sarah has knowledge of the stolen funds.

The search leads Sarah into a courtroom where lynch law threatens to explode, to a remote Indian village to rescue her son, and, finally, to a sanatorium where she finds the clue that leads her to her husband and allows her to Return to the Bosque.

I selected 1876 for the setting of *Return to the Bosque*. It was an interesting year for the United States and Texas:

 -The U.S. celebrated its centennial
 -Rutherford B. Hayes became president without a majority vote
 -Texas ratified its present constitution
 -Texas A&M opened
 -The Winchester Model 1876 rifle was issued
 -Custer's Last Stand took place at Little Big Horn
 -The Great Southern Buffalo Herd was nearly decimated
 -And, the railroad, stalled near Dallas, continued to Fort Worth

Against that historical setting, I wrote my story of Sarah Whitman's search for her missing husband accompanied by her daughter, her son, and her pet dog.

After several months my restless feet decided I needed a break from writing, volunteering, and playing golf.

Candy, Holly, and I headed north to Idaho for a family visit. My son, Alan, and his wife Donna joined us in Idaho and we drove up into Canada. Crossing over Kootenay Lake (for some reason the Canadians use Kootenay instead of Kootenai on the name of the river that flows through Bonners Ferry, Idaho), we looped back across southern British Columbia.

While visiting family in Idaho, we went to our old homestead on Camp Nine Road where I grew up. Someone had purchased the property a few years before and completely renovated the house and turned the barn into living quarters. They also tore down the old outhouse that had withstood years of summer heat and winter snows.

As I stood in the yard, memories flooded over me. I could picture Dad working in his strawberry patch and Mom hanging washing on the clothesline.

And I recalled the Sunday afternoon dinners when all the family (including my married brothers and sisters and their families) would congregate for fried chicken and adult conversation while us kids tore around the place playing outdoor games like Hide and Seek and Ante-I-Over, which was a game where you had a team on either side of the house and tossed a baseball over the roof. If the other team caught it, they could sneak around the house and hit us with the ball. If they didn't catch it, they had to toss it back over to us.

I remember seeing my older sister Penny, who died in 1991, drive up into the yard with her husband, Wayne, and her children, Ken, Karen, and Duane. She was a gentle soul who used to send me care packages when I was in the Air Force. I think she thought GI's needed shaving tools like they did during the Second World War.

As I stood in the yard, I could see the window over the kitchen sink I broke with a snowball I threw at my brother Floyd and missed during one of our winter kid wars. Floyd had an artistic talent he probably inherited from Mom. He passed away in 2008 after years of suffering with emphysema caused by getting hooked on cigarettes when he was a teenager. That was long before the Marlboro Man admitted he caught lung cancer from a lifetime of smoking and the tobacco companies finally admitted there was a link between their products and cancer.

As I looked toward the huge barn Dad had built (now remodeled into a house), I remember the day my brother-in-law (I better not name him) poured beer into the gullet of one of our male chickens. The poor creature spun around several times before falling to the ground. We thought he was dead, but after a few minutes he scrambled to his feet and hopped off into the barn.

While we were there during that visit Candy and I went huckleberry picking with my brother Charlie and his wife Lilly. Idaho huckleberries are sweet and about as large as a thumbnail, unlike the bitter, tiny ones that grow in the south. It was a family ritual when I was growing up to drive up into the mountains to gather huckleberries each fall. Mom made luscious jams and pies from them.

On the way down the mountain, Charlie drove with Lilly sitting beside him. Candy and I were in the back seat. All of a sudden, Lilly reached over and whacked Charlie on his shoulder. Candy looked at me in wonder. Then Lilly slapped Charlie again.

"What's up?" I asked.

"Charlie is falling asleep," Lilly said. "I think you better drive."

Charlie had a medical condition called narcolepsy where he would fall asleep without warning. After dozing for a few minutes he would wake up and be alert, but you never knew when he would go out. I've seen him fall asleep standing up in the middle of a sentence.

When we met our Illinois cousins for the first time in 2002, Charlie went with us. While he was talking to one of them sitting on a porch, he fell asleep. I had to explain that he wasn't being rude, he just couldn't help it.

When I was a young teenager, Charlie drove a logging truck up and down steep, narrow mountain roads. Whoa! What an occupation for someone with narcolepsy. He would hire me to ride with him to keep him awake while speeding down the one lane dirt roads winding above cliffs hundreds of feet high. I'm surprised my hair didn't turn white at an early age.

Charlie also had another distinguishing feature: he was a born story teller. He could not only tell stories, but unlike many who could, he told hilarious stories. If anyone questioned the veracity of the tales, he would smile and say, "Truth is stranger than fiction."

One of my favorite stories from Charlie was about the time he was an army private in the Korean War in the early 1950's. He was driving a jeep along a one lane dike road through a flooded rice paddy one day. Over half-way to the next cross road he met a jeep coming at him. The vehicle was flying the flag of a two-star general.

When the two jeeps met bumper to bumper, the general stood up and ordered Charlie to get off the road so he could pass. "But sir," Charlie said. "I'll have to back up a long way. You only have to go back a little to the cross road."

The general, enraged now, barked, "I told you to get off the road, private. I don't care how far you have to back up."

Charlie said he turned the steering wheel and backed his jeep down the bank into the deep water. As the vehicle sank down into the soft bottom and the water came up over the hood and above his waist, he stood up, saluted, and said, "Sir, the road is yours."

At one of our family Sunday dinners Charlie was bragging about being able to drive anything with a motor. Mom, who was normally very quiet, pointed at her washing machine. "Let's see you drive that," she said with a smile.

Charlie did have a talent that as a sojourner I could relate to. Someone asked him if he had ever been lost. "Lost!" He answered.

"Of course not. If I was ever lost, I wouldn't be here would I?"

Charlie passed away in 2009 but his stories are embedded in my memory. Along with Dad and Bob, he was my male idol during my entire life.

IUniverse, who published my book *Weep Without Tears*, agreed to put *Return to the Bosque* into both print and e-books. They also recommended a photograph from their archives to use for the cover illustration. It showed a woman holding a baby and standing next to a young girl and a large dog. They were in a field of cotton with a small house and some trees in the background. The woman, while appearing worried, has a look of determination on her face as she stands beside her family and pet.

The book became available on Amazon, Barnes and Noble, and other internet print publishers as well as on Kindle and Nook as an e-book. Positive reviews came in rapidly, and I attended a number of book signings and presentations in Fort Worth and other parts of Texas.

The great science fiction author, Ray Bradbury, wrote, "You have to know how to accept rejection and reject acceptance." I took the first part of his advice to heart, but I do appreciate the acceptance my books have had over the years.

I established a web site (kenmiller-books.com) through *Go Daddy* to add visibility to my books. My brother, Jerry, who lives in Seattle and is retired from Boeing Aircraft Company, wrote several interesting and imaginative short stories, which I put on the site.

The next, and final chapter, of this memoir will cover the sequel to *Return to the Bosque* and the 2015 Miller Family Reunion in Coeur d' Alene, Idaho.

Chapter 27
She's Squirting Oil

I received a number of queries about what happened to Sarah Whitman and her family after my novel *Return to the Bosque* was released. That novel ended with Sarah finding the remains of her father in west Texas nearly three years after her husband was murdered in Fort Worth. She was led to her father's bones lying near a river by several of the Comanche Indian chief Quanah Parker's warriors, and she gathered them up and returned them to her Bosque River ranch for burial next to her mother in their family cemetery.

I decided to pick up the story with Sarah's son Jody when he is a teenager. While visiting Fort Worth, he is beaten unconscious and his girlfriend violated when they witness the brutal whipping of a young woman by Whit Anson and Captain Oliver Lewis, owners of saloons and brothels in the notorious red light district known as "Hell's Half Acre."

As Jody grows into adulthood, that horrific incident continues to haunt him, his friends, and his family. When his best friend is murdered and the woman he loves savagely beaten, he challenges Anson to a fight in "Hell's Half Acre." When Anson is shot to death, Jody is charged with murder, and the only one who can attest to his innocence is Captain Lewis' daughter Deschanses.

A final showdown with Captain Lewis brings Jody to the edge of an evil abyss. If he crosses over and exacts his revenge, he will become as malevolent as Lewis.

I titled the novel *Beware the Abyss*. The name was based on the quotation from the 19th century German philosopher Friedrich Nietzsche, "Beware that when fighting monsters, you yourself do not become a monster. For when you gaze long enough into the abyss, the abyss gazes also into you."

My grandson, Cole, provided the cover photograph. The book was published by Create Space an Amazon company in 2014 and became available in printed copies from numerous on-line publishers and as an e-book from Nook and Amazon Kindle.

I've been asked many times about my writing process; how do I translate ideas into printed words. As a voracious reader and vivid dreamer, I've always found a way to jot down many of my thoughts. I started with notebook entries and my first attempt at manuscript writing was done on a Smith Corona mechanical typewriter.

What a pain those old machines were. The keys, which were mounted on the ends of slender arms raising and lowering had a habit of sticking together resulting in no or double strikes on the paper wound around a roller. And heaven help you if you made a typo error. It had to be corrected by erasing or blotting out with white ink or correction tape. The smudges on the paper left a horrible mess. The page looked like it had been dropped on the floor of a chicken house below a bunch of roosting hens with diarrhea.

Mechanical typewriters were invented in the 1860's and Mark Twain submitted the first book, *Life on the Mississippi*, to a publisher on one in 1883. Ernest Hemingway, one of the all-time greats of American literature, was reported to write standing up with a Royal typewriter.

Electric typewriters were introduced in the 1960's, which replaced the type bars with a spherical element (or type ball) slightly smaller than a golf ball, with reverse-image letters molded into its surface. They used a system of latches, metal tapes, and pulleys driven by an electric motor to rotate the ball into the correct position and then strike it against the ribbon and platen. My first one was the IBM Selectric, which was a huge step up from the ancient Smith Corona.

Then in the 1970's, word processors came into vogue. They made entries and corrections a lot easier. But the quantum leap in taking ideas and translating them into the printed word arrived when personal computers became cheap enough for the average person to buy in the 1980's. They were a blessing in disguise; correcting misspelling, double words, grammar errors, and making formatting easy.

General Dynamics started a computer buy program in the early 1980's to encourage its employees to become computer literate. They financed the personal computers at no interest. A number of us took advantage of the program including myself and the co-worker, John, whose desk was next to mine.

We both bought a TRS-80 home computer, which was one of the earliest mass produced personal computers. The TRS stood for the manufacturer Tandy Radio Shack. It used a modified RCA black and white television for a monitor (very poor picture quality) and a floppy disc drive. It did not have an audio system and the only sounds were an irritating buzz from the power supply as it threatened to blow up in your face and start your eyebrows on fire.

The MS-DOS operating system required the operator to type in commands rather than clicking on icons, which came later on Apple computers first. With only 16 kilobytes of internal memory and 85 kbs on the floppy discs, it was severely limited in performance. There was a crude word processor, a basic spread sheet program, and limited games (Black Jack and Ping Pong to name a few).

But it was really exciting for me and John to have our own computer. We couldn't wait to set it up at home and start using it. The systems were delivered to us on a Friday afternoon. As soon as we got home we both became immersed in the new world of electronics.

I asked John on Monday how he enjoyed the new computer.

"Well," he said. "I snatched it out of the box as soon as I got home and started playing with it. Damn MS-DOS is hard to use. The operating manual is thicker than a technical publication for the F-16. But I couldn't put it down. When my wife told me it was time for dinner, I snapped at her to leave me alone. A couple of hours later I heard a knock on my door. I looked up as she opened it. My God! She was standing there in a sexy negligee holding a glass of wine. 'John,' she said. 'There's some things that damn computer can't do for you.'"

John smiled as he continued, "I shut that sucker down and didn't turn it on again until Sunday afternoon when my wife went to visit her mother."

What a difference in today's computers. My iMac has 8 gigabytes (billions) of internal memory and 1 terabyte (trillion) of built in hard disc memory compared to the tiny amount on the TRS-80. It also has a surround sound audio system and a high definition color monitor. And it doesn't make any threatening sounds while it's working.

Today I use Microsoft Word for my writing projects. My Dad always said that to operate something, you had to be smarter than it. Well my computer is certainly smarter than me. Thank goodness for that. Any errors in my writing is because it doesn't want take me out of the creative process, and so it allows me to make some mistakes.

I'm sure we aren't far from the day when a smart computer will create audio, video, and printed media (which will be presented digitally as e-books since paper is quickly being phased out as a form of preferred media) and authors like me will be dinosaurs.

I've always been an avid reader of *Writer's Digest*, which is a monthly magazine with great insights into writing including articles from other authors. For marketing ideas and publisher contacts, I use the periodical *Writer's Market*.

I joined a local writer's group many years ago. I highly recommend that for any prospective author. The personal interaction with others pursuing the same craft is invaluable. The experience with my group resulted in my novel *Weep Without Tears* winning the Lu Spurlock

Black Gold Writing Award for an outstanding novel at the Fourth Annual Texans Writing to the World Writing Conference.

About the time *Beware the Abyss* was published, I received an email from my sister Katie's daughter Margaret who lives in Idaho. She suggested that it was time for another Miller family reunion, since the last one was over ten years before. I agreed with her and the planning for the event began.

We agreed the reunion should take place in Idaho and finally decided that Coeur d' Alene would be the best place for several reasons. My oldest sister, Eileen, was in a nursing home there, and it would give most of us an opportunity to visit her since she wasn't able to travel.

Coeur d' Alene, on the shores of the lake sharing its name, is a beautiful and friendly city with a population of just over 40,000 and is located conveniently close to Spokane, Washington about 30 miles to the west with its large airport. To the east looms the high passes and towering peaks of the Continental Divide of the Rocky Mountains. Just up the interstate lies the old mining town of Wallace, Idaho where the visually stimulating movie about a volcano explosion *Dante's Peak* starring Pierce Brosnan and Linda Hamilton was filmed using local scenery.

Coeur d' Alene brought back many memories to me of the time I spent there at North Idaho College in the late 1950's. Over my years as a sojourner I stopped by many times on visits to my parent's house north of Bonners Ferry. I recall the small, easily walkable campus on the shore of the lake, the friendly atmosphere of students (most of them from small towns like me), and the experienced and professional faculty.

It was a great reunion at the park. Joe and Alice came from Australia. My other siblings Danny, Carole, and Katie and their families were there. I met an extended family of nieces and nephews I had never met before. I thought about our Miller Family Tree on Ancestry. The Miller heritage that has passed down through the ages from the 14th century in Switzerland has produced many heirs that will continue to expand the family in the centuries to come.

My niece, Debby, and her mother drifted apart after her father, Bob, passed away. I have a photo of them hugging each other for the first time in several years. I also talked with my brother Charlie's widow, Lilly, who I hadn't seen since his death.

Several of us were able to spend some time with our sister Eileen at her nursing home nearby. She was as beautiful as ever. Although she now in a wheel chair, she's very active as the home has a lot of activities to keep her busy. Her daughters, Drexel and Ruth, and her grand-daughter, Michelle, often visit her.

I remember the times I stopped by her home near Athol, Idaho on my way to Bonners Ferry. She knew I missed Mom's biscuits (fluffy and soft, made from scratch with yeast to make them rise, and warm smelling fresh from the oven). When she saw me pull up in her yard, she would start making the biscuits for me. We would set at her table and eat them with coffee as we talked about the family and old times together.

The day after the reunion, Alan and I went on to Bonners Ferry to spend some time there. Several of us visited the Grand View Cemetery and the graves of most of our departed family members: Dad, Mom, Penny, Charlie, Floyd, Clifford, Paul, Lavina, and John. Only Bob and Leonard do not rest there atop the hill overlooking the Kootenai River valley.

Lying on top of Penny's grave were several copper pennies. Her real name was Verna Lee, but everyone called her Penny because of her beautiful copper colored hair. I took a penny out of my pocket and dropped it on the flat headstone.

Carole's husband, Don Nystrom, said quietly, "It came up tails."

"Yes," I said. "Heads is for males and tails for females."

"I didn't know that," Don said.

"I didn't either," I said. "I just made it up."

I turned away so he wouldn't see the tears in my eyes as I thought about Penny. She was the best big sister a boy who grew up in North Idaho and later sojourned around the world could have. Warm and smiling, she always made sure I ate well when I visited her and her family. When I was in the military, she sent me gift packages containing items she thought every serviceman would need.

During our family reunion in 2004 at the Twin Rivers Resort near Bonners Ferry, Penny's family (she passed away in 1991) wore purple shirts and dresses in her honor. That was her favorite color.

Shortly after the event I took a photograph of the Moyie River, which flows into the Kootenai River near where we had the reunion. It wasn't until I returned to Texas and was reviewing the pictures I had taken that I noticed a bright and distinctive orb in the photo. The orb was a deep purple. Hmm! Maybe it was a sign that Penny was looking in on our reunion.

Some people believe that orbs are more than dust particles or drops of moisture on the camera lens (that was the only photo I took of many in Idaho that had an orb in it). They think they are proof of guardian angels, captured on camera. When these "spirit orbs" or "angel orbs" appear near a single person or a group of people in a photo, it's a sign that they are blessed with the goodness, positive energy, and protection of angels. When orbs appear in a particular location, it's also a sign that angels are hovering nearby and the location is particularly blessed.

Clifford's and Paul's graves were especially difficult to visit. They both died so young and while still in good health: Clifford at 18 and Paul at 19.

Clifford, the youngest of our parents 17 children, was always outgoing and ebullient (cheerful and full of energy). He called me several times the summer before he died in 1969. I was assigned to the Apollo Program and he was fascinated with it. He wanted to know in detail what I was doing and what the astronauts were up to. He said his dream was to be one of them.

Clifford worked for a crop duster marking fields working out of the airport just north of Bonners Ferry that year. The pilot had an old open cockpit bi-wing Stearman aircraft like the one that chased Cary Grant across a field in the classic movie *North by Northwest*.

He kept pestering the pilot to let him ride with him until he did one day. After they landed, the pilot had to go to town for some reason. While he was gone, Clifford climbed in the airplane, took it off, flew around, and landed it back safely. This was after only one flight where he observed what the pilot was doing, no ground school, and no flying lessons.

After Clifford died from a gunshot accident late that year, Mom told me a large group from the local Mennonite Church (practitioners of the Anabaptist religion) came into the yard at dusk just before Christmas and sang carols in commemoration of Clifford. Mom said she and Dad were so choked with emotion they weren't able to thank them as they should have. I found out later that Clifford's girl friend was a Mennonite.

Paul was just over two years younger than me. He was a quiet and conscientious boy with Mom's peculiar smile. He was planning to go to college at the University of Idaho in Moscow after high school when I was assigned by the U.S. Air Force to attend Washington State University (WSU) at Pullman, Washington.

I asked Dad which side of the field would he sit at when the Idaho Vandals played the WSU Cougars in football. Dad thought about it for a moment, and then he answered, "I'll sit on each side for one half of the game. I don't want to show favoritism to any of you boys."

Unfortunately, Paul never made it to the University of Idaho. He was killed in a logging accident during the summer of 1961. The tragedy was especially difficult for Dad because he was working nearby when the bulldozer skidding logs crushed Paul and he couldn't do anything to stop it.

I have been blessed to be in such a large and close family. The love, friendship, and support has been wonderful. Unfortunately, with the great blessings have come great sorrows. I have experienced the death of both parents and seven of my brothers and sisters (Leonard died in 1935 before I was born).

I remember standing beside Dad at Penny's funeral service in 1991 when he said with tears in his eyes, "My children should not be dying before me. I wish I could have changed places with anyone of them."

After returning from the reunion this summer, I began work on my memoir in earnest. Most of the writing has come easily as I resurrected memories from thoughts, notes, books, and photos. Some of it has been difficult as I re-visited the tragedies in my life. But through it all, I have persevered.

Choosing a song to paraphrase my life was an easy choice. I have to pick *My Way* a song popularized by Frank Sinatra. Its lyrics were written by Paul Anka.

> I've lived a life that's full.
> I've traveled each and every highway;
> And more, much more than this,
> I did it my way.
>
> Regrets, I've had a few;
> But then again, too few to mention.
> I did what I had to do
> And saw it through without exemption.
>
> I've loved, I've laughed and cried.
> I've had my fill; my share of losing.
> And now, as tears subside,
> I find it all so amusing.
>
> I planned each charted course;
> Each careful step along the byway,
> And more, much more than this,
> I did it my way.
>
> For what is a man, what has he got?

If not himself, then he has naught.
To say the things he truly feels;
And not the words of one who kneels.
The record shows I took the blows –
And did it my way!

I did it my way. Now it's time to end *Tales of a Sojourner*. What is in my future? I hope a number of years of good health and positive experiences for me and my family. My daily mantra is, "I am blessed. Today I will focus on all that is right in my life."

There are some advantages to getting older as I have. I get a senior discount at the Fort Worth Zoo and the Japanese Gardens. I developed cataracts, and my senior Medicare and Tri-Care for Life (compliments of retiring from the military) medical coverage paid for their removal and for lens implants, letting me get rid of glasses and contacts lens. For the first three months after the operation, I would waken in the mornings and reach over to the bedside table for my glasses, which weren't there.

I have had some health issues, as can be expected over a long lifetime, but I can't complain. As Mark Twain said, "The only way to keep your health is to eat what you don't want, drink what you don't like, and do what you'd rather not."

My friend, Al Hatsell, addressed advancing age by telling me, "You know you're getting old when a bowel movement feels better than an orgasm."

I want to pass on Mark Twain's comment about reading a book, perhaps this memoir, "Persons attempting to find a motive in this narrative will be prosecuted; persons attempting to find a moral in it will be banished; and persons attempting to find a plot in it will be shot."

And I had a dream the other night that would make a great novel. It was about ...

As Al would say, "Shut her down, she's squirting oil."

Appendix
Author Listing

I have included in this appendix (section of additional matter at the end of a book, not that tiny superfluous body organ that gets infected and causes great pain in the stomach) a listing of some of the authors in alphabetical order who have influenced me over my lifetime. While I have read many of the classic writers of literature, I've only listed a few here. As Mark Twain said, "Classics are books people mention but rarely read." I have read those I list below.

Louisa May Alcott (1832 – 1888) One of the great women pillars of American literature. The author of over 30 books including *Little Women* and its sequels, most of them are based on incidents from her real life in the mid-1800's.

Hans Christian Anderson (1805 – 1875) Although a prolific writer of plays, travelogues, novels, and poems, Andersen is best remembered for his fairy tales. Andersen's popularity is not limited to children; his stories, called "fairy tales" express themes that transcend age and nationality. His tales, which have been translated into more than 125 languages, have become culturally embedded in the world's collective consciousness. While readily accessible to children, they present lessons of virtue and resilience in the face of adversity for mature readers as well. Some of his most famous fairy tales include *The Emperor's New Clothes*, *The Little Mermaid*, *The Nightingale*, *The Snow Queen*, *The Ugly Duckling*, and many more. His stories have inspired ballets, both animated and live-action films, and plays.

Isaac Asimov (1920 – 1992) A science fiction writer who, along with Robert A. Heinlein and Arthur C. Clarke, was considered one of the "Big Three" science fiction writers during his lifetime. Asimov's most famous work is the *Foundation* Series; his other major novels are the *Galactic Empire* series and the *Robot* series. The *Galactic Empire* novels are set in earlier history of the same fictional universe as the *Foundation* series. Later, beginning with *Foundation's Edge*, he linked this distant future to the Robot and Spacer stories, creating a unified future history for his stories. I started reading Asimov early in high school and devoured every one on his books that I could find in the Bonners Ferry Library and through other sources later in life. He is an intelligent writer with a clear vision of the future of the human race.

The Bible A collection of texts sacred in Judaism and Christianity. It was written at different times by different authors in different locations. Jews and Christians consider the Bible to be a product of divine inspiration or an authoritative record of the relationship between God and humans. There is no single Bible: many Bibles have evolved, with overlapping and diverging contents. The Christian Old Testament overlaps with the Hebrew Bible known in Judaism as the *Tanakh* and the Greek *Septuagint*. The New Testament is a collection of writings by early Christians, consisting of narratives, letters, and apocalyptic writings. Among Christian denominations there is some disagreement about the contents of the canon, primarily in the *Apocrypha*, a list of works that are regarded with varying levels of respect. The *King James Version* Bible, also known as the *Authorized Version*, is an English translation of the Christian Bible for the Church of England that begun in 1604 and completed in 1611. Millions of people for thousands of years have found guidance, comfort, and solace in the Bible. I have read it completely through many times and referred to parts of it often when seeking comfort. I have also studied translations of religious writings forming the basis of other than Christian religions, including the Jewish *Torah*, the Muslim *Koran*, the *Book of Mormon*, the Buddhist *Dharma*, and others. Many of them believe their sacred texts are divinely or supernaturally revealed or inspired, like the Bible is to Christians.

Ray Bradbury (1920 – 2012) American fantasy, science fiction, horror, and mystery fiction author. Widely known for his dystopian novel *Fahrenheit 451* as well as his science fiction and horror story collections *The Martian Chronicles* and *The Illustrated Man*, Bradbury was one of the most celebrated 20th and 21st century American genre writers. Recipient of numerous awards, including a 2007 Pulitzer Citation, Bradbury also wrote screenplays and television scripts, including *Moby Dick* and *It Came from Outer Space*. Many of his works were adapted to comic book, television, and film formats. On his death in 2012, *The New York Times* called Bradbury "the writer most responsible for bringing modern science fiction into the literary mainstream."

Bill Bryson (1951 –) Bryson is my favorite non-fiction author. A best selling Anglo-American author of humorous books on travel, as well as books on the English language and science. Born in the United States, he was a resident of Britain for most of his adult life. Bryson came to prominence in the United Kingdom with the publication of *Notes from a Small Island*, an exploration of Britain, and its accompanying television series. He received widespread recognition again with the publication of *A Short History of Nearly Everything*, a book widely acclaimed for its accessible communication of science. If you want to understand what you are, where you fit into the cycle of life, how large the universe is, how tiny cellular life is, how old the earth and the universe are, and other easily understood scientific facts, put this book on your bucket list. He also writes insightful and humorous travelogues. Two that stand out to me are *A Walk in the Woods* about hiking the Appalachian Trail, which was recently made into a movie starring Nick Nolte and Robert Redford, and *In a Sunburned Country*, a must read for Aussies and those interested in the unique and fascinating country of Australia.

Pearl Buck (1882 – 1973) An American writer and novelist. As the daughter of missionaries, Buck spent most of her life before 1934 in China. Her novel *The Good Earth* was the best selling fiction book in the United States in 1931 and 1932 and won the Pulitzer Prize in 1932. In 1938, she was awarded the Nobel Prize in Literature for her rich and truly epic descriptions of peasant life in China and for her biographical masterpieces. She was the first American woman to win the Nobel Prize for Literature. I read *The Good Earth* as a high school class assignment and made my first book report on it.

James Lee Burke (1936 –) The Cajun novelist who is a rare winner of two Edgar Awards. (The awards, named after Edgar Allan Poe are presented by the Mystery Writers of America to honor the best mystery fiction, non-fiction, television, film, and theater annually.) Twenty of his many novels feature one of the most acclaimed characters in American fiction: Cajun detective Dave Robicheaux. If you want to smell the warm odor of swamps, hear the cries of waterfowl and the grunts of alligators, and see the golden rays of the sun peering through the cypress trees of the misty Louisiana bayou country, read Burke. You will fall in love with his books.

Edgar Rice Burroughs (1875 – 1950) An American writer best known for his creations of the jungle hero Tarzan and the heroic Mars adventurer John Carter. *Tarzan of the Apes*, published in 1912, was one of his most successful series. He also wrote popular science fiction and fantasy stories involving Earthly adventurers transported to various planets (notably Barsoom, Burroughs's fictional name for Mars, and Amtor, his fictional name for Venus), lost islands, and the interior of the earth in his *Pellucidar* stories, as well as westerns and historical romances. Many of his stories were published in *The Argosy* magazine, which was popular during the mid to late 1900's. In a *Paris Review* interview, Ray Bradbury said, "Edgar Rice Burroughs never would have looked upon himself as a social mover and shaker with social obligations. But as it turns out – and I love to say it because it upsets everyone terribly – Burroughs is probably the most influential writer in the entire history of the world. By giving romance and adventure to a whole generation of boys, Burroughs caused them to go out and decide to become special."

Lewis Carroll (1832 – 1898) Charles Dodgson, better known by his pen name Lewis Carroll, was an English writer, mathematician, logician, Anglican deacon, and photographer. His most famous writings are *Alice's Adventures in Wonderland*, its sequel *Through the Looking-Glass*, which includes the poem *Jabberwocky*, and the poem *The Hunting of the Snark*, all examples of the genre of literary nonsense. He is noted for his facility at word play, logic, and fantasy. There are societies in many parts of the world dedicated to the enjoyment and promotion of his works and the investigation of his life.

Miguel de Cervantes (1547 – 1616) A Spanish novelist, poet, and playwright, his major work, *Don Quixote*, considered to be the first modern European novel, is a classic of Western literature, and is regarded among the best works of fiction ever written. I've often used Don Quixote's jousting with windmills as a metaphor (figure of speech that identifies something as being the same) when I've had to confront difficult government regulations, persons of authority, company's customer service phone support, and hard to install computer programs.

Agatha Christie (1890 – 1976) An English crime novelist, short story writer, and playwright. She is best known for the 66 detective novels and 14 short story collections she wrote about the investigative work of Hercule Poirot, Jane Marple, Parker Pyne, Harley Quin, and Tommy and Tuppence Beresford. She also wrote the world's longest running play, a murder mystery, *The Mousetrap*. In 1971 she was made a Dame for her contribution to literature. The *Guinness Book of World Records* lists Christie as the best selling novelist of all time. Her novels have sold roughly 2 billion copies, ranking her third behind only Shakespeare's works and the Bible. She is one the most translated individual authors – at least 103 languages. *And Then There Were None* is Christie's best selling novel, with 100 million sales to date, making it the world's best selling mystery ever, and one of the best selling books of all time. What a delightful writer Christie is with insights into the human character that rivals those of Shakespeare at time. Her novels are still a joy to read today in our world of instant gratification, hover crafts, drones, cell phone texting, and fast food addiction. Try her, I think you will like her.

Tom Clancy (1947 – 2013) The master of the techno-thriller genre, he was known for his technically detailed espionage and military science storylines set during and after the Cold War. Seventeen of his novels were bestsellers, more than 100 million copies of his books are in print, and a number of movies and video games were based on his writing.

Arthur C. Clarke (1917 – 2008) He is a British-Sri Lankan science fiction writer, science writer, futurist, inventor, undersea explorer, and television series host. He is perhaps most famous for being co-writer of the screenplay for the movie *2001: A Space Odyssey*, widely considered to be one of the most influential films of all time. His other science fiction writings earned him a number of Hugo and Nebula awards, which along with a large readership made him one of the towering figures of science fiction. For many years Clarke, Robert Heinlein, and Isaac Asimov were known as the "Big Three" of science fiction. I consider Clark the dean of science fiction authors. He is the most readable and scientifically correct writer I have ever read. I discovered his novel *Childhood's End* (published in 1953) in the town library. The story follows the peaceful alien invasion of Earth by the mysterious Overlords, whose arrival begins decades of apparent utopia under indirect alien rule, at the cost of human identity and culture. It made me a lifetime reader of Clarke.

James Clavell (1921 – 1994) An Australian born British novelist, screenwriter, director, and World War II veteran and prisoner of war. Clavell is best known for his epic Asian Saga series of novels and their televised adaptations, along with the films *The Great Escape* and *To Sir, with Love*. Clavell's first novel, *King Rat*, was a semi-fictional account of his prison experiences in China during the Second World War. When the book was published it became an immediate best seller and adapted for film. His next novel, *Tai-Pan* took place in Hong Kong, as told via the character who was to become Clavell's heroic archetype, Dirk Struan. Struan's descendants would inhabit almost all of his forthcoming books. *Tai-Pan* was adapted as a film in 1986. Clavell's third novel, *Shōgun*, is set in 17th century Japan and relates the story of an English navigator, based on William Adams. When the story was made into a TV series in 1980, it became the second highest rated mini-series in history with an audience of over 120 million. Clavell's fourth novel, *Noble House*, became a number one best-seller, and is one of my favorites.

Pat Conroy (1945 –) A *New York Times* bestselling American author who has written several acclaimed novels and memoirs. Two of his novels, *The Prince of Tides* and *The Great Santini*, were made into Oscar nominated films. He is recognized as a leading figure of late 20th century Southern literature. I have enjoyed all his books. One of my favorites is *The Water Is Wide*, which was based on his experiences as a teacher in a one-room schoolhouse on remote Daufuskie Island, South Carolina. The book won Conroy a humanitarian award from the National Education Association and was made into a feature film, *Conrack*, starring Jon Voight in 1974.

James Fenimore Cooper (1789 – 1851) A prolific and popular American writer of the early 19th century his historical romances of frontier and Indian life in the early American days created a unique form of American literature. Before embarking on his career as a writer he served in the U.S. Navy as a Midshipman, which greatly influenced many of his novels and other writings. He wrote numerous sea stories and his best known works are five historical novels of the frontier period known as the *Leatherstocking Tales*. *The Last of the Mohicans* is often regarded as his masterpiece. I brought this book home from high school one Friday afternoon. After dinner and the evening chores (milking and feeding cows, gathering eggs, and carrying wood down to the basement furnace), I started reading it. After everyone else went to bed, I sat up in Dad's chair and read all night long by lamp light. Early in the morning when Mom got up to put coffee on the stove and start breakfast, I was still awake and reading. She didn't say anything; just brought my breakfast on a tray so I could go on with the book. I finished it around noon and the grand adventure story stayed in my mind for many days. It transported me from the mountains of Idaho in the mid 1950's to the verdant forests of the North East during the French and Indian wars of the late 1700's.

Stephan R. Covey (1932 – 2012) An American educator, author, businessman, and keynote speaker, his most popular book was *The Seven Habits of Highly Effective People*. I first read it soon after I went to work for General Dynamics. It is a must have primer for anyone who wants to become a success in business, public relations, or personal relationships.

Clive Cussler (1931 –) An American adventure novelist and underwater explorer, his thriller novels, many featuring the character Dirk Pitt, have reached *The New York Times* fiction best seller list more than 20 times. Cussler is the founder and chairman of the real life National Underwater and Marine Agency, which has discovered more than sixty shipwreck sites and numerous other notable underwater wrecks. He is the sole author or lead author of more than 60 books. I especially like the early novels about Dirk Pitt. They are full of adventure and based on interesting true historical events.

Charles Dickens (1812 – 1870) An English writer and social critic, he created some of the world's best known fictional characters and is regarded as the greatest novelist of the Victorian era. His works enjoyed unprecedented popularity during his lifetime, and by the twentieth century critics and scholars had recognized him as a literary genius. His novels and short stories enjoy lasting popularity, many of them made and re-made into major Hollywood movies and television specials. His 1843 novella, *A Christmas Carol*, remains popular and continues to inspire adaptations in every artistic genre. *Oliver Twist* and *Great Expectations* are also frequently adapted, and, like many of his novels, evoke images of early Victorian London. His 1859 novel, *A Tale of Two Cities*, set in London and Paris, is his best known work of historical fiction.

E. L. Doctorow (1931 –) An American author, editor, and professor, best known internationally for his works of historical fiction, he has been described as one of the most important American novelists of the 20th century. He wrote twelve novels, three volumes of short fiction and a stage drama. They included the award-winning novels *Ragtime*, *Billy Bathgate*, and *The March*. These, like many of his other works, placed fictional characters in recognizable historical contexts, with known historical figures, and often used different narrative styles. His stories were recognized for their originality and versatility, and Doctorow was praised for his audacity and imagination. What a pleasure to read. I eagerly look forward to his new releases.

F. Scott Fitzgerald (1896 – 1940) An American novelist and short story writer, whose works are the best of writings about the Jazz Age, he is widely regarded as one of the greatest American writers of the 20th century. Fitzgerald is considered a member of the "Lost Generation" of the 1920s. He wrote four novels: *This Side of Paradise*, *The Beautiful and Damned*, *The Great Gatsby* (his best known), and *Tender Is the Night*. Fitzgerald also wrote numerous short stories, many of which treat themes of youth and promise, and age and despair. When I read his novels, or watch the movies made from them, I'm taken back to the carefree days of the 1920's when America was in a period of peace and prosperity between the war days of WWI and the looming financial disasters resulting in the Great Depression of the 1930's.

Ian Fleming (1909 – 1964) an English author, journalist, and naval intelligence officer, best known for his James Bond series of spy novels. While working for Britain's Naval Intelligence Division during the Second World War, Fleming was involved in planning for intelligence units. His wartime service and his career as a journalist provided much of the background, detail, and depth of the James Bond novels. Fleming wrote his first Bond novel, *Casino Royale*, in 1952. It was a success, with three print runs being commissioned to cope with the demand. Eleven Bond novels and two short story collections followed between 1953 and 1966. The novels revolved around James Bond, an officer in the Secret Intelligence Service, commonly known as MI6. Bond was also known by his code number, 007, and was a commander in the Royal Naval Reserve. The Bond stories rank among the best-selling series of fictional books of all time, having sold over 100 million copies worldwide. Fleming died at the age of 56 from the ravages of being a heavy life long smoker and drinker, both characteristics he imbued James Bond with. President John F. Kennedy said Fleming was his favorite writer. He was often seen carrying a James Bond book around with him. The Fleming books are great escape fiction for me. Any time I feel stressed out, I just pick up one of the Bond series and am instantly taken into the world of subterfuge and international espionage that existed during the Cold War period of the 1950's and 1960's.

C. S. Forester (1899 – 1966) An English novelist who rose to fame with tales of naval warfare, his most notable works were the 12 book *Horatio Hornblower* series, depicting a Royal Navy officer during the Napoleonic wars, and *The African Queen*, which was made into an Academy Award winning movie starring Humphrey Bogart and Katherine Hepburn.

John Gray (1951 –) An American relationship counselor, lecturer and author. In 1992 he published the book *Men Are from Mars, Women Are from Venus*, which became a best seller and formed the central theme of all his subsequent books and career activities. The book has sold more than 50 million copies and was the highest ranked work of non-fiction of the 1990s, spending 121 weeks on the bestseller list. The book states that most common relationship problems between men and women are a result of fundamental psychological differences between the sexes, which the author exemplifies by means of his eponymous metaphor: that men and women are from distinct planets—men from Mars and women from Venus—and that each sex is acclimated to its own planet's society and customs, but not to those of the other. There is an old adage that says sinners make the best preachers; they have been through a crucible of fire. I think I have been through a crucible of fire when it comes to personal relationships. So perhaps I can pass on some advice to help others in their relationships: buy two copies of this book now! Read one yourself and give one to your partner. After you both have read it, sit down and discuss the differences and the similarities between yourselves. I guarantee it will bring you and your companion closer.

John Grisham (1955 –) An American bestselling writer, attorney, politician, and activist best known for his popular legal thrillers. His books have been translated into 42 languages. The master of courtroom and lawyer fiction, his books have sold over 275 million copies worldwide. Grisham is one of only three authors to sell 2 million copies on a first printing; the others are Tom Clancy and J.K. Rowling, the author of the *Harry Potter* series. Grisham's first bestseller was *The Firm*; which sold more than seven million copies. The book was adapted into a feature film of the same name, starring Tom Cruise. Eight of his other novels have also been adapted into films: *The Chamber, The Client, A Painted House, The Pelican Brief, Skipping Christmas, The Rainmaker, The Runaway Jury,* and *A Time to Kill*. I came under his spell when I read his book *One L*, about the travails of a first year law student. Since then, I have read every novel he has written.

A.B Guthrie (1901 – 1991) An American novelist, screenwriter, historian, and literary historian who won the Pulitzer Prize for fiction in 1950 for his novel *The Way West*. *The Big Sky*, *The Way West*, and *Fair Land, Fair Land* are a trilogy, starting in the 1830's about Mountain Men trappers, then continuing with settlers traveling the Oregon Trail, and onward to the development of Montana up through the cattle empires of the 1880's. I've reread his books several times. His description of action scenes is only matched by the great South African author Wilbur Smith. He evokes a sense of sight, sound, smell, and feel that is truly amazing.

H. Rider Haggard (1856 – 1925) An English writer of adventure novels set in exotic locations, predominantly Africa, and a pioneer of the Lost World literary genre. My favorite book is his epic tale of African adventure and survival *King Solomon's Mines*, which was made into one of my all time favorite movies starring Stewart Granger and Deborah Kerr.

David Halberstam (1934 – 2007) An American journalist and historian, known for his work on the Vietnam War, politics, history, the Civil Rights Movement, business, media, American culture, and later, sports journalism. He won a Pulitzer Prize for International Reporting in 1964. In 2007, while doing research for a book, Halberstam was killed in a car crash. *The Best and the Brightest* (1972) is an account of the origins of the Vietnam War. The focus of the book is on the erroneous foreign policy crafted by the academics and intellectuals who were in John F. Kennedy's administration, and the disastrous consequences of those policies in Vietnam. The title referred to Kennedy's "whiz kids"—leaders of industry and academia brought into the Kennedy administration—whom Halberstam characterized as arrogantly insisting on "brilliant policies that defied common sense" in Vietnam, often against the advice of career U.S. Department of State employees. This book was one of my references while I was writing my novel that took place in Vietnam, *Evening of Pale Sunshine*.

Ernest Haycox (1899 – 1950) A prolific author of Western fiction, he published two dozen novels and about 300 short stories, many of which appeared first in pulp magazines in the early 1920s. During the 1930s and 40s, he was a regular contributor to *Collier's Weekly* from 1931 and *The Saturday Evening Post* from 1943. Fans of his work included Gertrude Stein and Ernest Hemingway, and the latter once wrote, "I read *The Saturday Evening Post* whenever it has a serial by Ernest Haycox." His story *Stage to Lordsburg* was made into the movie *Stagecoach*, directed by John Ford and featuring John Wayne in the role that made him a star. The novel *Trouble Shooter*, originally serialized in *Collier's*, was the basis for the movie *Union Pacific*, starring Barbara Stanwyck and Joel McCrea. Haycox, Max Brand, Zane Grey, and Luke Short, were some of Dad's favorite western authors. When I was growing up in Idaho, after he would finish reading one of their books, I would snatch up one of their novels, read it, and then return it to the box beside his living room chair.

Ernest Hemingway (1899 – 1961) An American novelist, short story writer, and journalist. He had a strong influence on 20th century fiction, while his life of adventure and his public image influenced later generations. Hemingway produced most of his work between the mid-1920s and the mid-1950s, and won the Nobel Prize in Literature in 1954. He published seven novels, six short story collections, and two non-fiction works. Many of his works are considered classics of American literature. Shortly after the publication of *The Old Man and the Sea* in 1952, Hemingway went on safari to Africa, where he was almost killed in two successive plane crashes that left him in pain and ill health for much of his remaining life. Hemingway had permanent residences in Key West, Florida, and Cuba, and in 1959, he bought a house in Ketchum, Idaho, where he committed suicide in the summer of 1961. I really enjoyed his novels, *The Sun Also Rises*, *A Farewell to Arms*, *For Whom the Bell Tolls*, and *Islands in the Stream*.

James Hilton (1900 – 1954) An English novelist best remembered for several best sellers, including *Lost Horizon* and *Goodbye, Mr. Chips.* The name Shangri-La from *Lost Horizon* has become a byword for a mythical utopia, isolated from the world. After the Doolittle Raid on Tokyo, when the fact that the bombers had flown from an aircraft carrier remained highly classified, U.S. President Franklin D. Roosevelt told the press facetiously that they had taken off from Shangri-La. Roosevelt named his Maryland presidential retreat Shangri-La. (Later, President Dwight D. Eisenhower renamed the retreat Camp David after his grandson.) *Lost Horizon*, made into an Academy Award winning movie starring Ronald Colman in 1937, has remained one of my favorites.

John Irving (1942 –) An American novelist and Academy Award winning screenwriter, he achieved critical and popular acclaim after the international success of *The World According to Garp* in 1978. Some of Irving's novels, such as *The Cider House Rules*, *A Prayer for Owen Meany*, and *A Widow for One Year*, have been bestsellers. Five of his novels have been adapted to film.

Dr. Gregg D. Jacobs A Sleep Medicine doctor who developed a cognitive behavioral therapy (CBT) program for insomnia. His very readable book, *Say Goodnight to Insomnia* will help you eliminate sleeping pills, establish sleep promoting habits, change negative thoughts into positive thoughts about sleep, and implement relaxation and stress reduction techniques. It works folks!! My insomnia, which I had for years, is a thing of the past thanks to this book.

Elmer Kelton (1926 –) an American journalist and author, known particularly for his Western writing. Three of his novels have been featured in *Reader's Digest Condensed Books*. Eight Kelton novels, *Buffalo Wagons*, *The Day the Cowboys Quit*, *The Time It Never Rained*, *Eyes of the Hawk*, *Slaughter*, *The Far Canyon*, *Many a River*, and *The Way of the Coyote*, have won Spur Awards from the Western Writers of America. Peers in the WWA also named him as the greatest Western Writer of All Time. *The Good Old Boys* was made into the Turner Network Television TV movie starring Tommy Lee Jones. In 1977, Kelton received an Owen Wister Award for lifetime achievement (named for Owen Wister, the author of *The Virginian*).

Ken Kesey (1935 – 2001) An American novelist, essayist, and counter-cultural figure, he considered himself a link between the Beat Generation of the 1950s and the hippies of the 1960s. His most notable novels were *One Flew Over the Cuckoo's Nest*, made into the award winning movie starring Jack Nicholson, and *Sometimes a Great Notion*, which also became a movie starring Paul Newman. An acknowledged drug user, Kesey was arrested a number of times for possession of marijuana and experimental drugs. But what a writer he was.

Stephen King (1947 –) An American author of contemporary horror, supernatural fiction, suspense, science fiction, and fantasy, his books have sold more than 350 million copies, many of which have been adapted into feature films, miniseries, television shows, and comic books. King has published 54 novels, including seven under the pen name Richard Bachman, and six non-fiction books. He has written nearly 200 short stories, most of which have been collected in book collections. Many of his stories are set in his home state of Maine. He is the master of the Horror Fiction genre. I enjoyed some of his early books, notably *The Shining*, *The Stand*, *Misery*, and *The Green Mile*. When he wrote many of his later novels, in my estimation, his word processor suffered from diarrhea; he took pages to say what he could have said in a paragraph or a few words. King's addictions to alcohol and other drugs were so serious during the 1980s that, as he acknowledged in *On Writing* in 2000, he can barely remember writing *Cujo*. Shortly after the novel's publication, King's family and friends staged an intervention, dumping on the rug in front of him evidence of his addictions taken from his office including beer cans, cigarette butts, cocaine, Xanax, Valium, and marijuana. As King related in his memoir, he then sought help, quit all drugs (including alcohol) in the late 1980s, and has remained sober since. The first novel he wrote after putting his addictions behind him was *Needful Things*.

Rudyard Kipling (1865 – 1936) An English short story writer, poet, and novelist, his works of fiction include *The Jungle Book*, *Kim*, and many short stories, including *The Man Who Would Be King*, which was made into a wonderful movie starring Sean Connery and Michael Caine. His poems include the great *Gunga Din*. He is regarded as a major innovator in the art of the short story; his children's books are classics of children's literature; and one critic described his work as exhibiting "a versatile and luminous narrative gift."

Harper Lee (1926 –) An American novelist widely known for her novel *To Kill a Mockingbird*, published in 1960. It was immediately successful, winning the Pulitzer Prize, and has become a classic of modern American literature. The plot and characters are loosely based on her observations of her family and neighbors, as well as on an event that occurred near her hometown of Monroeville, Alabama in 1936, when she was 10 years old. The novel deals with the irrationality of adult attitudes towards race and class in the Deep South of the 1930s, as seen through the eyes of two children. Though Lee published only this single book for half a century, she was awarded the Presidential Medal of Freedom for her contribution to literature. Lee assisted her close friend Truman Capote in his research for his book *In Cold Blood*. *To Kill a Mockingbird* was made into an award winning movie starring Gregory Peck with a riveting courthouse trial scene that has become a classic.

Jack London (1876 – 1916) An American author, journalist, and social activist, he was a pioneer in the world of commercial magazine fiction, and became one of the first writers to obtain worldwide celebrity and a large fortune from his fiction alone. He wrote some of my favorite adventure novels: *The Call of the Wild* and *White Fang* set in the Klondike Gold Rush of the late 1880's, and *Sea Wolf*, a sailing ship adventure made into several movies over the years. Unfortunately, London died when he was only 40 years old so his literary output is sadly limited. If you want to know what it is like for a person to freeze to death (in excruciating physical and psychological detail) read his short story, *To Build a Fire*, about a lone traveler trying to survive in the wilds of the Yukon during a winter with temperatures more than 30 degrees below zero.

Norman Mailer (1923 –) An American novelist, journalist, essayist, playwright, filmmaker, actor, and political activist. His novel *The Naked and the Dead* was published in 1948. His best known work was widely considered to be *The Executioner's Song*, which was published in 1979, and for which he won one of his two Pulitzer Prizes. In addition to the Pulitzer Prize, his book *Armies of the Night* was awarded the National Book Award. Along with Truman Capote, Hunter Thompson, and Tom Wolfe, Mailer is considered an innovator of creative nonfiction, a genre sometimes called New Journalism, which uses the style and devices of literary fiction in fact based journalism. I was really impressed with his novel of warfare in the Pacific during World War II, *The Naked and the Dead*. Although it is a story of the horror, brutality, and anguish of war, it rises above that and addresses the close knit comradeship of the American soldiers, which was their only hope for survival.

David McCullough (1933 –) An American author, narrator, historian, and lecturer. He is a two-time winner of the Pulitzer Prize and the National Book Award and a recipient of the Presidential Medal of Freedom, the United States' highest civilian award. His first book was *The Johnstown Flood*; and he has since written nine more on such topics as Harry S. Truman, John Adams, the Brooklyn Bridge, and the Wright brothers. McCullough's two Pulitzer Prize winning books, *Truman* and *John Adams*, have been adapted by HBO into a TV film and a miniseries, respectively. Reading a biography about a politician who has been pushing up daisies for several centuries has to be boring, right? Well read *John Adams*, and meet an exciting, sensitive, and perceptive person who helped shape our great country into what it is today.

John D. McDonald (1916 – 1986) An American writer of novels and short stories, known for his thrillers, he was a prolific author of crime and suspense novels, many of them set in his adopted home of Florida. His best known works include the popular and critically acclaimed Travis McGee series, and his novel *The Executioners*, which was filmed twice as *Cape Fear*. MacDonald was named a grandmaster of the Mystery Writers of America, and the winner of a U.S. National Book Award. Stephen King praised MacDonald as "the great entertainer of our age, and a mesmerizing storyteller." If you want some escape fiction or a book to read on an airplane or at the beach, pick up one of the many Travis McGee novels. You won't be disappointed.

Rod McKuen (1933 –) An American singer, songwriter, musician, and poet. He was one of the best-selling poets in the United States during the late 1960s. Throughout his career, McKuen produced a wide range of recordings, which included popular music, spoken word poetry, film soundtracks, and classical music. He earned two Academy Award nominations and one Pulitzer nomination for his music compositions. His poetry deals with themes of love, the natural world, and spirituality. McKuen's songs sold over 100 million recordings worldwide, and 60 million of his poetry books were sold as well. I bought several copies of his poetry over the years. My favorite is *Lonesome Cities*, which provided the lyrics for one of Frank Sinatra's best selling albums of the same name.

Larry McMurtry (1930 –) An American novelist, essayist, bookseller, and screenwriter whose work is predominantly set in either the old West or in contemporary Texas. His novels include *Horseman, Pass By*, *The Last Picture Show*, and *Terms of Endearment*, which were adapted into films earning 26 Academy Award nominations. His 1985 Pulitzer Prize winning novel *Lonesome Dove* was adapted into a television miniseries that earned 18 Emmy Award nominations, with the other three novels in his *Lonesome Dove* series adapted into three more miniseries earning eight more Emmy nominations. McMurtry also co-wrote the screenplay for *Brokeback Mountain*, which won a number of awards. One of my all time favorite novels is *Lonesome Dove*. I have read it at least five times over the years since it was first published. And I have watched the remarkable movie starring Robert Duval, Tommy Lee Jones, and Diane Lane at least that many times. A remarkable writer who makes scenes and characters come alive and overwhelming, he is a must read on any bucket list.

James Michener (1907 – 1997) An American author, who was born in the same year as my mother, of more than 40 books, the majority of which were fictional, lengthy family sagas covering the lives of many generations in particular geographic locales and incorporating solid history. Michener was known for the popularity of his works; he had numerous bestsellers and works selected for Book of the Month Club. He was also known for his meticulous research. Michener's novels include *Tales of the South Pacific*, for which he won the Pulitzer Prize for Fiction in 1948, *Hawaii*, *The Drifters*, *Centennial*, *The Source*, *The Fires of Spring*, *Chesapeake*, *Caribbean*, *Caravans*, *Alaska*, *Texas*, and *Poland*. His non-fiction works include *Iberia*, about his travels in Spain and Portugal; his memoir *The World Is My Home*; and *Sports in America*. His first book was adapted as the popular Broadway musical *South Pacific* by Richard Rodgers and Oscar Hammerstein, and later as a great film by the same name. One of my all-time favorite writers. I especially like *Hawaii*, *Alaska*, and *Space*. I use his superb memoir, *The World Is My Home*, as a model for this book.

Margaret Mitchell (1900 – 1949) an American author and journalist. One novel by Mitchell was published during her lifetime, the American Civil War era novel *Gone with the Wind*, for which she won the National Book Award for Most Distinguished Novel of 1936 and the Pulitzer Prize for Fiction in 1937. Her novel became one of the greatest movies of all time starring Clark Gable and Vivien Leigh. At the age of 48, she was killed by an automobile while crossing a street in Atlanta to talk to her publisher about a new novel she was writing.

Patrick O'Brian (1914 – 2000) An English novelist and translator, best known for his series of sea novels set in the Royal Navy during the Napoleonic Wars and centered on the friendship of English naval captain Jack Aubrey and the Irish physician Stephen Maturin. The 20 novel series, the first of which is *Master and Commander* (made into a great movie starring Russell Crowe), is known for its well-researched and highly detailed portrayal of early 19th century life aboard English ships of state as well as its authentic and evocative language. I chanced upon O'Brian's books at a garage sale a few years ago where I bought nine books of the series for $5. O'Brian is head and shoulders above most modern day authors in his ability to tell a rip roaring sea adventure story.

Boris Pasternak (1890 – 1960) A Russian poet, novelist, and literary translator. In his native Russian, Pasternak's first book of poems, *My Sister, Life*, is one of the most influential collections ever published in the Russian language. Outside of Russia, Pasternak is best known as the author of *Doctor Zhivago*, a novel which takes place between the Russian Revolution of 1905 and the First World War. Due to the novel's independent minded stance on the socialist state, *Doctor Zhivago* was rejected for publication in the USSR. The manuscript was smuggled to Milan and published in 1957. Pasternak was awarded the Nobel Prize for Literature in 1958, an event which both humiliated and enraged the Communist Party of the Soviet Union, which forced him to decline the prize, though his descendants were later to accept it in his name in 1988. What a great epic novel of adventure and love *Doctor Zhivago* is. I have read it many times over my life and it always thrills and entrances me. It was made into a classic movie, which won many well deserved Academy Awards starring Julie Christie and Omar Sharif.

Harvey Penick (1904 – 1995) An American golf professional and coach, who taught many Hall of Fame players. Late in life, he became a best selling writer. He was inducted into the World Golf Hall of Fame in 2002, seven years after his death. In 1992, he co-authored (with Bud Shrake) *Harvey Penick's Little Red Book*, which is filled with insightful, easily understood anecdotes. It became the largest selling golf book ever published. While Penick was a strong all-around teacher of the game, he was perhaps the most gifted instructor of the mental game who ever lived. One of Penick's students was the Hall of Fame golfer Ben Crenshaw of Texas. Penick died a few days before the 1995 Master's Tournament in Augusta, Georgia. Crenshaw cut out several days of practice rounds to attend his funeral. Then, that momentous Sunday, he made a long putt on the 18th green to win the coveted Green Jacket. Sinking to his knees, he cried as he paid homage to his long time mentor and friend Penick.

Edgar Allan Poe (1909 – 1949) An American writer, editor, and literary critic, Poe is best known for his poetry and short stories, particularly his tales of mystery and the macabre. Widely regarded as a central figure of Romanticism in the United States and American literature as a whole, he was one of the country's earliest practitioners of the short story. Poe is generally considered the inventor of the detective fiction genre and is further credited with contributing to the emerging genre of science fiction. He was the first well known American writer to try to earn a living through writing alone, resulting in a financially difficult life and career. Like Jack London, he died at the early age of 40 years. But during his brief literary career, he produced a number of stories that are still enjoyed by readers and were made into movies.

Mario Puzo (1920 –1999) An American author, screenwriter, and journalist. He is known for his novels about the Mafia, most notably *The Godfather*, which he later co-adapted into a three-part film saga. He received the Academy Award for Best Adapted Screenplay for the first film in 1972 and Part II in 1974. Puzo also wrote the original screenplay for the 1978 Superman film. I include Puzo in my list of influential authors because of the all-time great *Godfather* movies adapted from his books.

Robert Ruark (1915 – 1965) an American author, syndicated columnist, and big game hunter. Ruark grew up in Wilmington, North Carolina, which was the setting for one of my favorite books he wrote, *The Old Man and the Boy*. It is a great human interest story about a young boy and the relationship he develops with his grandfather through their hunting and fishing expeditions. Ruark's first bestselling novel was *Something of Value*, which describes the Mau Mau Uprising by Kenyan rebels against British rule. It was adapted into a successful 1957 movie. *Uhuru* (the Swahili word for freedom) was his novel with a similar theme. Both of his Africa novels were extremely enjoyable.

Richard Russo (1949 –) An American novelist, short story writer, screenwriter, and teacher. Russo was born in Johnstown, New York. His 2001 novel *Empire Falls* received the 2002 Pulitzer Prize for Fiction. His book *Nobody's Fool* was made into a 1994 film of the same title, starring Paul Newman. A great writer, he reminds me of Thomas Wolfe in his ability to create sympathetic characters who you would like to have as friends in your life.

Carl Sagan (1934 – 1996) An American astronomer, cosmologist, astrophysicist, astrobiologist, author, and science communicator in astronomy and other natural sciences. His contributions were central to the discovery of the high surface temperatures of Venus. He is best known for his contributions to the scientific research of extraterrestrial life, including experimental demonstration of the production of amino acids from basic chemicals by radiation. Sagan assembled the first physical messages that were sent into space: The Pioneer plaque and the Voyager Golden Record, universal messages that could potentially be understood by any extraterrestrial intelligence that might find them. He narrated and co-wrote the award winning 1980 television series *Cosmos: A Personal Voyage*. The most widely watched series in the history of American public television, *Cosmos* has been seen by at least 500 million people across 60 different countries. He also wrote the science fiction novel *Contact*, which was the basis for the 1997 movie.

Jeff Shaara (1952 –) An American novelist and the son of Pulitzer Prize winning author Michael Shaara. He wrote *Gods and Generals* and *The Last Full Measure*, which are the prequel and sequel, respectively, to his father Michael's award-winning Civil War novel *The Killer Angels*. Jeff followed his father's footsteps upon the latter's death, writing historical fiction and documenting the American wars and their most historically relevant characters. Jeff has written thirteen *New York Times* bestselling novels. He completed a trilogy in 2010 about World War II in the European and North African theaters. A fourth WWII novel, titled *The Final Storm*, covers the end of the war in the Pacific, and was released on May 17, 2011.

William Shakespeare (1582 – 1616) An English poet, playwright, and actor, widely regarded as the greatest writer in the English language and the world's pre-eminent dramatist. He is often called England's national poet, and the "Bard of Avon." His works consist of 38 plays, 154 sonnets, and two long narrative poems. His plays have been translated into every major living language and are performed more often than those of any other playwright. I think Shakespeare was the greatest writer in history. No one expressed the drama and comedy of the human condition any better than he did.

Nevil Shute (1899 – 1960) an English novelist and aeronautical engineer who spent his later years in Australia. Twenty-four of his novels and novellas have been published. Many of his books were filmed, including *Lonely Road*, *Landfall*, *Pied Piper*, *On the Beach*, *No Highway*, and *A Town Like Alice*. Although I have read several of his books, I include him on this list for one that stands out to me: *On the Beach*. A 1957 post-apocalyptic novel, it details the experiences of a group of people in Melbourne, Australia as they await the arrival of deadly radiation spreading towards them from the northern hemisphere following a nuclear war a year previously. As the radiation approaches, each person deals with their impending death in different ways. It was made into a fascinating movie starring Gregory Peck.

Wilbur Smith (1933 –) A South African novelist of historical fiction about the development of Africa across three centuries, as seen from the viewpoints of both black and white families. He gained a film contract with his first published novel *When the Lion Feeds*. This encouraged him to become a full time writer, and he developed three long chronicles of the South African experience which all became best sellers. His work includes much authentic detail about the areas in and around Africa and covers the many wars that have ravaged Africa over the centuries. His 35 published novels have sold more than 120 million copies. Smith will always remain one of my favorite tellers of adventure stories. Stephen King wrote about him, "He is the best historical novelist. You can get lost in his books and misplace all of August." His Egyptian series, which includes *River God* and *The Seventh Scroll* are riveting tales of ancient Egypt. His trilogy *Birds of Prey*, *Monsoon*, and *Blue Horizon* caused me several sleepless nights when I couldn't stop reading them. He is certainly not a cure for insomnia.

John Steinbeck (1902 – 1968) An American author of 27 books, including 16 novels, six non-fiction books, and five collections of short stories. He is widely known for *Tortilla Flat* and *Cannery Row*, the multi-generation epic *East of Eden*, and the novellas *Of Mice and Men* and The *Red Pony*. The Pulitzer Prize winning *The Grapes of Wrath*, widely attributed to be part of the American literary canon, is considered Steinbeck's masterpiece. In the first 75 years since it was published in 1939, it sold 14 million copies. It won the National Book Award and Pulitzer Prize for fiction, and was cited prominently when Steinbeck was awarded the Nobel Prize in 1962. One of my favorite books, I have read it numerous time.

Robert Louis Stevenson (1850 – 1894) a Scottish novelist, poet, essayist, and travel writer. His most famous works are *Treasure Island*, *Kidnapped*, and *Strange Case of Dr. Jekyll and Mr. Hyde*. If anyone got through their childhood years without meeting this great adventure teller, I feel sorry for them. I remember reading *Treasure Island* over one weekend when I was about 13 years old only interrupted by chores and meals.

J.R.R. Tolkien (1892 – 1973)   An English writer, poet, and university professor who is best known as the author of the classic fantasy works *The Hobbit, The Lord of the Rings,* and *The Silmarillion*. His classic stories of the Middle Earth are epic adventures rarely matched in literary history. *The Lord of the Rings* and *The Hobbit* were made into the blockbuster movies filmed in New Zealand. My sister Carole visited the Hobbit Village there and returned to Idaho with the intention of building an underground Hobbit room near her house.

Leo Tolstoy (1828 – 1910) A Russian writer who is regarded as one of the greatest authors of all time. Born to an aristocratic Russian family in 1828, he is best known for the novels *War and Peace* and *Anna Karenina*, often cited as pinnacles of realist fiction. He first achieved literary acclaim in his twenties with his semi-autobiographical trilogy, *Childhood, Boyhood,* and *Youth,* and *Sevastopol Sketches*, based upon his experiences in the Crimean War. The dean of Russian writers, his novel *War and Peace* was responsible for me establishing a New Words Room in my minds eye. I read it as a teenager and came across a number of new words I had not seen before. I put them in the Room until I could look them up in a dictionary and understand their meaning, then I would let them out.

Mark Twain (1835 – 1910) Samuel Clemens, better known by his pen name Mark Twain, was an American author and humorist. He wrote *The Adventures of Tom Sawyer* and its sequel, *Adventures of Huckleberry Finn*, the latter often called "The Great American Novel." Twain grew up in Hannibal, Missouri, which provided the setting for *Huckleberry Finn* and *Tom Sawyer*. He later became a riverboat pilot on the Mississippi River before heading west to Nevada. In 1865, his humorous story, *The Celebrated Jumping Frog of Calaveras County*, was published. It brought him international attention, and was even translated into classic Greek. His wit and satire, in prose and in speech, earned praise from critics and peers, and he was a friend to presidents, artists, industrialists, and European royalty. What a great, perceptive writer and most enjoyable to read. Don't miss reading some of his short stories; they are wonderful.

Leon Uris (1924 – 2003) A United States Marine and author, known for his historical fiction and the deep research that went into his novels. His best known work may be *Exodus*, which was published in 1958. *Exodus* illustrated the history of Palestine from the late 19th century through the founding of the state of Israel in 1948 from a Zionist point of view. It was a worldwide best seller, translated into a dozen languages, and was made into a feature film in 1960, starring Paul Newman. His novel *Topaz* was adapted for the screen and directed by Alfred Hitchcock in 1969. If you want to understand what has caused the conflicts in Ireland between the Catholics and Protestants over the centuries, read his great novel *Trinity*.

A.E. Van Vogt (1912 – 2000) A Canadian born author regarded as one of the most popular and influential science fiction writers of the mid-twentieth century: The Golden Age of the genre. His plots are marvels of interlocking pieces, often ending in real surprises and shocks, and genuine paradigm shifts, which are among the hardest conceptions to depict. And the intellectual material of his fiction, and the observations on culture and human and alien behavior, reflect a probing mind. Each tale contains a new angle, a unique slant, that makes it stand out. I started reading Van Vogt as a teenager and was enthralled by his novels *The World of Null-A*, *The Voyage of the Space Beagle*, and *The House That Stood Still*.

H.G. Wells (1866 – 1946) a prolific English writer in many genres, including the novel, history, politics, social commentary, textbooks, and rules for war games. He is now best remembered for his science fiction novels, and Wells is called the father of science fiction, along with Jules Verne and Hugo Gernsback. His most notable science fiction works include *The Time Machine*, *The Island of Doctor Moreau*, *The Invisible Man*, and *The War of the Worlds*, all made into successful Hollywood movies (several times over). I especially liked the 1960 version of *The Time Machine* starring the fine Australian actor Rod Taylor who was also in another favorite movie of mine, the Alfred Hitchcock classic *Birds*.

P.G. Wodehouse (1881 – 1975) An English author and one of the most widely read humorists of the 20th century. Born the son of a British magistrate based in Hong Kong, after leaving school he was employed by a bank but disliked the work and turned to writing in his spare time. His early novels were mostly school stories, but he later switched to comic fiction, creating several regular characters who became familiar to the public over the years. They include the feather brained Bertie Wooster and his sagacious valet, Jeeves; the immaculate and loquacious Psmith; Lord Emsworth and the *Blandings Castle* set; the *Oldest Member*, with stories about golf; and *Mr. Mulliner*, with tall tales on subjects ranging from bibulous bishops to megalomaniac movie moguls (He was a master in the use of alliteration). If you want to read really humorous writing, delve into any of the Jeeves stories. I laughed every time I would read one of Wodehouse's golf stories from *Oldest Member*. It is difficult to find anyone today who can write with his innate sense of humor; Bill Bryson comes as close as anyone.

There are more I could have included in the expanded area above, but in the interest of space I will add a briefer list of additional authors who impressed me:

Margaret Atwood, Dan Brown, Dee Brown, Barbara Cartland (The greatest author you have probably never heard of. She wrote an astounding 723 romance novels that sold over one billion copies to make her the third biggest seller in history behind Shakespeare and Agatha Christie), Michael Chrichton, Winston Churchill, Robin Cook, Bryce Courtenay, Nelson DeMille, James Dickey, T.S. Eliot, Ralph Waldo Emerson, Edna Ferber, Ken Follett, Diana Gabaldon, Zane Grey, Arthur Hailey, Alex Haley, Aldous Huxley (the author of the magnificent novel *Brave New World*, and whom my Australian niece, Kaylin, named her pet dog after), James Jones, Dean Koontz, Louis L'Amour, C.S. Lewis, Ken Miller (Oops! Where did this author's name come from?), Ogden Nash, Richard North Patterson, Ellery Queen, Marjorie Kinman Rawlings (*The Yearling*), Ann Rice (the queen of the vampire genre), Harold Robbins, J.K. Rowling (*Harry Potter* series), Rod Serling (*Twilight Zone*), Dr. Seuss, Sidney Sheldon, Mickey Spillane, Booth Tarkington (*Penrod and Sam*), Gore Vidal, Irving Wallace, Morris West, Thomas Wolfe (both of the well known authors with that name), and Herman Wouk.

I could continue and fill many more pages with authors who I have enjoyed and who have had an influence on my life, because I have read many thousands of articles, books, short stories, and treatises (written works dealing formally and systematically with a subject), but I will stop here.

I leave you with Mark Twain's warning, "Be careful about reading health books, you may die of a misprint."

About the Author

Ken Miller is the author of four internationally acclaimed historical novels: *Evening of Pale Sunshine*, *Weep Without Tears*, *Return to the Bosque*, and *Beware the Abyss*.

He is a former U.S. Air Force officer and aerospace manufacturing executive. In addition to assignments around the globe, Ken supported the NASA Apollo Manned Lunar Program and was a reporting officer for Project Bluebook, the official Unidentified Flying Object (UFO) reporting agency. Recipient of two Air Force Commendation Medals and the Bronze Star Medal while in the service, he has lived in many of the United States, and the countries of Iceland, Vietnam, Thailand, and Taiwan. His worldwide travels have taken him to all 50 of the United States, 45 countries, and numerous territories.

The 9th of 17 children of Charles and Ruth Miller, he was raised in North Idaho, and now lives in Fort Worth, Texas. A former host of the Friends of the Fort Worth Library monthly book forum, he is an active leader in book discussion groups, public library support, and genealogical and historical research.

Cole Miller, who provided the cover photo, is Ken's grandson. He attends college in Austin, Texas. He is an experienced and talented photographer, computer designer, and web business developer.

Ken Miller's Historical Novels

Evening of Pale Sunshine

Occasionally love awakens in us passions that transcend time and place, and the loss of loved ones. *Evening of Pale Sunshine* is the story of such a love; a love between two people who think they have lost everything only to find that they have so much to live for: with each other. Assisted by a rag tag army consisting of a little orphan girl, a legless beggar, and an enemy spy Captain Paul Hansen searches through a war-torn city to rescue his love, Linh Than, from her brutal captors on an *Evening of Pale Sunshine*.

"An epic and heart rending story of the conquering spirit of love overcoming insurmountable obstacles."   - *Southwest Life Magazine*

"A war story and a love story set in Saigon during the chaotic years of the Vietnam War.   - *Joseph E. Ruffa, SgtMajor, U.S.M.C. (Ret)*

Weep Without Tears

A stirring adventure story of love, faith, and courage in the face of persecution and impending death. This sequel to *Evening of Pale Sunshine* is set in the turbulent post-year times of the 1970's. An exhilarating tale of a courageous young orphan boy, a man fighting for his life from a debilitating injury, and the woman who will unite them at the risk of losing the one she loves.

Winner of a Lu Spurlock Black Gold Writing Award for a novel at the fourth annual *Texans Writing to the World Writers Conference*.

"Ken Miller writes with authority in this critically acclaimed sequel to *Evening of Pale Sunshine*. The inspirational journey will keep you turning the pages."   - *Laurie Moore, Edgar Nominated author of Constable's Apprehension*.

Return to the Bosque

To protect her family, Sarah Whitman is forced to kill two intruders at her ranch who are fleeing from the law after a government robbery. Those murders haunt her as she searches for her missing husband in the raw frontier town of Fort Worth, Texas during the post-Civil War era. Accompanied by her teenage daughter, infant son, and their pet dog, Sarah is aided in her quest by a saloon madam, a Shakespeare quoting newspaper owner, a young deputy marshal, an alcoholic attorney, and, through it all, the memories of her deceased father.

"*Return to the Bosque* is an episodic tale of a wife, Sarah Whitman, in search of her missing husband in post-Civil War Texas. The story moves quite briskly, bringing the reader along with Sarah as she encounters a world of Comanches, gamblers, prostitutes, unlikely heroes, and dangerous killers. Along the way, the reader enjoys humor, tragedy, peril, redemption, and a truly memorable dog." - Scott R. Lucado, author of Never Too Busy For You

Beware the Abyss

Beware the Abyss is the sequel to the historical novel *Return to the Bosque*. Teenager Jody Whitman is beaten unconscious and his girl friend violated when they witness the brutal whipping of a young woman by Whit Anson and Captain Oliver Lewis, owners of saloons and brothels in Fort Worth, Texas' notorious red light district known as the Acre. When his best friend is murdered and the woman he loves is savagely beaten, he challenges Anson to a fight in the Acre. Charged with murder, the only one who can attest to his innocence is Captain Lewis' daughter, Deschanses. A final showdown with Captain Lewis brings Jody to the edge of an evil abyss. If he crosses over, he will become as malevolent and cold hearted as Lewis.

"Ken Miller is a brilliant writer who manages to capture the sights, sounds, and characters in this time period. He continues the saga of Sarah Whitman and her family 20 years later when her son, Jody, seeks adventure in Fort Worth, Texas only to find himself in danger. I encourage you to read this page turner. By the way, the striking cover was designed by Cole Miller. - *Candace Gillen, Texas Book Reviewer*

Made in the USA
Charleston, SC
26 February 2016